Oh, you must live in Columbia!

The origins of place names in Columbia, Maryland

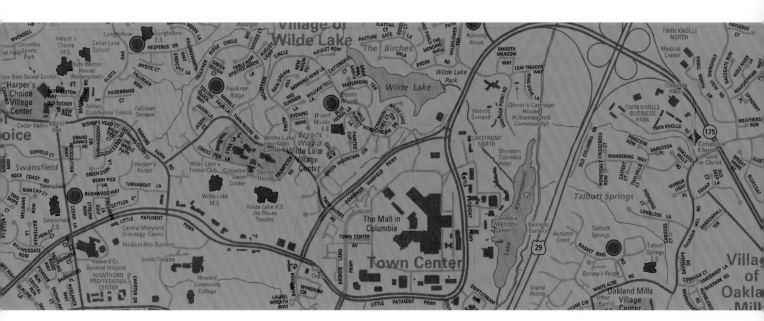

Missy Burke, Robin Emrich and Barbara Kellner

Published by Columbia Archives
Columbia, Maryland

Printed in United States

Book design by Patrick Mullaly

For information about Columbia Archives
Telephone: 410 715 3103
Email: Columbia.archives@columbiaassociation.com
10227 Wincopin Circle
Columbia, MD 21044

Contents

Permissions

For work of Robert Frost

A Leaf Treader, West-Running Brook, A Prayer in Spring, The Death of the Hired Man, The Tuft of Flowers, Wild Grapes, Mowing, The Peaceful Shepherd, The Star-Splitter, New Hampshire, A Star in a Stoneboat, The Last Mowing from THE POETRY OF ROBERT FROST edited by Edward Connery Lathem. Copyright 1923, 1928, 1969 by Henry Holt and Company, copyright 1936, 1951, 1956, 1962 by Robert Frost, copyright 1964, 1967 by Lesley Frost Ballantine. Reprinted by permission of Henry Holt and Company, LLC.

For work of Robinson Jeffers

The Inquisitors, The World's Wonder, The Torch-Bearers' Race, copyright 1925 and renewed 1953 by Robinson Jeffers, *Tor House,* copyright 1928 and renewed 1956 by Robinson Jeffers, *The Deer Lay Down Their Bones,* copyright 1925, 1929 & renewed 1953, 1957 by Robinson Jeffers, *Summer Holiday,* copyright 1925 & renewed 1953 by Robinson Jeffers, *An Artist, Morro Bay, Soliloquy,* copyright 1928 & renewed 1956 by Robinson Jeffers, *Continent's End,* copyright 1924 and renewed 1952 by Robinson Jeffers, *Roan Stallion,* copyright 1925, 1929 & renewed 1953,1957 by Robinson Jeffers, *Their Beauty Has More Meaning, Carmel Point,* copyright 1954 by Robinson Jeffers, *To the Stone Cutters,* copyright 1924 & renewed 1952 by Robinson Jeffers, *Love the Wild Swan,* copyright 1935 and renewed 1963 by Donnan Jeffers and Garth Jeffers, *Animals,* copyright 1951 by Robinson Jeffers, *Original Sin,* copyright 1925, 1929 & renewed 1953, 1957 by Robinson Jeffers, *Night,* copyright 1925 and renewed 1953 by Robinson Jeffers, *Vulture,* copyright ©1963 by Garth Jeffers and Donnan Jeffers, *Birds and Fishes,* copyright ©1963 by Steuben Glass, *The Bed by the Window,* copyright 1925, 1929 & renewed 1953, 1957 by Robinson Jeffers, *The Purse Seine,* copyright 1938 & renewed 1966 by Donnan Jeffers and Garth Jeffers, *Return,* copyright 1935 & renewed 1963 by Donnan Jeffers and Garth Jeffers, *Rock and Hawk,* copyright 1934 and renewed 1962 by Donnan Jeffers and Garth Jeffers, *Calm and Full the Ocean, The House Dog's Grave,* copyright 1941 by Robinson Jeffers and renewed 1969 by Donnan Jeffers and Garth Jeffers, *The Love and the Hate, Birds,* from SELECTED POETRY OF ROBINSON JEFFERS by Robinson Jeffers copyright 1925, 1929 & renewed 1953, 1957 by Robinson Jeffers. Used by permission of Random House, Inc.

Tamar, In the Hill at Newgrange, The Beak of Eagles, Margrave, Subjected Earth, Hands, Watch the Lights Fade, Give Your Heart to the Hawks, The Love and The Hate, The Inhumanist, Cawdor, Prelude, The Loving Shepherdess, The Women at Point Sur, Granddaughter, October Evening, Oysters, The Broken Balance, Red Mountain, Birds, The Treasure, Gray Weather, The Coast Road, Joy, The Maid's Thought, Passenger Pigeons, Flight of Swans, Thurso's Landing, Decaying Lambskins, Ghosts in England,
What's the Best Life, On an Anthology of Chinese Poems, Natural Music, Oh Lovely Rock, Patronymic, The Wind Struck Music, Divinely Superfluous Beauty, The Unformed Volcanic Earth, The Storm Blowing. Adapted from Robinson Jeffers, *The Collected Poetry of Robinson Jeffers* by Tim Hunt. Copyright© by the Jeffers Literary Properties.

For work of Ogden Nash

It's Snug to be Smug, New Yorker 1936 Copyright© 1936 by Ogden Nash, *The Tale of Custard The Dragon,* Child Life 1936 Copyright© by Ogden Nash. Used by permission Curtis Brown, Ltd.

For work of Carl Sandburg

Excerpt from *Bird Footprint* in HONEY AND SALT, copyright ©1958 by Carl Sandburg and renewed 1986 by Margaret Sandburg, Helga Sandburg Crile and Janet Sandburg, reprinted by permission of Houghton Mifflin Harcourt Publishing Company. Excerpts from *Love is a Deep and a Dark and a Lonely, The Evening Sunsets Witness and Pass On* in HONEY AND SALT, copyright©1960 by Carl Sandburg and renewed 1988 by Margaret Sandburg, Helga Sandburg Crile and Janet Sandburg, reprinted by permission of Houghton Mifflin Harcourt Publishing Company. Excerpt from *Little Word, Little White Bird* and in HONEY AND SALT, copyright ©1961 by Carl Sandburg and renewed 1989 by Margaret Sandburg, Helga Sandburg Crile and Janet Sandburg, reprinted by permission of Houghton Mifflin Harcourt Publishing Company. Excerpts from *Honey and Salt, Old Music for Quiet Hearts, Deep Sea Wandering, Lesson, Child Face and Fame If Not Fortune* in HONEY AND SALT, copyright ©1963 by Carl Sandburg and renewed 1991 by Margaret Sandburg, Helga Sandburg Crile and Janet Sandburg, reprinted by permission of Houghton Mifflin Harcourt Publishing Company. Excerpt from *Old Deep Sing-Song* from WIND SONG, copyright ©1958 by Carl Sandburg and renewed 1986 by Margaret Sandburg, Janet Sandburg and Helga Sandburg Crile, reprinted by permission of Houghton Mifflin Harcourt Publishing Company. Excerpts from *Without Notice Beforehand and Redhaw Rain* in GOOD MORNING, AMERICA, copyright ©1928 and renewed 1956 by Carl Sandburg, reprinted by permission of Houghton Mifflin Harcourt Publishing Company. Excerpts from the following are in public domain; first appeared in CORNHUSKERS, CHICAGO POEMS, SLABS OF THE SUNBURNT WEST AND SMOKE AND STEEL by Carl Sandburg, published by Houghton Mifflin Harcourt Publishing Company. *Caboose Thoughts* From CORNHUSKERS, *Fog* From CHICAGO POEMS, *At a Window* From CHICAGO POEMS, *Half Moon in a High Wind* From SMOKE AND STEEL, *For You* From SMOKE AND STEEL, *Prairie* From CORNHUSKERS, *Balloon Faces* From SMOKE AND STEEL, *Between Two Hills* From CHICAGO POEMS, *Chords* From SMOKE AND STEEL, *The Windy City* From SLABS OF THE SUNBURNT WEST, *Slabs of the Sunburnt West* From SLABS OF THE SUNBURNT WEST, *Haze* From SMOKE AND STEEL, *Honey and Salt* From HONEY AND SALT, *Moon Riders* From
SLABS OF THE SUNBURNT WEST, *Panels* From SMOKE AND STEEL

For work of William Carlos Williams

Tree and Sky, by William Carlos Williams, from COLLECTED POEMS: 1909-1939 VOLUME I, copyright© 1935 by William Carlos Williams. Reprinted by permission of New Directions Publishing Corp. Sales Territory: U.S./Canadian only. *BlueFlags, Complaint, Dawn, Della Primavera Transportata al Morale: April, Fish, Good Night, January Morning, Primrose, Spring and All (VIII) At the Faucet of June, St. Francis Einstein of the Daffodils, Struggle of Wings, Sub Terra, The Birds, The Bull, The Descent of Winter, The Flowers Alone, The Trees, These, Trees, Wild Orchard, Winter, Winter Sunset,* By William Carlos Williams, from COLLECTED POEMS:1909-1939, VOLUME I, copyright 1938 by New Directions Publishing Corp. Reprinted by permission of New Directions Publishing Corp. Sales Territory: U.S./Canadian rights only. *Sparrows Among Dry Leaves,* By William Carlos Williams, from COLLECTED POEMS 1939-1962, VOLUME II, copyright ©1944 by William Carlos Williams. Reprinted by permission of New Directions Publishing Corp. Sales Territory: U.S./Canadian rights only.

For Longfellow Stamp

Henry Longfellow Stamp Design ©2007 United States Postal Service. All Rights Reserved. Used with Permission.

For *The Boondocks*

The Boondocks ©1999 Aaron McGruder. Dist. By Universal Press Syndicate. Reprinted with permission. All rights reserved.

For Edwin Warfield Photograph
Courtesy of the Collection of the Maryland State Archives
Artist: Thomas Cromwell Corner (1865-1938)
Title: Edwin Warfield (1860-1920)
Date: 1907
Medium: Oil on canvas
Dimensions: 48X48
Accession number:MSA SC 1545-1124

For George Dobbin Photograph

Courtesy of the Collection of the Maryland State Archives
Special Collections (Judge James F. Schneider Collection)
Habana, Judge George W. Dobbin, c. late 19th century
Accession number: MSA SC 5598-4-200

For The Moon is a Gong Image

Papers of John Dos Passos, MSS 5950, Special Collections, University of Virginia Library.
By permission of Lucy Dos Passos Coggin.

For Dorsey Hall and Hickory Ridge Photographs

Courtesy of University of Maryland Libraries.
Series VIII, Celia Holland Papers, Special Collections.

Acknowledgements

The task of creating a book on the origin of Columbia place names proved complex and took longer than anyone would have imagined at the outset. It involved three primary people and each, understandably, had her own concept of the finished product. The overriding goal, however, was clear: compile the most accurate account of the street naming process and the derivation of each and every name. The entries have been checked and rechecked. We felt very strongly about being as complete and accurate as possible understanding that this book would become the definitive story and reference for years to come. Each author has individuals who were helpful during the process and so we include a three-part author's note and acknowledgments.

Missy Burke

Having the opportunity to see an idea actually become a book is always exciting, but in the case of *Oh, you must live in Columbia!*, the final product would never have been possible without the help of many people. We owe much to Evelyn Menzies Chisolm, Nancy Miller and Scott Ditch for the time and attention they gave on the phone, through e-mails and in person to share their memories. Their stories and recollections made the days of early Columbia come alive. Dave Forester also lent invaluable insights into both the more recent naming and the overall process.

Many thanks to the patience of Dick Jordan, CAD Administrator and Address Coordinator at the Howard County Police Department and Karen Stires, Land Acquisitions Agent at the Howard County Department of Public Works who gracefully endured repeated phone calls, visits and questions. The marvelous staff at the Howard County Library was ever supportive and always ready to help, especially Susan Cooke, who repeatedly found volumes that no one else could find! Robert Kafka and Robert Brophy were kind enough to lend their expertise in everything 'Jeffers' when obscure information eluded us. Thank you to Robert Slavinski at the Howard County GIS for his research and production of maps. We are indebted, also, to Jerry Brock, Lesa Borg, Richard Wilson, Howard Phillips, Kent Rayburn, Nadine Klatt, Pat Marlatt and many others for taking time to add to our story.

Warm thanks go to Brita Stennes Stewart and Judy Barrett for their stories and unsolicited interest and support.

Finally, I extend my personal thanks to Cathy Rosenheim, whose boundless enthusiasm jump-started this project!

Robin Emrich

Working on this book has been the greatest sleuthing job I have ever had. As a lifelong fan of a good mystery, I am forever grateful to Barbara and Missy for bringing me on board and giving me the opportunity to practice what I read. My fact finding skills greatly benefitted from Professor Marilyn White's instruction on how to turn the unknown into the known. Because Professor Frank Burke shared his passion for documents and the stories that lay within them, I found myself returning to The Rouse Company (TRC) records many times in search of the stories they would reveal. To those in TRC who thought to save the records documenting the naming process and donate them to the Columbia Archives, I am truly indebted. Nancy Miller's donation of index cards containing place name information, was, for me, the moment this project began. Over the years, Nancy and later Evelyn Chisolm answered questions that arose with such clarity that, at times, it seemed as if only days rather than decades had passed since the names were chosen. Early on, Dave Forester donated documents from his name-generating days as a development director that were chock-full of information needed to solve many naming mysteries, and give fresh clues to others.

I am fortunate to live in Howard County where the public libraries have rich collections, easy-to-use electronic databases, and speedy interlibrary loans. The Howard County Historical

Ron Rizzolo, were extremely helpful in finding collections that told the stories behind the local history place names.

I am grateful to all of the subject experts, colleagues, friends and family members who willing, and sometimes unwittingly, revealed clues in conversations and e-mails with me. In particular, thanks go out to the following: Lisa Long, curator at the Redwood Library, who gave insight on Longfellow's round tower; Lee Glazer, curator at the Freer and Sackler Galleries, who tracked down information on the more obscure Whistler etchings and taught me some etching lingo; John L. Due who generously shared the history of his home and neighboring properties; and Susan Schubel and Carl Katenkamp, in Howard County Government, who enabled my quest to view and study the 1961 Howard County road map. Had we not talked to two former Howard County Government officials, Tom Harris and Granville Wehland, in the waning hours of this project our entries on the Howard County roads would have been woefully inadequate. Granville Wehland has remarkable recall of naming stories for each street he recorded when generating the 1961 road map. I relied on local historian Joetta Cramm for her knowledge on specific place names, and had her give a final review of all historically-based place names. Often Mary Mannix, director of the Maryland Room, Frederick County Public Library, was the person I turned to first when stumped on local history questions, because of her amazing ability to get me the information needed, or at the very least give me a contact or resource that would.

Lucy Dos Passos Coggins, daughter of John Dos Passos, graciously gave us permission to use the "Moon is a Gong" image, and shared wonderful memories on her family's connections with James Rouse and Columbia.

Jeannette Lichtenwalner very capably organized call-outs and images, acted as a sounding board for ideas, and, perhaps most important to me, endured the tedium of final accuracy checks of each book entry with me, without ever a complaint.

Special thanks go to my mother, who enjoys a good mystery too, and to my father, whose passion for history and literature probably took me down the road I am on. Lars, my husband, and Lauren, my daughter, saw me through this project with their unending love and support, and they even did some of the street sign checks! I couldn't ask for more.

Barbara Kellner

I have learned much from the joint writing project and thank my fellow authors, especially Robin Emrich who is the best fact-checker, researcher I know. Michele Krupka, Ann Blimmel and Susan Thorton Hobby gave valuable proof-reading assistance. It was a wonderful experience to meet Evelyn Menzies Chisolm and I thank her for reaching back into her memory time and again as we searched for answers. This also goes for Scott Ditch, Nancy Miller, Dave Forester, Tom Harris, and Sonny Wehland. Thanks too to Phyllis Kepner Reinhard, Dick Lewis and Gail Holliday who graciously permitted us to use their material adding color and character. Gordon Katz visited the Columbia Archives to research the history of the Columbia post office and ended up giving us information we could use including the images of old Columbia postmarks that he had collected in his research. Mary Louise DeSarran at Maryland Historical Trust and Jennie Levine at University of Maryland Special Collections Libraries were helpful and gracious providing historic photographs.

Patrick Mullaly, who designed the book, is the most patient, accommodating artist anyone could wish to have involved in a project. His dedication to Columbia and this project was very meaningful. For helping me navigate through the legal issues of copyright I am indebted to David Johnstone and the Washington Area Lawyers for the Arts. Finally, the book would not have been possible without the support of Leslie Barnett and Michelle Miller of the Columbia Association who continued to believe in the project and supported the decision to commit time to it.

Great Blue Heron photo by Michael Oberman

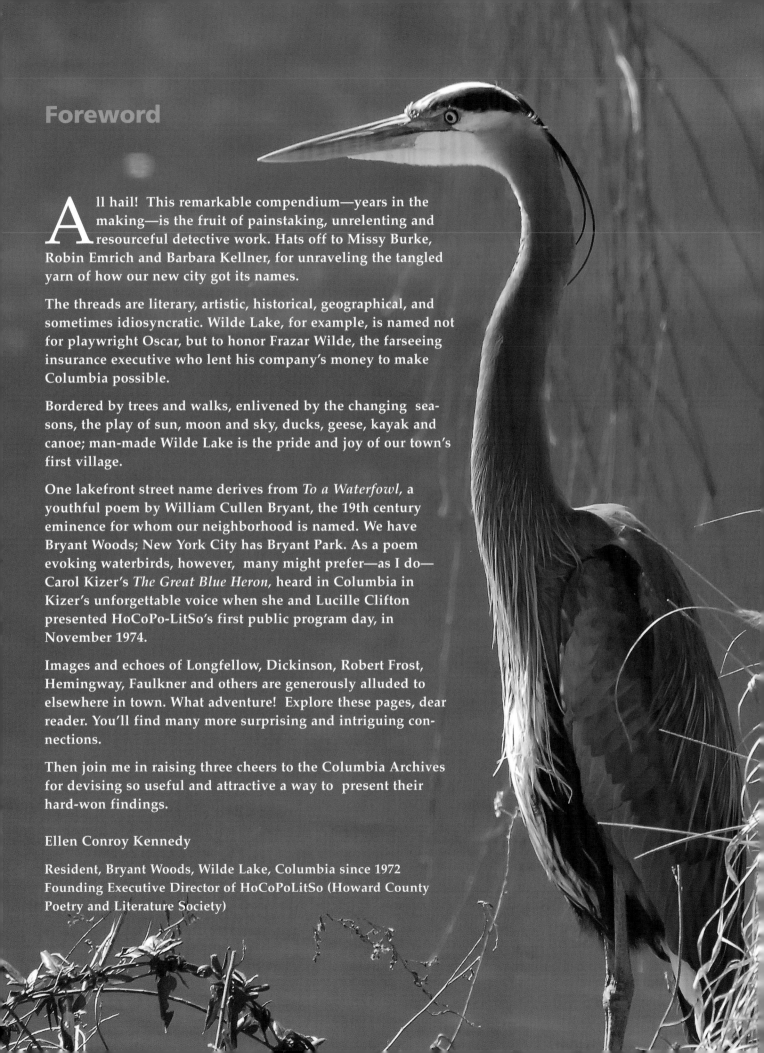

Foreword

All hail! This remarkable compendium—years in the making—is the fruit of painstaking, unrelenting and resourceful detective work. Hats off to Missy Burke, Robin Emrich and Barbara Kellner, for unraveling the tangled yarn of how our new city got its names.

The threads are literary, artistic, historical, geographical, and sometimes idiosyncratic. Wilde Lake, for example, is named not for playwright Oscar, but to honor Frazar Wilde, the farseeing insurance executive who lent his company's money to make Columbia possible.

Bordered by trees and walks, enlivened by the changing seasons, the play of sun, moon and sky, ducks, geese, kayak and canoe; man-made Wilde Lake is the pride and joy of our town's first village.

One lakefront street name derives from *To a Waterfowl*, a youthful poem by William Cullen Bryant, the 19th century eminence for whom our neighborhood is named. We have Bryant Woods; New York City has Bryant Park. As a poem evoking waterbirds, however, many might prefer—as I do— Carol Kizer's *The Great Blue Heron*, heard in Columbia in Kizer's unforgettable voice when she and Lucille Clifton presented HoCoPo-LitSo's first public program day, in November 1974.

Images and echoes of Longfellow, Dickinson, Robert Frost, Hemingway, Faulkner and others are generously alluded to elsewhere in town. What adventure! Explore these pages, dear reader. You'll find many more surprising and intriguing connections.

Then join me in raising three cheers to the Columbia Archives for devising so useful and attractive a way to present their hard-won findings.

Ellen Conroy Kennedy

Resident, Bryant Woods, Wilde Lake, Columbia since 1972
Founding Executive Director of HoCoPoLitSo (Howard County Poetry and Literature Society)

COMMUNITY RESEARCH AND DEVELOPMENT, INC.

INTRA-OFFICE MEMORANDUM

January 4, 1966

TO: James W. Rouse

FROM: W. E. Finley

. . . .

The Names are great. The Depts. are I have passed a few comments along to Scott in his absence J

RE: Columbia Naming System – First Phase

Scott Ditch and his staff have produced a unique and thoughtful set of names for the major elements of the first two villages which, I believe, should be adopted with few exceptions. As is apparent, he has attempted to reach into the cultural life of America, as well as the historic background of Howard County, Maryland.

Historic names like Governor Warfield, Van Devanter (U.S. Supreme Court Justice and Howard County resident), Robert Oliver (miller at the original Oakland Mill) have been used for the major thoroughfares.

We recommend that the first village be called Wilde Lake Village because of the visual and prestige importance of the lake as the focal point of the first village. This would result in the shopping and   center being known as Wilde Lake Center, and the junior and   probably named accordingly.

The north   is named after the works of
                                                                 A.

TO: William E. Finley

CC: W. Scott Ditch

FROM: E. Menzies

                                                                 APRIL

SUBJECT: Golf Course Names–Clari

en Bryant, and each of the
neighborhood is named for
and thereby thrown in for fun.

was presumably the first
no objection to the use
atapsco, Patuxent,
However, my reaction
of the downtown with
ng ability for the
he fact that Goi is
the view across
important vista.
naw downtown can

The following is a list of Golf Course names and

MEMORANDUM FROM

Tall Tuft - The Tuft of Flowers

Low Bough - A Dream

Wayside Nook - In Neglect

Sunset Bird - Looking to

Terr - O

First

A Dream Party

Sunset Lin

Hobbit's Glen Golf Club-

Spring Pools Golf Club

Indian Cab

A Hobbit is described in J.
as little people who love p
earth. They like to l
They like good ti
to hurry.

Introduction

Imagine placing a catalog order, giving your address and being asked to repeat it. Certainly that has happened to many Columbians. But imagine the surprise of one Columbia resident when she gave her address and the catalog order-taker said, "Oh, you must live in Columbia."

Like the city's curling culs-de-sac and community mailboxes, Columbia's street names require a bit of work from city residents, but deliver something more than a code for the mail carrier. Michael Chabon, the Pulitzer Prize-winning author raised in Columbia, loved those names. For him, "They were like magic spells, each one calibrated to call into being one particular stretch of blacktop, sidewalk and lawn, and no other."[1]

Magic or not, Columbia street names have the power to spark imagination, confuse, amuse and, in at least one case, turn an everyday citizen into a community activist. How did Columbia get these names? What is real and what is myth about Columbia's fanciful names?

Behind most place names there is a meaning, even if it is as simple as a numbering system. What do these names say about the community? A quick search on the Internet will reveal that San Francisco street names introduce a short history of the city, from early explorers like Ortega, to the gold rush era names of Sutter and Geary. In Cleveland, one can trace the pattern of early immigration with its British, French and German named streets. In Los Angeles, local figures are honored. There is, for example, Chandler

Boulevard named for Los Angeles Times publisher, Harry Chandler, and Mulholland Drive named for William Mulholland, the engineer who worked on the Los Angeles Aqueduct. For more information, the American Name Society, founded in 1951 to promote the study of names and naming practices, has an interesting website. (www.wtsn.binghamton.edu/ANS/)

But Columbia, Maryland, was different. It didn't grow slowly, it wasn't discovered, and while the early settlers called themselves pioneers, they moved onto already built and named streets. Columbia's neighborhood design, with a reliance on few through streets and many culs-de-sac, meant there were an exceptionally large number of thoroughfares. They all needed names—good names, James Rouse, Columbia's visionary founder, insisted. "Names are a part of design, of the environment, of the atmosphere in which people live. They should have integrity, interest and beauty. It is worth the time and the effort to produce good names. Our names should be distinguished. We should not accept less."[2]

The challenge began with finding the right person for the job. The sheer enormity of planning, engineering and building Columbia held top priority with all of the people involved in the project. Naming more than one thousand streets was only a tiny cog in the complex machine of the city-making project. No one on the small staff had the job title or description of "street-namer." The assignment landed on the desk of Scott Ditch, director of marketing for The Rouse Company (TRC).

In the summer of 1963, a couple of months before James Rouse announced plans to build a city in Maryland, he traveled to Europe with his family. On the itinerary were visits to Garden Cities in England and New Towns in Scandinavia to gather information for the monumental planning process that he was about to initiate.

Among the cities Rouse visited was Basildon, England. In his diary of the trip Rouse observed, "Very interesting street and place names throughout the town. These were the responsibility of one man who took a great interest in researching the Essex lore and coming up with the names. . . Instead of calling everything a street or a way, there were a wide variety of names that might be applicable for our use in Cross Keys or elsewhere."

"Couldn't you have prepared, fairly simply, a map of Columbia that would indicate all of the roads, lakes, public places, etc. that require names. Couldn't we distribute it with a description of the places involved and offer a reward for any successful names," Rouse wrote to Ditch in October 1965. "Clearly we must have names and soon," he continued. "Clearly we have a serious internal congestion in developing acceptable names. I worry about settling in desperation on some kind of arbitrary naming system. It may be beyond the capacity of anyone to produce a large number of names, but many individuals might each have a good idea for something."[3]

Ditch describes the years leading up to the opening of Columbia as "beyond hectic." He had joined TRC in 1963 not knowing the full extent of his job responsibilities but certainly, street naming wasn't part of the job description at the time. His responsibilities included promoting the community of Cross Keys that TRC was developing in north Baltimore, preparing for the opening of Columbia,

Scott Ditch, Director of Marketing, The Rouse Company, had primary responsibility for developing the street naming system.

producing a variety of annual reports, publishing the bi-monthly company newsletter and overseeing the leasing brochures for TRC's shopping malls. His first desk was literally in a hallway in TRC's Saratoga Street office, and he recalls moving his office space ten times in a year! The organization was growing so rapidly that employees had shifting functions and quickly changing job descriptions. Meetings, creative or otherwise, were often held on the fly while standing near a desk or passing in a hallway.

In spite of the rapid, nearly overwhelming pace, Ditch and his staff welcomed the street naming challenge. The first "opportunity," as Rouse often defined a challenge, was to comply with a policy that had recently been established by the Baltimore Regional Planning Council and the United States Post Office to prohibit the duplication of street names within Howard County, or in the adjacent counties of Anne Arundel and Baltimore and Baltimore city. While that restriction dramatically reduced the pool of street name possibilities, it also forced a creative process that fit well into the planning of Columbia itself. Columbia was making headlines in the field of urban planning. A fresh approach to names with the same headline catching appeal seemed appropriate. "We decided from the very beginning that names for things in Columbia should be different – not for the sake of being different, but because most places have such a bland, ho-hum system," Ditch said in 1968.[4]

Ditch wanted a way to name streets that celebrated the ground-breaking spirit of the new city. "Inherent in Columbia's ideals and goals was the concept of 'The Next America,' a truly better approach to the development of a city, but also a concept that celebrated the best of the American ideals."[5] Ditch recalled that Rouse talked about having uplifting themes celebrating American achievements, but not war or technological or commercial advancements. During a series of informal conversations, Ditch presented to Rouse the idea of mining the works of American poets and authors. Rouse warmed to the idea and encouraged Ditch to develop it. Unsure whether or not this plan could work, Ditch turned to his staff, primarily Evelyn Menzies, a research assistant working on annual reports and other market research projects, who was also an avid student of literature and an amateur poet. "I was presented with a conundrum, and I ran with it," recalls Menzies. "Overnight I went from a financial researcher to a creative researcher."[6] Menzies understood that a naming system based on such an innovative idea would be exclusive to Columbia and could potentially offer names that fit Rouse's goal to be distinguished and beautiful, and also simple and clear. Only one question remained: Would it work?

Menzies began spending a lot of time in the poetry section at the Enoch Pratt Library in Roland Park, near her home. Relying on her own broad literary background, Menzies brought sensitivity and a depth of knowledge to the task. She recalls enjoying this part of the job immensely. "Imagine, getting paid for reading!"[7]

Ditch and Menzies also tackled the history of the land itself, using the few books on Howard County history that were available in the mid-1960s, including *The Founders of Anne Arundel and Howard Counties, Maryland,* by J. D. Warfield,

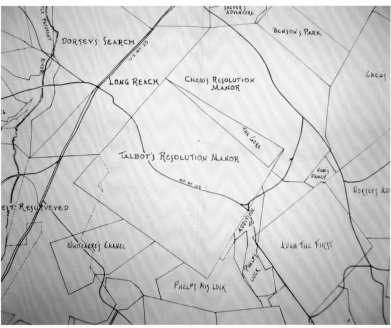

which was published in 1905 and reprinted in 1967.

By January 1966, the street naming system was in place. William Finley, Columbia project director, confidently told Rouse that "Scott Ditch and his staff have produced a unique and thoughtful set of names for the major elements of the first two villages. As is apparent, he has attempted to reach into the cultural life of America, as well as the historic

TOP
Evelyn Menzies sat down with WBAL-TV's Bob Coltman on May 25, 1967 when the subject of Columbia and its street names was "breaking news."

BOTTOM
A portion of Dr. Dorsey's Howard County Land Grant Map. The Charter of Maryland in 1632 gave Lord Baltimore the authority to assign or grant land to anyone who wanted to purchase it. This practice continued until the Revolutionary War.

background of Howard County, Maryland. Historic names like Governor Warfield … and Robert Oliver have been used for the major thoroughfares."[8] Authors for the first two neighborhoods were selected: William Cullen Bryant for the first and William Faulkner for the second. "The names and the system are great," Rouse responded to Finley, pleased that a system was finally in place.

A January 26, 1966, *Baltimore Evening Sun* article with a somewhat unfortunate headline made the system public and brought some interesting consequences. The headline was "Unusual Street Names Sought for Columbia." While the text correctly explained that the staff was taking care of finding these names, the headline grabbed attention and a number of people sent letters to the company suggesting some very unusual names indeed. Noting that some places would be built for children's activities, it was suggested that roads be named "Roller Skate Road, Bicycle Lane or Coasting Hill."[9] "Skunk's Misery" was another suggestion, " in case you have too many streets for the names you think up."[10]

With development proceeding and hundreds of roads on the map, Menzies was busy reading and identifying possible names—sometimes not quickly enough. In December 1966, as the steel framework was going up on Town Center's first buildings and construction was under way in Wilde Lake, Rouse was asking Ditch again about names—specifically names for buildings such as the apartments in Wilde Lake and The Exhibit Center. Everyone involved in the Columbia project was juggling many jobs. Ditch's office was putting out press releases, brochures, an exhibit and slide show. Rouse was patient, but persistent.

"That's gotta be in Columbia."

When queried by his very efficient secretary, Nancy Allison, whether she should forget about following up with Ditch, his answer was a quick "No."[11]

At about this time, coincidentally and quite fortunately, Caleb Dorsey, a man whose ancestors settled in the area in the 1600s, was completing eight years of extensive research on the pre-revolutionary land grants of the county. In 1968 he produced a map, *Original Land Grants of Howard County, Maryland.* "The original names turned up by Dorsey proved fascinating to the namers of Columbia's streets and villages," Menzies wrote in 1969 in *Columbia,* a magazine published by TRC. Once Dorsey's map was available, many neighborhood and village names were chosen from this pool. In Wilde Lake and Harper's Choice, neighborhood names reflected the literary sources. Oakland Mills was being named about the time the map came out. Memos indicate that initially neighborhood names were to follow that pattern—namely Winterfields and Christina, both pulled from Andrew Wyeth works. But subsequent memos show the switch to Steven's Forest and Talbott Springs, which were drawn from the land grant map.

"Acceptance of the naming system was not easy or universal," Ditch recalled. "To some, the names seemed long and cumbersome. Green Mountain Circle, Pasture Gate Lane and Willow Bottom Drive took up a large space on envelopes and required extra writing when filling out forms with tiny spaces … In time, however, people came to enjoy the reactions … when explaining that they lived on Proud Foot Place or Rain Dream Hill. 'That's gotta be in Columbia,' was more frequently than not the response. Thus it was that a distinctive system took hold, a system that not only satisfied the stringent and necessary requirements of the postal authorities, but also celebrated the depth and breadth of American arts and letters."[12]

Long lists of street names and a formal process for how they would be approved and assigned followed. All names chosen by "Miss Columbia," as Menzies came to be called, were passed through a series of approvals starting with Ditch and ending with Rouse. The Howard County Planning Commission got to weigh in; they checked for duplication and rejected others for various reasons. Names also went to the Post Office for review and approval. Goldsmith Road, Geranium Court, Homer Place and Blackberry Lane were among the names rejected by the Post Office as being in use or too similar to existing names in surrounding areas. Once the names were approved, a street name "bank" was ready for dissemination. Ditch was the keeper of the name list in the early years. Project directors or others in the planning and design department submitted requests for names and were given several choices. Once names were selected they were submitted to Rouse for final approval. Getting his approval was not always routine. When seeing Harper's Choice Gardens, Oakland Mills Gardens and Oakland Gardens as the name choices for apartments, he made his opinion clear. "This is dull, unimaginative and inappropriate. Where are the gardens? Why the repetitious use of a meaningless word in a title? … it may be boring to have to pay attention to this one [detail] but NAMES ARE IMPORTANT."[13]

Menzies continued as chief researcher and compiler of names until 1969 when she left TRC. By then she had put her stamp on the villages of Wilde Lake,

Harper's Choice, Oakland Mills and Long Reach. Robinson Jeffers, whose work inspired almost all the names in Long Reach, proved to be one of Menzies's favorites. "His words were so colorful, that pulling long lists of names was easy,"[14] she said. Her choices did not go unnoticed by at least one Long Reach child who never knew her. Michael Chabon lived first in Harper's Choice and then in Long Reach. In a recent interview he remarked that names like Margrave Mews and Drystraw Drive were musical and alliterative. "The woman, God bless her, she had an ear for language … without regard for whether it sounded dignified or sensible or intelligible. She went for the sound."[15]

Long Reach was among the first assignments for Kay Sarfaty, who took on the street-naming role in 1970. Like Menzies, it was part of her marketing department position. Qualifications? She liked to read. Like Menzies, she found Jeffers a rich source. As Long Reach continued to develop, so did the pattern of Jeffers-inspired streets. Sarfaty called her street-naming duties fun. "I'm going to have a ball naming a neighborhood after Samuel L. Clemens … He wrote enough and used colorful language," she noted in one of the many articles about street names that appeared through the years.[16]

The naming process usually proceeded fairly smoothly; however, it wasn't always perfectly routine. Some builders seemed less than enamored with the individual names. When submitting choices to one builder, Sarfaty pleaded, "No raised eyebrows please. You don't know what we have to go through to get acceptable names for the post office."[17]

Lesa Borg became the official name lady in 1981. By then the pace of development

"…NAMES ARE IMPORTANT."

had slowed and she was spending only about eight hours a year researching street names. But Borg may have inadvertently perpetuated the often-repeated myth of the little old lady hired to name streets. A 1985 *Columbia Magazine* article bold-faced this quote: "Many people imagine me as some funny old lady, sitting in a rocking chair with her bottle of Jack Daniels, and just naming streets when she feels mellow enough." Reading to the end of the article clears up the image. "'So the myths can be put to rest,' Borg concludes with a smile, 'I'm just a regular person, not some eccentric old lady.'"[18]

"Here comes the street name lady," is how Nancy Miller recalls being greeted at the Howard County Planning and Zoning office. Miller, who had been with TRC since the mid-1970s, was assigned the naming duties when Borg retired in the mid-1980s. It was a very small piece of her job and she, like those before her, often took poetry books home at night. "A glass of wine or two eased the creative process," joked Miller.[19] Long lists of possible names got a second reading in the morning before they were sent to the development director for review. "We really wanted to find nice names, it was important to us," she noted.[20]

One of Miller's biggest naming challenges was River Hill. Whitman was difficult because his freestyle verse did not present a large number of colorful phrases. In contrast, as the neighborhood of Kendall Ridge in Long Reach continued to be developed, Miller went back to Robinson Jeffers. As Menzies and Sarfaty had found, his language lent itself to the process.

By the mid-1990s, with the completion of the street naming in River Hill, the once-arduous process of finding and approving street names was winding down. Names for pockets of new streets were apparently being pulled from old lists. Names in Town Center, for example, bear this out. Responsibility for finding names continues to fall to the developer, now General Growth Properties (GGP) which acquired TRC in 2004. Nancy Tucker, senior community development representative, holds the street naming position. In assigning names to Snowden Overlook, an area of Long Reach that began development in 2006, Tucker continued to follow the Jeffers theme. In addition, perhaps in a bow to the large number of names that his works inspired, GGP named one of the streets in Gateway Overlook, a commercial center not far from Long Reach, Robinson Jeffers Drive.

Articles about street names appear in the local papers with some regularity—each new reporter apparently finds the names enticing and each gives the story a slightly different spin. In 2000, Laura Vozzella, writing in the *Baltimore Sun,* became so interested in the poetry of Jeffers and the namesake streets in Long Reach, that she devoted most of her story to his work. Vozzella's story caught the eye of Washington's Channel 9 WUSA and Joan Gartlan came to Columbia to do a feature. But perhaps the most widely read piece about street names came in the form of a syndicated comic strip.

In 1999, Aaron McGruder, creator of *The Boondocks*, portrayed his character Riley making new street signs because he just couldn't live on something like Timid Deer and he couldn't sit idle when "those poor people have to live on Rustling Leaf Drive …"[21] Few in the national audience likely knew that Rustling Leaf, while drawn from literature, is a real place in Columbia. McGruder knew because he grew up in Columbia's Owen Brown village and graduated from Oakland Mills High School. "Columbia is in some ways the inspiration for Woodcrest, the fictional home of the 'Boondocks' characters."[22]

Hickory Ridge resident Paige Murphy didn't read *The Boondocks*, but she thought the name of her street definitely needed changing. She, like Riley, took things into her own hands, but in her own way. Murphy moved onto Satan Wood Drive in Hickory Ridge in 2000. She didn't really like the name but lived with it for a few years before the comments of catalog order-takers and out-of-town friends called her to action.

Murphy's first stop was the Columbia Archives. She wanted to confirm the story told to her by neighbors that the street name was a misspelling; that the intended name was Satinwood derived from an Amy Lowell poem "A Pantomime in One Act." Columbia Archives showed her the poem and the original list indicating Satinwood. That was all she needed. "I was determined to make the change happen," said Murphy, "even after finding out that it would cost the homeowners a couple of thousand dollars."[23] Murphy waged a campaign, calling on local politicians to help her. In the end, it wasn't the politicians, but the

press and the Internet, that brought the story into the limelight and caught the attention of GGP who offered to pay for the name change. In May 2005 a new street sign was hammered onto its post and the old sign became an artifact for the Columbia Archives collection.

Those blue street signs—bearing a name worthy of changing or those worthy of the ages—are emblematic of Columbia. James Rouse once said that humans "will rise to the big, dramatically good plan—they will yawn at the timid, the cautious, the unconvincing."[24] The street names in The Next America inspire no yawns. They're not timid. Perhaps there's magic in the lyrical labels that mark our streets.

RIGHT

The opening of Columbia's first post office on August 15, 1966 was reason for celebration. Raising the flag are James Clark, state senator; Willard Rouse, vice president of The Rouse Company and Jim Rouse's brother; Charles Miller, Howard County commissioner; John Shallcross, HRD manager of land management; and John Slayton, Columbia Association manager. The post office opened before any new structures were built in Columbia; it utilized a stone house that was once a blacksmith shop for Oakland Manor. The building has been completely renovated and is privately owned and located on Hyla Brook Road in The Birches in Wilde Lake.

BELOW

James Rouse mailed a first day cover to himself and to a number of others including Lawrence O'Brien, Postmaster General of the United States.

First day of postmark use   August 15, 1966

COLUMBIA

BALTIMORE

COLUMBIA

WASHINGTON D.C.

COLUMBIA, MD
AUG
15
1966
A.M.
21043

REGISTER
VOTE

5¢ POSTAGE

Mr. James W. Rouse
1 Overlook Lane
Baltimore, Maryland 21210

How Did Columbia Get Its Name?

How did Columbia, Maryland, marketed as "The Next America," and innovative in so many ways, end up with one of the most popular names in the country? More than 20 American cities or towns are named Columbia and there are dozens more townships. Columbia's creators—like most parents—found that choosing the perfect name is not easy.

Finding a name for the town was a frequent agenda item at weekly Columbia planning meetings. Scott Ditch was asked to "seek out a useful name with an historical connotation that would be part of the tradition of Howard County."[25] Ditch did an exhaustive study of Howard County and Maryland history and brought a great number of choices to the table. At various times Carrollton, Snowden, Broken Land, Patuxent, Dorsey's Forge, White Wine and Claret, Meridian, Wellspring and Columbia were on the list as possible names. Columbia had historical context. In 1874 a Columbia post office had been established to serve the small community that straddled Columbia Turnpike. Located near the junction of present day Route 29 and Route 108 the post office was in operation until 1912 when service was discontinued and transferred to Ellicott City. The name, however, lived on in place names such as the small development called Columbia Woodlands that was built in the early 1930s near the Allview Public Golf Course and Columbia Hills that was developed in the late 1950s.

The name Columbia was generally in the lead during the discussions at those weekly planning meetings but it had "not set anyone on fire."[26] One concern was the popularity of the name. The possibility of confusion and misdirected mail was discussed: Columbia MO looked very close to Columbia MD. Clearly the creative planning team was not coming up with the right answers when it came to a name.

After one such meeting, Rouse wrote to Sam Neel, a close friend and TRC board member. "Do you have any names that are better than Columbia?" he asked. "We have tried hundreds but are eager to receive other nominations. This [Columbia] has the advantage of being consistent with the location of the property on 'Columbia Pike.' It tends to establish it as relating to the District of Columbia and as Columbia, Maryland. It identifies it as being between Baltimore and Washington. It also has an onward and upward flag-waving note. This is not fixed—but it is the leading candidate at the moment."[27]

The Columbia development team was working at full throttle—studying the

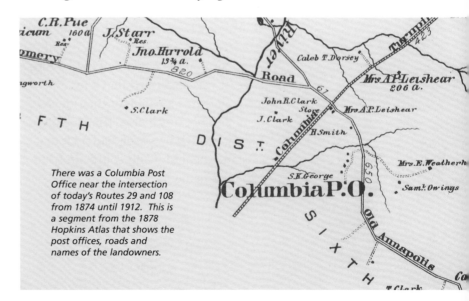

There was a Columbia Post Office near the intersection of today's Routes 29 and 108 from 1874 until 1912. This is a segment from the 1878 Hopkins Atlas that shows the post offices, roads and names of the landowners.

land, mapping and sketching, distilling ideas—working toward a deadline to publicly unveil a comprehensive, if not final, design concept. By the end of March the list of names had been whittled down to Columbia, Meridian and Wellspring. Those three names were brought to a staff meeting and put to a vote. Columbia came off first. "But then on asking for a show of hands on the question, 'Are you satisfied to name it Columbia?' only two or three of the 12 present raised their hand. Thus the community continued namelessly on."[28]

On a trip to New York in May 1964, "Rouse was congratulated by Burnham Kelly, Dean of Architecture at Cornell University, on the new town not having a name. It was suggested that a lot of developers had a name for their development, and not much else. The Howard County project, however, had a lot of substance behind it and could afford to wait for a name."[29]

The search for a name continued. Wallace Hamilton, who was chronicling the planning process, made this observation in a June 17 entry. "There is some thought at the present time that, at the time of the presentation of the plan, the project will be called Howard New Town: and that, as the new town matures, the New Town will be dropped, and the name Howard retained as the final name. But since New York, New Haven, New Bedford and many other "New" east coast towns have been maturing for about three hundred years predictions are risky."

The one name that was never raised was anything that included "Rouse." Reston, a Virginia new town founded in April 1964 is named for its founder Robert E. Simon. It was just not in Jim Rouse's personality to want something named for him.

By late summer of 1964 the model of town center and adjacent villages was under construction and the script and marketing pieces were being prepared for a formal presentation of the plan scheduled for November. "The clock wound down to late October. The galleys for the presentation binders and the newspaper insert were being set. The press materials were moving into type in preparation for the grand unveiling of the new city. It had to have a name . . . Jim Rouse was informed that printing of all materials must go forward without delay. 'What about the name?' he asked. 'We have nothing new to offer' was the response. 'We've written in Columbia.' 'Then Columbia it is,' he directed. And so it was."[30]

Size, Color and Shape Matter!

Size, color and shape matter. Columbia street signs have been blue and uniquely sized—a rather stubby 24"x14" rectangle—since Columbia began. They were carefully designed, as was every aspect of the new town, and they immediately identified the streets within Columbia's "New Town Zoning." If a street was an "outparcel" that is, land that had not been acquired by the developer, not included in the zoning designation and not put under the Columbia Association assessment, the street sign was green as were other Howard County street signs. The Rouse Company designed the signs which were made by Shannon-Baum of Eldersburg, Maryland. The sign size was unique to the Baltimore area when it was first done for Columbia although it had been used in other locations. The typeface, side mount design and the wooden post were all new for their time. Shannon Baum came to call the design "Columbia style."

By the 1980s responsibility of sign making had been transferred to Howard County. The Rouse Company got out of the sign business and purchased a sign-making machine for the County. Over the years things began to change. Brown signs began popping up on signposts. In Columbia, as is the case in most new home building projects, the developer builds the roads. When the area is complete and residents start moving onto those roads they are dedicated to the County which is then responsible for maintaining them. There are exceptions, of course. Some roads can't be dedicated because they're too short, too narrow, or

New signs with larger lettering are replacing older signs to comply with federal standards. Metal poles are being used rather than wooden ones and signs are no longer printed on both sides. (2007) Photograph courtesy of William Santos.

Original Columbia street signs were mounted on square wooden poles with distinct mounting.

Metal poles that last longer began replacing wooden posts in the 1990s. Photograph courtesy of William Santos.

Original-style Columbia street sign mounted on metal pole.

they are actually part of a parking lot in a townhouse or condominium development. In that case they become private roads. Howard County decided that those roads needed to be identified as such so it began to change the blue signs on those streets to brown signs. Brown signs identify private roads throughout Howard County. However, you could still count on the size to identify the new town. That changed in 2004.

Mark DeLuca, Chief of Traffic Engineering at the Howard County Bureau of Highways, shed light on the changes. New federal guidelines for road signage have been mandated within the last several years prompted by the country's growing aging population. To comply, Howard County began conducting sign tests using different fonts and sizes to improve visibility and finally moved to a new standard sign—a 9-inch blade with 6 inch type. Columbia's distinctive signs are still the norm but they all will be phased out as old signs need to be replaced and as the County moves to full compliance with the standards by 2012.

But there are more changes in street signs. Green rectangular signs now mark intersections on Route 175. More confusing, perhaps, are the green street signs that appear in neighborhoods that are Columbia. Street signs in Snowden Overlook, the new section of Kendall Ridge in Long Reach are green. DeLuca explained that the roads in this community, which will be gated, are private and street signs were installed by the developer!

Do size and color and shape still matter? Not as much as they once did.

Street Names Can Be Fun

The literary and artistic works that inspire Columbia's street names have inspired many in Columbia to decorate, celebrate and write. Parade floats have capitalized on the theme, as have block parties.

Ralph Treitel, a long-time resident of Harper's Choice and founder, poet, and editor of the original *Little Patuxent Review* published from 1977-1980, had a little poetic fun adapting Longfellow's poem *The Arrow and the Song*.

> *I shot an arrow into the air:*
> *It sailed across the Columbia Fair*
> *And reached its zenith in the sky*
> *On the Longfellow Fourth of July!*

Phyllis Kepner, a long-time resident who wrote for the *Columbia Flier*, had a little fun herself when she was covenant advisor for Owen Brown and felt the need to vent her creative side. In 2002 she offered to write a Christmas poem for *The Observer*, the Owen Brown newsletter. Kepner remembers how the poem below was penned. "The list of street names was a heavily used tool as it was referenced almost daily when residents had questions or complaints. Reading over the list I just started writing using the street names. It came together quickly." It has become an Owen Brown tradition to reprint the poem in the December issue of *The Observer*.

An Owen Brown Holiday
The reindeer have no Elkhorns,
    and Dasher *isn't* Green,
But we still all will Hopewell
    For a perfect winter scene.
When Christmas comes to Owen Brown,
    we'll have A Giant *party,*
    And make the Cradlerock *until*
    Each Gentlefolk *feels hearty.*
With Banjo Court *and* Bugledrum,
    A Windharp's Gentle Way,
And Harpstring, Farbell *and* Windbell
    The Merry *songs we'll play.*
While Madrigals *hum* Robin Songs
    Along with Minstrels *merry,*
And Curtsey *low with green* Bendboughs
    All laden with red berries.
Fruitgifts *and* Candleshine *aglow*
    will fill the Lacelike *table*
    Garlands *of* Scarlet Petals
    will hang along the gable.
The Oaken Door *holds* Winter Roses
    On a Dewlit *wreath*
While Peace Chimes *ring*
As Younghearts *sing upon the steps*
    beneath.
A Deep Calm *lies upon the ground,*
A Snowman's *holding* Court,
    As each one raises a Deep Cup
    Of Fairmead *or of* Port.
This Homespun *holiday soon comes*
    To a Sleepsoft Gracious End
As Happy Hearts *meet* Rising Moons
    And Setting Stars *descend.*

Start a stamp collection

The Longfellow stamp is the 23rd issue in the U.S. Postal Service's Literary Arts Series. Faulkner, Hemingway, Fitzgerald and Nash are other literary figures whose works inspired Columbia street names and are part of the series. Through the years other postage stamps have been issued honoring literary figures and artists who are represented in Columbia. These include Twain, Whittier, Whitman, Riley, Audubon, Whistler and Jeffers. Try collecting stamps or first day covers of your favorite figure. Henry Longfellow Stamp Design ©2007 United States Postal Service. All Rights Reserved. Used with Permission.

Create a Decorating Theme

It all started with one photograph in 1987. Colette Roberts now has 85 swan pictures hanging in her home on Swan Point Way. Many are on this wall in what is sometimes referred to as the "Swan Room," aka the powder room. Roberts told Columbia Archives that most pictures are of local swans on Lake Elkhorn, including Patty who resided there for many years. But, "when you start collecting, friends and family tend to add to your collection. When they travel they bring me photos and other collectibles." In addition to the photos, Roberts counts more than 25 kitschy items including perfume bottles and soaps. Has she started a trend in Swan Point? Roberts said she gets quite a few comments from the neighbors and a few people have picked up on her idea. "No one has taken it quite as far as I have," she said.

A collection of frogs felt right at home at the Bush Family home on Treefrog Place.

Brigid Daly, of Raccoon Court, poses with a sampling of her raccoon collection.

Oh, you must live in Columbia! for people who win in the "best," "most creative," "most recognizable," etc. categories!

• Most of the street names in Macgill's Common are derived from American folk songs found in the body of work collected by Alan Lomax. Whether you live in Macgill's Common or not, why not throw a "Lomax Tune Party?" Listening to the songs may start your guests talking, or maybe even dancing or singing along! They may even develop an appreciation for that part of our American culture that Lomax sought to preserve.

• Stage a road rally! Send teams of two or four into Columbia equipped with a map and clues to different street names. (The order of the clues will be different for each team, but they will all eventually end up in the same place!) Finding each of the names and following each street eventually leads to a prize!

• Have a birthday party honoring your favorite poet or artist. Find out where he or she lived and other biographical information. Print out copies of some poems and have guests make up their own street names.

16

Navigating

Finding your way around Columbia without a map is possible—but not simple. It is much the same for *Oh, you must live in Columbia!* You can flip through the book, but to find the most direct route and make your ride more enjoyable, it is best to have a road map. This section covers the basic layout of the book, provides a key for the information found in the place name entries, and offers tips on how you can quickly get to the information you want to know.

The main part of the book is set up by villages and neighborhoods—much like Columbia itself. Each chapter covers one village, and the neighborhood listings divide the chapters into sections. Most street names appear under the neighborhood listings. Village community centers and main village thoroughfares are the exceptions. Since these features do not belong to any one neighborhood, they are listed directly under the village name preceding the neighborhood listings. If a street crosses village or neighborhood lines, it is listed in all relevant sections.

The book places the villages in alphabetical order, the neighborhoods in alphabetical order under each village, and the streets in alphabetical order under each neighborhood. That means the arm-chair traveler choosing the comprehensive tour of Columbia's place names will start with the Village of Dorsey's Search, moving on to the Village of Harper's Choice, and so on through the villages until reaching the Village of Wilde Lake (note: Town Center is placed

between River Hill and Wilde Lake). Since TRC was responsible for naming more than just the residential streets, the last chapter completes the tour with the names of Columbia's business and industrial centers and their streets.

To find your own street, or any street, you can turn directly to the village and neighborhood where it is located. If, for example, you know that Centre Stone Ring is in the Village of Hickory Ridge in the Hawthorn neighborhood, you can turn to it directly. Village identifiers are found at the bottom of each page to speed your search along.

If you cannot recall the neighborhood or the village, don't despair! There is an index in the back of the book listing every street and place name included in the book. Additional help can be found in the enhanced bibliography preceding the index. The bibliography is split into two sections—one for place names derived from literary and artistic works selected by TRC, and one for the general and historically based place names found in Columbia. In the literary and artistic section, the referenced sources list the titles of the poems, stories, folk songs, paintings, and etchings chosen by TRC with the corresponding street names that were derived from them. A location code is attached to each place name to identify where in Columbia it can be found. These features make the bibliography unique and hopefully helpful in answering questions like: how many streets are named from Whitman's poem "Song of Myself"? how many different Longfellow poems

---

Navigating Legend

[1] Most probably true

[2] A good educated guess

✱ Street existed before Columbia

A mystery . . .
   We really tried but we
   have no good clues

DEFINITIONS

Poets often use words that are not commonly used. Definitions of some of these words are highlighted.

were used? or how many different neighborhoods have street names derived from Sandburg's poems?

Understanding the Entries

Research to find the origin of place names began with memorandums, index cards, and other documents created by TRC and now in the Columbia Archives collection. Not all place names had complete citation information; some documents revealed only an author's or a painter's name, and some had nothing but the place name. Extensive research ensued to verify the origins for all Columbia place names. Place name entries with definitive origins appear in the text without any coding. This includes not only entries that had complete citations from TRC, but also those entries based on searches that resulted in only one possible origin. For some place names enough information was gleaned from documents and searches to render a most probable origin. These entries are followed by a [1] next to the place name. Other searches were inconclusive and the entries are based on primary source clues, some research, and a gut feeling. These entries are followed by a [2]. Place name entries that simply record "A mystery . . ." indicate that no good clues surfaced to identify the origin. Alternatively, some place name searches suggested several works could be the origin. Since no clues emerged identifying which one was the origin, all works are listed without coding. Perhaps the multiple listings will serve as starting points for future research into the precise origins. The coding system is a way for readers to assess how closely the information in the place name entries captures the intent of TRC people who chose the names.

The information gathered during the research process was arranged into a set format to present the findings as consistently as possible. At the minimum, the entries begin with information identifying the creator and the title of the work of origin behind the place name. For many literary-based names, an additional selection of verse, lyric or prose containing the place name phrase was included. The selection is italicized to indicate that it comes directly from the source, and all indentations, unusual spellings, and punctuations are retained. In cases where words were italicized in the original source, the entry selection has those words in Roman typeface. Often the exact wording of the entry only matches the exact source referenced (see bibliography for more). If other sources are used, titles, verse and/or prose may vary from the entry selection. Some place names are intentional variations by the "street namers" who played with the words in the works by using alternate spellings, reversing the word order, etc., to create a pleasing sound for the place name. The citation line is used to note variations from the exact verse, prose, or title of the work. If the place name is derived from the title of the work or a main character found in the work, a descriptive note often takes the place of a selection from the source.

TRC is The Rouse Company. To develop Columbia, TRC created a subsidiary called Howard Research and Development (HRD). TRC is used most often in the book. However, HRD is used where job titles or functions are exclusive to the subsidiary.

Examples of literature-based entries (key on right side column):

ENTRY:	Key:
Blue Barrow Ride	**Street Name (main entry)**
From Holmes poem *Spring Has Come:*	Source poet and poem cited (see bibliography)
The scarlet shell-fish click and clash	*Quote in exact format as the source cited, i.e.,*
In the blue barrow where they slide;	*indentations and punctuations as found.*
Larkspring Row	**Street Name (main entry)**
Variation of "lark has sprung" found in	Variation note and source poet and poem cited
Holmes poem *After a Lecture on Wordsworth:*	(see bibliography)
Up to the clouds the lark has sprung	*Quote in exact format as the source cited, i.e.,*
Still trilling as he flies;	*indentations and punctuations as found.*
Purple Twilight Way 1	**Street Name [accuracy code] (main entry)**
From Holmes poem *The Last Reader:*	Source poet and poem cited (see bibliography)
But spreading purple twilight still	*Quote in exact format as the source cited, i.e.,*
High over memory's shadowed hill.	*indentations and punctuations as found.*
Ram's Horn Row	**Street Name (main entry)**
The phrase "ram's horn" is found in two	Descriptive note indicating that the poet is
Holmes poems: *A Song for the Centennial*	known, but two poems were found with
Celebration of Harvard College, 1836, and *Two*	the phrase and no documents to indicate
Sonnets: Harvard 1. "Christo Et Ecclesiæ," 1700.	which one was **the** poem.
Tarkington Place	**Street Name (main entry)**
From Nash poem title *Tarkington, ThouShould'st*	Descriptive note indicating that phrase is part
Be Living in This Hour.	of title.
Brett Lane	**Street Name (main entry)**
Lady Brett Ashley is a main character in	Descriptive note indicating character name
Hemingway's *The Sun Also Rises.*	from novel is the basis of the street name.

> **ELLIPSES . . .**
>
> In the poetry selections, ellipses are used exclusively when the source work has additional text on the same line.

The artistic-based place names of Columbia usually came from artwork titles or variations of them. The visual nature of the source dictated the use of descriptive information on the artwork. Accuracy codes, variation notes and additional descriptive statements follow the same format as those in the literary-based entry key.

ENTRY:	KEY:
Green Dory Lane	**Street Name (main entry)**
From Homer painting *The Green Dory,*	Source artist and artwork cited,
watercolor on paper, 1880, Museum of Fine	medium used, date, owner (when known).
Arts, Boston, MA.	

TRC chose historic names, typically with local connections, to form some of Columbia's more prominent place names. Many of the village, neighborhood, community center, and even several street names can trace their origins to historic figures, historic homes, and original land grants. In general, the entries based on historic names are very descriptive reflecting the research involved in going beyond a name found on memoranda to the interesting facts behind the name. Most of these entries have endnotes documenting the sources used in conducting the research. Accuracy codes follow the same format as those in the literary-based entry key.

ENTRY:

Majors Lane 1

An early list of possible names for Long Reach had Major's Choice, an original land grant patented to Edward Dorsey in 1688, slated as a neighborhood name. Although the name was never used for that purpose, Majors Lane, a variation of the namesake, did find its way into Jeffers Hill.[72]

KEY:

Street Name [accuracy code] (main entry)
Descriptive note giving background on the historical name and some information on TRC's possible use of the name. Ends with endnote.

Several other types of entries appear in the book—those based on inventors, those named by builders and developers other than TRC, those that existed in Howard County before Columbia was developed and those that are from TRC but without any good clues to date on their origin. Most of these types follow a format similar to the historical entries, with some exceptions that are handled by coding (e.g., a road that was developed before Columbia and is signified by an ✸). The four sample entry types follow the four types mentioned.

ENTRY:

Albert Einstein Drive
Albert Einstein (1879-1955). Physicist whose work included quantum theory, theory of relativity, and the well-known equation relating mass and energy, $E = mc^2$. Einstein was awarded the 1921 Nobel Prize in Physics.[126]

KEY:

Street Name (main entry)
Inventor name (dob-dod). Descriptive note on what inventor is known for inventing. Ends with endnote.

El Camino 1
Named by the builder to create a Spanish theme for Capistrano Villas. The names of the model homes were Sonoma, Carmel, and the San Franciscan.

Street Name [accuracy code] (main entry)
Descriptive note on builder named theme.

Cedar Lane ✸
The onetime country road rolling between Routes 32 and 108 had Bassler family farms on either side and was lined with cedar trees that gave the road its name. The Rouse Company acquired 68 acres of land from Clarence Bassler in 1963, . . . name-inspiring cedar trees along Cedar Lane, particularly on the northern segment that connects to Rivendell.[38]

Street Name [preCol code] (main entry)
Descriptive note on background information on history of the road and any connection with TRC and the development of Columbia. Most end with an endnote.

Brentwood Lane
A mystery . . .

Street Name (main entry)
No good clues available at present to determine origin of name.

Now that you have your road map, sit back and plan your tour of the place names of Columbia, Maryland. We hope you enjoy the trip!

The name of the village is from an original land grant titled Dorsey's Search patented to John Dorsey in 1696 for 479 acres.[31]

Linden Hall   1

The name of the village community center is from the Holmes poem *Musa*:
Come while their balms the linden-
*   blossoms shed!—*
*   Come while the rose is red,—*
*   While blue-eyed Summer smiles*
On the green ripples round yon sunken piles.

Columbia Road/Columbia Pike   ✱

On January 6, 1810, Maryland's General Assembly passed "an act to incorporate a Company to make a Turnpike Road from near Ellicott's lower Mills towards George-Town, in the District of Columbia." It would be several years before construction was completed on the Columbia Turnpike Road, the commonly used name derived from the southern terminus, the District of Columbia. During the early part of the 20th century, advances in railroad lines and the inception of the State Highway Commission were making companies like The Columbia Turnpike Road Company obsolete. Over the years, the State assumed maintenance of the road, the turnpike apparatus was removed, and the name became Columbia Road—although some still refer to it as Columbia Pike, a remnant of its historical past.[32]

Dorsey Hall

The 18th century home known as Dorsey Hall is the origin of the neighborhood name, preserving the name of the prominent Howard County Dorsey family in the new town of Columbia. Built on land granted to the Honorable John Dorsey in 1695, the house remained in the Dorsey family until the 20th century. In the late 1960s, The Rouse Company purchased the house as part of the larger tract that became the neighborhood. The Rouse Company did some renovation work but for many years it was vacant. Developers Richard Talkin and Donald Reuwer purchased the house in 2000 and restored it, incorporating it into the development of a small office complex. Dorsey Hall was listed on the National Register of Historic Homes in 2001.[33]

Dorsey Hall in 1980. In 2001 it was showcased as the Historic Ellicott City Decorator Show House and afterward became the centerpiece of an office complex. It is located at 5100 Dorsey Hall Drive. Courtesy of University of Maryland Libraries.

The street names in Dorsey Hall are derived primarily from the work of Oliver Wendell Holmes, 19th century author and poet.

Alpine Rose Bend
From Holmes poem *A Song of Other Days:*
As o'er the glacier's frozen sheet
  Breathes soft the Alpine rose,
So through life's desert springing sweet
  The flower of friendship grows;

Blue Barrow Ride
From Holmes poem *Spring Has Come:*
The scarlet shell-fish click and clash
  In the blue barrow where they slide;

Brentwood Lane
A mystery . . .

Bright Bay Way
From Holmes poem *A Rhymed Lesson (Urania):*
Turned to soar upwards, when his glance
  revealed
A calm, bright bay enclosed in rocky bounds,
And at its entrance stood three sister
  mounds.

Dorsey Hall neighborhood sign, 2007.

Bright Rocket Way
From Holmes poem *An After-Dinner Poem (Terpsichore):*
Small room for Fancy's many-chorded lyre,
For Wit's bright rockets with their trains of
  fire,

Broken Lute Way
From Holmes poem *Variations on an Aria:*
The broken lute, the harp unstrung,—
  We listen and we look for these.

Chariot's Flight Way
From Holmes poem *Les Bohémiens:*
Love, without his torch, at night,
Binds us to his chariot's flight.

Coattail Court
From Holmes poem *A Song for the Centennial Celebration of Harvard College, 1836:*
And when at length the College rose,
  The sachem cocked his eye
At every tutor's meagre ribs
  Whose coat-tails whistled by:

Dancing Sunbeam
Variation of "sunbeam dancing" found in Holmes poem *Vestigia Quinque Retrorsum:*
Whose smile is that? Its pattern Nature gave,
A sunbeam dancing in a dimpled wave;

Dorsey Hall Drive
See neighborhood name.

Eagles Wing Court
From Holmes poem *Song at the Hunt:*
Our hearts, without the "Eagles Wing"
  Have flown across the waters

Firefly Way
From Holmes poem *Penitentia:*
By all the firefly sparks that fill
The twilight groves of Shady hill,—
(Faint emblems of the gleams that flit
And sparkle through a woman's wit,)

Fragile Sail Way

From Holmes poem *A Modest Request,
Complied with After the Dinner at
President Everett's Inauguration:*
*While at his feet the hoarse and blinding gale
Strews the torn wreck and bursts the
   fragile sail,*

Gray Rock Drive ✳

Long before the debate on whether Gray
Rock Drive would run uninterrupted
from Frederick Road to Columbia Road,
an historic house and farm covering
almost 400 acres of land came to be
known as Gray Rock [or Grey Rock].
Well-known Howard County families
lived and worked on the property over
the years, including Dorseys, Pues,
Mackubins, Herberts, Sloatfields, and
Millers. In the late 1970s the Millers
started planning a residential development on the old farm land. At first, Gray
Rock Drive lay in two segments, one running south from Frederick Road through
Gray Rock Farm, and one running north
through the Dorsey Hall neighborhood,
with about 1,000 feet of land in-between.
The segments were connected by 1994,
but still laid impassable by a blockade of
cement barricades. The barricades came
down in 1996.[34]

Hallowed Stream

From Holmes poem *To Julia Ward Howe:*
*Hold out thy hand! these scanty drops
Come from a hallowed stream,
Its sands, a poet's crumbling hopes,
Its mist, his fading dream.*

Hemlock Cone Way

From Holmes poem *The New Eden:*
*   Look where the laboring orchard groans,
And yields its beryl-threaded strings
   For chestnut burs and hemlock cones.*

*Gray Rock in May 1977. The
house is located on Angus
Valley Trail in Ellicott City.*
Photo on file at Maryland Historical
Trust Library.

Henhawk Court

From Holmes poem *After a Lecture on
Wordsworth:*
*Above, the hen-hawk swims and swoops,
   Flung from the bright, blue sky;
Below, the robin hops, and whoops
   His piercing Indian cry.*

Huckleberry Row ☐1

From Holmes poem *The Last Survivor:*
*Will it be a rich old merchant in a square-tied
   white cravat,
Or selectman of a village in a pre-historic hat?
Will his dwelling be a mansion in a marble-
   fronted row,
Or a homestead by a hillside where the
   huckleberries grow?*

Kingscup Court

Variation of "kingcups" found in Holmes
poem *After a Lecture on Wordsworth:*
*And daisies strew the banks along,
   And yellow kingcups shine,
With cowslips, and a primrose throng,
   And humble celandine.*

Larkspring Row

Variation of "lark has sprung" found in
Holmes poem *After a Lecture on
Wordsworth:*
*Up to the clouds the lark has sprung,
   Still trilling as he flies;*

Kingcups—Any of
various common
buttercups.

Dorsey Hall was a late addition to the Columbia map. The original land purchases for Columbia, and the New Town Zoning that guided its development, were concluded by 1965. The purchase of the 685 acres that became Dorsey Hall transpired in 1968. When Howard Research and Development (HRD) presented plans for the mixed use development of the property as part of the New Town Zoning district it met with some opposition from neighboring residential communities. During a several year process that included meetings with neighbors, HRD revised the plan, resulting in fewer housing units, larger lots and more open space.

Initial research for naming the streets in this new development led to a completely new theme that included breeds of cattle, horses and sheep. In a 1973 memo "name lady" Kay Sarfaty wrote "I went to this source as this is a bucolic county and I am sure that your intention in this area is to keep a countrified atmosphere." Dorsey Hall, with its predominance of single family homes and larger lot sizes, did preserve a more "countrified atmosphere" but did it without the help of farm animal street names.

Learned Sage
From Holmes poem *Les Bohémiens*:
Thine eye can never stir again,
*   Learned sage*
*   Of slenderest gauge,—*
Thine eye can never stir again
From thy old steeple's rusty vane.

Leyden Way
From Holmes poem title *Robinson of Leyden.* John Robinson of Leyden was an English Puritan pastor who fled with his congregation to the Netherlands, eventually settling in Leiden (or Leyden) in 1609. In 1620, part of his congregation left for America on the Mayflower. He is referred to in the poem as "the pastor."

Lilac Lane
From Holmes poem *Poetry: A Metrical Essay*:
Still following onward as the months unclose
The balmy lilac or the bridal rose;
And still shall follow, till they sink once more
Beneath the snow-drifts of the foreign shore,

Manorhill Lane
A mystery . . .

Maydew Mews Way
Variation of "Maydew" found in Holmes poem *Spring Has Come*:
The windows blush with fresh bouquets,
*   Cut with their Maydew on the lips;*

Morning Ride Court
From Holmes poem *Spring Has Come*:
The horseman, proud of streak and splash,
*   Creeps homeward from his morning ride.*

Mustering Drum
From Holmes poem *Lexington*:
As through the storm-clouds the thunder-
*   burst rolling,*
*   Circles the beat of the mustering drum.*

Oakview Court
A mystery . . .

Old Annapolis Road ✳
On the 1860 Martenet map this road is named "Road from Carroll's Manor to Annapolis City." "Carroll's Manor" refers to Doughoregan Manor, the home of Charles Carroll of Carrollton (1737-1832), a signer of the Declaration of Independence. Carroll's social and business life, particularly when he served as a Maryland Senator from 1777-1800 and Senate President from 1782-1783, required regular travel to Annapolis. Over time the road became known as Old Annapolis Road. Incidentally, Charles Carroll of Carrollton holds the distinction of having been the last living signer of the Declaration of Independence. Doughoregan Manor continues to be held by Carroll descendants.[35]

Old Dragon Path
Variation of "old dragoons" found in Holmes poem *An After-Dinner Poem (Terpsichore)*:
Poems that shuffle with superfluous legs
A blindfold minuet over addled eggs,
Where all the syllables that end in èd,
Like old dragoons, have cuts across the head;

Oxbow Court
From Holmes poem *After a Lecture on Wordsworth*:
With ox-bow curve and sinuous twist
*   It writhes to reach the Sound.*

Dragoon—A mounted infantryman of the 17th and 18th centuries, especially one armed with a carbine.

Purple Twilight Way $\boxed{1}$
From Holmes poem *The Last Reader*:
But spreading purple twilight still
High over memory's shadowed hill.

Ram's Horn Row
The phrase "ram's horn" is found in two
Holmes poems: *A Song for the Centennial*
Celebration of Harvard College, 1836 and
Two Sonnets: Harvard. 1. "Christo Et
Ecclesiæ," 1700.

Red Bandana Way
Variation of "red bandanna" found in
Holmes poem *A Rhymed Lesson (Urania)*:
I know full well what alderman has tied
His red bandanna tight about his side;

Scarlet Sage Court
From Holmes poem *Programme*:
From the June of long ago,
When the rose was full in blow,

Till the scarlet sage has come
And the cold chrysanthemum.

Seabird Way
From Holmes poem *A Rhymed Lesson*
(Urania):
When through thy shrouds the wild tornado
*   sings,*
And thy poor sea-bird folds her tattered
*   wings, —*
Oft will delusion o'er thy senses steal,

Smokey Wreath Way
Variation of "smoky wreath" found in
Holmes poem *The Steamboat*:
And many a foresail, scooped and strained,
*   Shall break from yard and stay,*
Before this smoky wreath has stained
*   The rising mist of day.*

Snowdrop Court
From Holmes poem *Spring Has Come*:
And first the snowdrop's bells are seen,
*   Then close against the sheltering wall*
The tulip's horn of dusky green,
*   The peony's dark unfolding ball.*

Somerset Lane
A mystery . . .

Speedwell Court
From Holmes poem *Robinson of Leyden*:
Before the Speedwell's anchor swung,
*   Ere yet the Mayflower's sail was spread,*
While round his feet the Pilgrims clung,
*   The pastor spake, and thus he said: —*

"Men, brethren, sisters, children dear!
*   God calls you hence from over sea;"*

Starwreath Way
Variation of "wreath of stars" found in
Holmes poem *The Last Survivor*:
He? Who? No voice may whisper what
*   wrinkled brow shall claim*
The wreath of stars that circles our last
*   survivor's name.*

Sunlit Passage
From Holmes poem *My Aviary*:
One glimpse of day, then black annihilation,—
*   A sunlit passage to a sunless shore?*

Sweet Bell Court
From Holmes poem *A Rhymed Lesson*
(Urania):
Hark! The sweet bells renew their welcome
*   sound:*
As one by one awakes each silent tongue,
It tells the turret whence its voice is flung.

Twilight Grove Court
From Holmes poem *Penitentia*:
By all the firefly sparks that fill
The twilight groves of Shady hill,—
(Faint emblems of the gleams that flit
And sparkle through a woman's wit,)

Ogden Nash, master of humorous poems and limericks, lived in The Village of Cross Keys in Baltimore, MD, a Rouse Company-built community that was a precursor to Columbia. Nash had been living in Cross Keys for four years when he penned a letter to James Rouse complaining about the deplorable television reception he had because covenants restricted roof antennae. "The frustration this causes is growing into fury," wrote Nash. This not so furious sounding verse ran in the community newsletter about a year later. It's not clear whether or not Nash's reception improved.

"My viewing has a restricted view:
Channels 13, 11, 2.
I hope that some day ere my burial
I'll be allowed a roof aerial."[36]

White Star Way
From Holmes poem *From an After-Dinner Speech:*
So let the heavenly splendors
Of truth's white star be found
Still shining fairest in us
While dark is all around!

Wild Filly Court
From Holmes poem *Spring Has Come:*
Wild filly from the mountain-side,
Doomed to the close and chafing thills,
Lend me thy long, untiring stride
To seek with thee thy western hills!

Wildwood Way
From Holmes poem *After a Lecture on Wordsworth:*
Our children know each wildwood smell,
The bayberry and the fern,
The man who does not know them well
Is all too old to learn.

Willow Bend
From Holmes poem *The Last Survivor:*
The willow bends unbroken when angry
tempests blow,
The stately oak is levelled and all its
strength laid low;

Willowgrove Drive
A mystery . . .

Thill—planks or thin stratum of fireclay.

Gail Holliday and the Columbia Neighborhood Posters

In 1967, as construction crews worked feverishly to ready Columbia for its first visitors and residents, a young graduate of California's Immaculate Heart College Art program and student of noted artist Sister Mary Corita, came to work for The Rouse Company. Soon brightly colored primitive style silk-screened posters began to appear. At first they were generic, The New City or wordless designs portraying cars and busses, houses and children. Soon there was special focus—a poster for every neighborhood. The posters became ubiquitous as neighborhoods grew and each one got Holliday's personal expression. Poster trees, hand-painted by Holliday, were erected in front of the Columbia Exhibit Center. The posters furthered the plan to create a sense of community and place within each neighborhood.

Holliday thrived in Columbia. She has said that Jim Rouse allowed her to grow by giving her the freedom to work independently. With minimal supervision she was asked to create the artistic expression of Columbia's goals. She was young and eager and inspired by the Columbia dream.

In 2007, in celebration of Columbia's 40th birthday, Holliday worked with General Growth Properties to reproduce some of the original neighborhood posters. With her permission these posters are reprinted here, sprinkled within their corresponding chapters.

Fairway Hills

The fairways of Allview Golf Course inspired the name of the neighborhood. Allview Golf Course opened as a public course in 1932. It was purchased by The Rouse Company in 1964 during the initial land acquisition phase and the operation continued under the management of the Columbia Association until 1985 when the construction of the interchange at Route 29 and Route 108 took some of the Allview Golf Course property and the course closed. By 1986 the soon to be built neighborhood was named Fairway Hills. A reconfigured, renovated and renamed golf course, Fairway Hills Golf Club, owned and operated by Columbia Association, opened in 1995.

The street names in Fairway Hills are derived from the work of Ogden Nash, a 20th century American poet.

April Journey [1]
"April" is found in several Nash poems, including one that alludes to a journey, *Drive Slow, Man Chortling, Or April 1941.*

Butler Court
From Nash poem *It's Snug to be Smug:*
*. . . but sometimes I wish I had the courage of
    a lion,*
*And then I could look life in the eye with a
    will of iron,*
*and to a goose, or a burglar, or even a butler,
    I wouldn't hesitate to say Boo!*

Chase Lions Way
From Nash poem *The Tale of Custard the Dragon:*

Belinda is as brave as a barrel full of bears,
*And Ink and Blink chase lions down the
    stairs,*
Mustard is as brave as a tiger in a rage,
But Custard keeps crying for a nice safe cage.

Tarkington Place
From Nash poem title *Tarkington, Thou Should'st Be Living in This Hour.*

LEFT
Fairway Hills neighborhood sign, 2007.

BELOW
The old fairways of Allview Golf Course inspired the neighborhood name.
Photo circa 1985.

From The Evening Sun, August 26, 1988. Courtesy of the Baltimore Sun Company, Inc. All Rights Reserved.

Harper's Choice is named for R. G. Harper Carroll, a Howard County farmer with ancestral lines to Charles Carroll of Carrollton, signer of the Declaration of Independence. The Rouse Company purchased portions of his family farm, Jericho, in several land transactions between 1962 and 1964. Harper died in December 1962 and it was the family's desire to have Harper's name included in some way in the new town. Rouse responded that they would "find an appropriate place to identify in Harper's memory."[37]

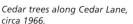

Cedar trees along Cedar Lane, circa 1966.

Cedar Lane ✱

The onetime country road rolling between Routes 32 and 108 had Bassler family farms on either side and was lined with cedar trees that gave the road its name. The Rouse Company acquired 68 acres of land from Clarence Bassler in 1963, followed by almost 140 acres from George Bassler in 1964. Part of the Basslers' land was developed into Harper's Choice Village Center. Shortly after the village center was completed, Cedar Lane was bisected in order to divert the heavier traffic flow to Harpers Farm Road which was designed for that purpose. Today, it is still possible to see some of the name-inspiring cedar trees along Cedar Lane, particularly on the northern segment that connects to Rivendell.[38]

Harper's Farm Road

Named to honor Harper Carroll, who with his wife, Muriel, sold a portion of their area farm to The Rouse Company. See village name.

Kahler Hall

The village community center is named for William C. Kahler. His widow, Katie Mae Kahler, was among the first group of area farmers to sell property to The Rouse Company beginning with a partial sale in November 1962, and subsequently selling almost 280 acres. Her property was located west of Cedar Lane and became the neighborhood of Swansfield. It was her wish that a street be named for her husband who passed away in the 1950s. While a street name did not fit the naming system, it was important to The Rouse Company to comply with Katie's

KAHLER HALL

NAMED IN HONOR OF

WILLIAM CHARLES KAHLER

A LIFELONG HOWARD COUNTY RESIDENT
WHO FARMED THE LAND ON WHICH
THIS BUILDING NOW STANDS

DEDICATED FEBRUARY, 1971

Plaque explaining the naming of Kahler Hall is inside the community center building near the courtyard entrance.

March 22, 1966

Dear Muriel:

Humiliation!

Your nice letter of February 19 became attached to a paper in my file, and thus has gone unanswered --- please forgive me.

Of course we will not name the Golf Course "Jericho" and I can well understand your desire that we not do so. Also, we will consider it an opportunity to find an appropriate place to identify in Harper's memory.

I have asked Scott Ditch to send you a copy of the plat as it now stands, indicating a first go-round, beginning an initial effort at a naming system for the golf course area. We will be glad to have your comments and criticism.

We are deeply grateful for your co-operation and friendly interest in Columbia. Please drop me a line whenever you have an idea, a question, or a complaint.

Best wishes.

Sincerely,

James W. Rouse

Mrs. R. G. H. Carroll, II
"Jericho" -- R.F.D. 4
Ellicott City, Maryland

:jw

Humiliation!

One of the first facilities built and needing a name was the golf course in Harper's Choice. In January 1966, Bill Finley happily told Jim Rouse that Scott Ditch had produced names for the first village and several other main streets and amenities. He reported that Ditch proposed to name the first golf course Club Jericho after Muriel Carroll's farm to the north. Soon after, the Baltimore Evening Sun *printed that information. Upon reading the article, Muriel Carroll wrote to Rouse politely requesting that they not use Jericho as it was her personal address. Rouse was happy to comply and sent her this letter.*[41]

Lightfoot Path

From Tolkien book *The Return of the King: And afterwards when all was over men returned and made a fire there and burned the carcase of the beast; but for Snowmane they dug a grave and set up a stone upon which was carved in the tongues of Gondor and the Mark:*

Faithful servant yet master's bane, Lightfoot's foal, swift Snowmane.

Manorstone Lane

Manorstone appeared on a list of potential street names for large lots in Dorsey Hall in February 1986. At the time, Douglas McGregor, an HRD senior vice president, requested that the name be reserved for the estate area of Hobbit's Glen North. In April 1993 that area, renamed Forest Glen, was being developed and Manorstone Gate topped the lists of both Dave Forester, HRD development director, and McGregor. As Forester stated, "Manorstone would reflect both the opulent houses in Forest Glen and the stone entrance and stone work on the road culverts crossing two streams within the property." By the time the street name was official, Gate was dropped and the approved name was Manorstone Lane.[42]

Northern Fences Lane

From Tolkien book *The Fellowship of the Ring:*
"I have returned from the Northern Fences," said the Elf, *"and I am sent now to be your guide again."*

Oakenshield Circle

Thorin Oakenshield, a dwarf, is a main character in *The Hobbit,* and is mentioned briefly in Tolkien book *The Fellowship of the Ring:*
As is told in The Hobbit, *there came one day to Bilbo's door the great Wizard, Gandalf the Grey, and thirteen dwarves with him: none*

other, indeed, than Thorin Oakenshield, descendent of kings, and his twelve companions in exile.

Proud Foot Place
From Tolkien book *The Return of the King*, under "Family Trees, Baggins of Hobbiton," which lists Hobbit family name, Proudfoot, starting with Bodo Proudfoot. The family name is mentioned several times, as well, at Bilbo's farewell party in Tolkien book *The Fellowship of the Ring*, such as the listing of attendees:
> . . . and a selection of Burrowses, Bolgers, Bracegirdles, Brockhouses, Goodbodies, Hornblowers and Proudfoots.

Ravenhill Row   1
Place name for an area on the southern ridge of Lonely Mountain, where the dragon, Smaug, lived as found in Tolkien book *The Hobbit*:
> They made their first camp on the western side of the great southern spur, which ended in a height called Ravenhill.

Ridermark Row
Variation of "Riddermark" found in Tolkien book *The Fellowship of the Ring*:
> "And I was glad, for in the Riddermark of Rohan the Rohirrim, the Horse-lords, dwell, and there are no horses like those that are bred in that great vale between the Misty Mountains and the White."

Rivendell
Place name where the elf, Elrond, lives, as found in Tolkien book *The Hobbit*:
> They asked him where he was making for, and he answered: "You are come to the very edge of the Wild, as some of you may know. Hidden somewhere ahead of us is the fair valley of Rivendell where Elrond lives in the Last Homely House."

In the trilogy, this is the place where the fellowship of the ring is formed.

Rushlight Path
From Tolkien book *The Fellowship of the Ring*:
> The Men of Bree seemed all to have rather botanical (and to the Shire-folk rather odd) names, like Rushlight, Goatleaf, Heathertoes, Appledore, Thistlewool and Ferny (not to mention Butterbur).

Shadowmere Mews
Mentioned in Bilbo's "Song of Eärendil" found in Tolkien book *The Fellowship of the Ring*:
> beneath the Hill of Ilmarin
> a-glimmer in a valley sheer
> the lamplit towers of Tirion
> are mirrored on the Shadowmere.

Silver Tree Place
From Tolkien book *The Two Towers*:
> Gondor! Gondor, between the Mountains
>   and the Sea!
> West Wind blew there; the light upon the
>   Silver Tree
> Fell like bright rain in gardens of the Kings
>   of old.

Southern Star Terrace
From Tolkien book *The Fellowship of the Ring*:
> ". . . all accounts agree that Tobold Hornblower of Longbottom in the Southfarthing first grew the true pipe-weed in his gardens in the days of Isengrim the Second, about the year 1070 of Shire-reckoning. The best home-grown still comes from that district, especially the varieties now known as Longbottom Leaf, Old Toby, and Southern Star."

Straight Star Place   1
Variation of "Straight Stair" found in Tolkien book *The Two Towers*:
> "Yes, yess, longer," said Gollum. "But not so difficult. Hobbits have climbed the Straight Stair. Next comes the Winding Stair."

After rejection of Jericho as the name for Columbia's first golf course Evelyn Menzies submitted a list of other possibilities including Hobbit's Glen, Spring Pools, Indian Cabins, Good Hours, Ash Lawn and Glimmerglass. When asked to explain the meanings she included the commonly used Tolkien description of a hobbit that appears in many additions of the book. Hobbits are "little people who love peace and quiet and good tilled earth. They like to laugh, eat six meals a day and drink. They like good times, bright clothes, but they never like to hurry." Explaining the other choices illustrates the various themes being explored for names. *Spring Pools* and *Good Hours* are poems by Robert Frost that got used as street names in Running Brook; Indian Cabins comes from directions in the survey of Doughoregan Manor; Ashlawn was the former home of President James Monroe; and Glimmerglass was the name of a lake in *The Leatherstocking Tales* by James Fennimore Cooper.[43]

Longfellow neighborhood sign, 2007.

OPPOSITE PAGE:
TOP-RIGHT—
The Round Tower in Newport Rhode Island, 2007. Photograph by Aime Clinkenbeard.

BOTTOM
The Longfellow Fourth of July Parade began in 1971. Street names have been a source of pride and inspiration for both participants and those who line the parade route. The Wreck of the Hesperus sailed in the parade in 1972.

Gerfalcon—Any of the large varieties of falcons of the Arctic, Asia and America, a gerfalcon is also known as a German hunting bird.

Fallriver Row Court
A partially armored skeleton discovered in Fall River, Massachusetts, in 1835, inspired Longfellow's poem, *The Skeleton in Armor.*

Gerfalcon Road
From Longfellow poem *The Skeleton in Armor:*
"Far in the Northern Land,
By the wild Baltic's strand,
I, with my childish hand,
    Tamed the gerfalcon;"

Harvest Moon Lane
From Longfellow poem *Autumn:*
Thy shield is the red harvest moon,
    suspended
    So long beneath the heaven's
        o'erhanging eaves;

Hesperus Drive
From Longfellow poem title *The Wreck of the Hesperus,* and found twice in verse, the first being:
It was the schooner Hesperus,
    That sailed the wintry sea;
And the skipper had taken his little daughter,
    To bear him company.

Hildebrand Court
Found twice in Longfellow poem *The Skeleton in Armor,* the first being:

When of old Hildebrand
I asked his daughter's hand,
Mute did the minstrels stand
    To hear my story.

Iron Pen Place
From Longfellow poem title *The Iron Pen.*

Killingworth Way
From Longfellow poem title *The Poet's Tale: The Birds of Killingworth,* and found three times in verse, the first being:
Thus came the jocund Spring in Killingworth,
    In fabulous days, some hundred years ago;

Light House Court
From Longfellow poem *The Lighthouse:*
The rocky ledge runs far into the sea,
    And on its outer point, some miles away,
The Lighthouse lifts its massive masonry,
    A pillar of fire by night, of cloud by day.

Mad River Lane
From Longfellow poem *Mad River:*
Why dost thou wildly rush and roar,
    Mad River, O Mad River?
Wilt thou not pause and cease to pour
Thy hurrying, headlong waters o'er
    This rocky shelf forever?

Mystic Court
From Longfellow poem *The Landlord's Tale: Paul Revere's Ride:*
And beneath him, tranquil and broad
    and deep,
Is the Mystic, meeting the ocean tides;

Open Window
From Longfellow poem title *The Open Window.*

Paul Revere Ride
From Longfellow poem title *The Landlord's Tale: Paul Revere's Ride,* and found four times in verse, the first being:
Listen, my children, and you shall hear
Of the midnight ride of Paul Revere,

Phantom Court

From Longfellow poem title *The Phantom Ship.*

Rondel Place

From Longfellow poem title *Rondel.* [written in French by Jean Froissart, translated by Longfellow]

Round Tower Place

In the Longfellow poem *The Skeleton in Armor*, "lofty tower" refers to the Round Tower in Newport, Rhode Island:
"There for my lady's bower
Built I the lofty tower,
Which, to this very hour,
Stands looking seaward."

Summer Day Lane

From Longfellow poem *A Summer Day by the Sea:*
O summer day beside the joyous sea!
O summer day so wonderful and white,
So full of gladness and so full of pain!

Three Kings Lane

From Longfellow poem title *The Three Kings,* and found three times in verse, the first being:
Three Kings came riding from far away,
Melchior and Gaspar and Baltasar;

Three Wise Men out of the East were they,
And they travelled by night and they slept
by day,
For their guide was a beautiful,
wonderful star.

Windmill Lane [1]

The Round Tower, a setting in the Longfellow poem *The Skeleton in Armor*, is believed by some to have been a windmill at one time.

Five Longfellow neighborhood streets are derived from the *The Skeleton in Armor,* a poem first composed in 1840: Fallriver Row Court, Gerfalcon Road, Hildebrand Court, Round Tower Place, and Windmill Lane.

The poem was inspired by two separate, yet believed by Longfellow to be connected, elements—the 1835 discovery of a skeleton in Fall River, Massachusetts, and the Round Tower, sometimes called the Old Wind-Mill, of Newport, Rhode Island. The skeleton and the tower both continue to be surrounded by mystery and a number of theories abound. But Longfellow wrote assuredly of the story in his journal. "This skeleton in armor really exists. It was dug up near Fall River, where I saw it some two years ago (when returning from Newport). I suppose it to be the remains of one of the old Northern sea-rovers, who came to this country in the tenth century. Of course I make the tradition myself; and I think I have succeeded in giving the whole a Northern air."[44]

Swansfield neighborhood sign, 2007.

Swansfield

The neighborhood name is drawn from the painting by James Abbott Whistler titled *"The Swan," Chelsea*, etching on paper, 1872, Smithsonian Institution, Freer Gallery of Art and The Hunterian Museum and Art Gallery, University of Glasgow.

The street names in Swansfield are drawn primarily from the titles of the works by Whistler, a 19th century painter and etcher, and Winslow Homer, a 19th century artist.

Battersea Lane
The old wooden Battersea Bridge in London was the subject of several Whistler etchings and paintings, for example: *Brown and Silver: Old Battersea Bridge*, oil on canvas, 1859-1863, Addison Gallery of American Art, Andover, MA.

Beaverkill Road ☐1
The street is named for an early American covered bridge that is likely to be the one located in Beaverkill State Park, Lewbeach, New York. The bridge was built in 1865 by John Davidson and spans 98 feet.[45]

Berrypick Lane
From two Homer paintings:
The Berry Pickers, watercolor and gouache over graphite, 1873, private collection.
The Berrypicker, watercolor, 1879, Hirschl & Adler Galleries, NY.

Billingsgate Row
From Whistler etching *Billingsgate,* 1859, The British Museum, UK, and Smithsonian Institution, Freer Gallery of Art.

Bishops Head Court
A mystery . . .

Bushwood Way
A mystery . . .

Eight Bells Lane
From Homer painting *Eight Bells,* oil on canvas, 1886, Addison Gallery of American Art, Andover, MA.

El Camino ☐1
Named by the builder to create a Spanish theme for Capistrano Villas. The names of the model homes were Sonoma, Carmel, and the San Franciscan.

Freshaire Lane
From Homer painting *Fresh Air,* watercolor over charcoal, 1878, The Brooklyn Museum, Brooklyn, NY.

Gloucester Road
From Homer painting *A Gloucester Farm,* oil on canvas, 1874, Philadelphia Museum of Art, Philadelphia, PA. This was an erroneous title for the painting, *A Temperance Meeting*, which also temporarily had the title of *Noon Time.*

Grand Banks Road
From Homer painting *Lost on the Grand Banks,* oil on canvas, 1885-1886, private collection.

Green Dory Lane
From Homer painting *The Green Dory*, watercolor on paper, 1880, Museum of Fine Arts, Boston, MA.

Gulf Stream Row
From two Homer paintings:
The Gulf Stream, oil on canvas, 1899, The Metropolitan Museum of Art, NY.
The Gulfstream, watercolor, 1889, The Art Institute of Chicago, Chicago, IL.

Harvest Scene
From Homer painting *Harvest Scene*, oil on canvas, ca.1873, The Metropolitan Museum of Art, NY.

Henley Court
A mystery . . .

High Tide Court
The periodical, *Every Saturday*, printed Homer's *High Tide*, which was a wood engraving of his painting *Eagle Head, Manchester, Massachusetts*, oil on canvas, 1870, The Metropolitan Museum of Art, NY. This often led to the Homer oil painting being misnamed *High Tide*.

Iron Crown Court
From Homer painting *Wreck of the Iron Crown*, watercolor on paper, 1881, private collection on extended loan to The Baltimore Museum of Art, Baltimore, MD.

Millbank Row
From Whistler etching *Millbank*, 1861, Smithsonian Institution, Freer Gallery of Art and The Hunterian Museum and Art Gallery, Glasgow.

Morning Glory Court
From two Homer paintings:
Morning Glories, oil on canvas, 1873, private collection.
Morning Glories, watercolor, 1873, private collection.

Neighborhood poster by Gail Holliday.

Old Tucker Row
The street is named for an early American covered bridge.[46]

Rock Coast Road
From Homer painting *Rocky Coast (Maine Coast)*, oil on canvas, ca. 1882-1900, Wadsworth Atheneum, Hartford, CT.

Rum Cay Court
From Homer painting *Rum Cay*, watercolor over graphite on off-white wove paper, 1898-1899, Worcester Art Museum, Worcester, MA.

Settler Place
From Homer painting *Old Settlers*, watercolor on paper, ca.1892, Museum of Fine Arts, Boston, MA.

Swansfield Road
See neighborhood name.

From The Howard Sun, February 2, 1990.
Courtesy of the Baltimore Sun Company, Inc.
All Rights Reserved.

The Bridle Path
From Homer painting *The Bridle Path, White Mountains,* oil on canvas, 1868, Sterling and Francine Clark Art Institute, Williamstown, MA.

Turnabout Lane
A mystery . . .

Two Ships Court
From Whistler etching *The Two Ships,* 1875.

Wineglass Court
From Whistler etching *The Wine-Glass,* 1858, Smithsonian Institution, Freer Gallery of Art and The Hunterian Museum and Art Gallery, Glasgow.

Woodcutter Way
From Homer painting *The Woodcutter,* watercolor on paper, 1891, private collection.

Woodenhawk Circle
A mystery . . .

Youngtree Court
From Whistler etching *The Young Tree,* ca.1886-1887, The Hunterian Museum and Art Gallery, Glasgow.

Hickory Ridge was an original land grant patented to Greenberry Ridgely and Richard Davis on September 17, 1753. As was the case for several village and neighborhood names that were drawn from the land grant map, the location of the original tract does not match the location of the namesake. The original tract was located near the intersection of Routes 108 and 216. The historic home of the same name is still standing on Highland Road.[47]

The Hawthorn Center
The village community center name comes from the Hawthorn neighborhood name.

Caravan Court
From Twain book *Tom Sawyer Abroad* in chapter title, *It's a Caravan,* and found several times in text, the first being:
"But they're camels, just the same. It's a caravan, that's what it is, and it's a mile long."

Charter Drive
A mystery . . .

Hickory Ridge Road
See village name.

Little Patuxent Parkway
Named for the Little Patuxent River that runs through Columbia.

Hickory Ridge, an historic home in private ownership, is located on Highland Road in Fulton. Photograph 1973. Courtesy of University of Maryland Libraries.

Clary's Forest

The neighborhood name is a variation of Clary's Forrest, an original land grant patented to John Clary in 1734 for 100 acres.[48]

The street names in Clary's Forest are derived primarily from the work of William Carlos Williams, a 20th century American poet.

Avalanche Way
Named by Sierra Villas builder, Mathews-Phillips, Inc., to create a ski resort theme.

Bare Bush Path 2
Variation of "bare brush" found in Williams poem *Tree and Sky:*
Again
the bare brush of
the half-broken
and already-written-of
tree alone

Broadcloth Way

From Dickinson poem 306 (*A Shady friend - for Torrid days -*):
The Vane a little to the East -
Scares Muslin souls - away -
If Broadcloth Hearts are firmer
Than those of Organdy -

Cadence Court

From Dickinson poem 378 (*Better - than Music!*):
Let me not spill - it's smallest cadence -
Humming - for promise - when alone -

Eden Brook Drive

Variation of "Brooks in Eden" found in Dickinson poem 378 (*Better - than Music!*):
Children - so - told how Brooks in Eden -
Bubbled a better - melody -
Quaintly infer - Eve's great surrender -

Farthest Thunder Court

From Dickinson poem 1665:
The farthest Thunder that I heard
Was nearer than the Sky
And rumbles still, though torrid Noons
Have lain their Missiles by -

First League

From Dickinson poem 143 (*Exultation is the going*):
Can the sailor understand
The divine intoxication
Of the first league out from Land?

Indian Pipe Court

From Dickinson poem 1513:
'Tis whiter than an Indian Pipe -
'Tis dimmer than a Lace -
No stature has it, like a Fog

Kindler Road ✱

The road is so named because it led to the home of Hans and Alice Kindler. Hans Kindler, cellist and founder and first conductor of the Washington National Symphony, and his wife Alice, an artist, purchased historic Iris Hill (aka Whitehall or Worthington's Quarters) in 1936. While the Kindlers lived there the access road to their home became known as Kindler's or Kindler Road. At the time it ran from Guilford Road or old Route 32 to Gorman Road. Hans died in 1949 and several years later Alice sold the home. The name of the road, however, stuck, and when the County assigned road names to their map in 1961, Kindler Road became the official name. In 1963, The Rouse Company purchased the home and the surrounding 162 acres. When Hurricane Agnes hit Howard County in 1972, flooding closed a portion of Kindler Road. To this day it remains as two disconnected segments—one that ends at First League and one south of the Middle Patuxent River that ends at Gorman Road. Now Iris Hill is accessed by Broadcloth Way.[62]

Lilac Sea

From Dickinson poem 1368:
Opon a Lilac Sea
To toss incessantly
His Plush Alarm

Little Bird Path

From Dickinson poem 314 (*"Hope" is the thing with feathers -*):
And sweetest - in the Gale - is heard -
And sore must be the storm -
That could abash the little Bird
That kept so many warm -

Mickey's Pride

Mildred (Mickey) Dunham was a Columbia "pioneer," the first director of Community Services for the Columbia Association and the first developer's representative for HRD, a position created in 1971. The developer's representative, according to Richard Anderson, a Rouse Company vice president, was "to stimulate and simplify communication between Columbia residents and the people who can best respond to their needs." When Dunham retired in 1981, the Kings Contrivance Village Board passed a resolution requesting a street in their developing village be named to commemorate "her fourteen years of tireless service to the residents of the entire community."[63]

Midas Touch

From Dickinson poem 1488:
One of the ones that Midas touched
Who failed to touch us all
Was that confiding Prodigal
The reeling Oriole -

Moon Portrait Way

Variation of "Portrait in the Moon" found in Dickinson poem 676:
You know that Portrait in the Moon -
So tell me Who 'tis like -

Narrow Wind Way

From Dickinson poem 1121 (*The Sky is low - the Clouds are mean.*):
A Narrow Wind complains all Day
How some one treated him

Mickey's Pride was named for Mickey Dunham, seen here speaking at the rededication of Slayton House on May 26, 1974. Joining her at the podium are Norma Rose, who was chair of the Wilde Lake Village Association and Pat Kennedy, who was president of Columbia Association.

New Grace Mews

From Dickinson poem 706 (*I cannot live with You -*):
Nor could I rise - with You -
Because Your Face
Would put out Jesus' -
That New Grace

Pink Wood

Variation of "woods are pink" found in Dickinson poem 24:
Frequently the woods are pink -
Frequently, are brown.

Red Cravat Court

From Dickinson poem 210:
If I shouldn't be alive
When the Robins come,
Give the one in Red Cravat,
A Memorial crumb -

Sandalfoot Way

Variation of "sandal on his foot" found in Dickinson poem 331 (*The only Ghost I ever saw*):
He had no sandal on his foot -
And stepped like flakes of snow -

Sandrope Court

Variation of "Ropes of Sand" found in Dickinson poem 931:
An Everywhere of Silver
With Ropes of Sand
To keep it from effacing
The Track called Land -

Dickinson neighborhood sign, 2007.

Second Time Lane

From Dickinson poem 378 (*Better - than Music!*):
'Twas'nt contained - like other stanza -
No one could play it - the second time -
But the Composer - perfect Mozart -
Perish with him - that keyless Rhyme!

Setting Sun Way

From Dickinson poem 479 (*Because I could not stop for Death -*):
We passed the Fields of Grazing Grain -
We passed the Setting Sun -

Silent Bird Court

Variation of "Bird the silence" found in Dickinson poem 1741 (*A lane of Yellow led the eye*):
If Bird the silence contradict
Or flower presume to show
In that low summer of the West
Impossible to know -

Single Wheel Path

From Dickinson poem 370:
Within my Garden, rides a Bird
Opon a single Wheel -
Whose spokes a dizzy music make

Stonebrook Lane

Named by Troutman Communities, builders of Stonebrook, the townhouse community located on this street.

Summer Leave Lane

From Dickinson poem 368 (*I envy Seas, whereon He rides -*):
The happy - happy Leaves -

That just abroad His Window
Have Summer's leave to play -

Sweet Hours Way

From Dickinson poem 1785:
Sweet hours have perished here,
This is a timid room -
Within it's precincts hopes have played
Now fallow in the tomb.

Water Lily Way

From Dickinson poem 148 (*Will there really be a "morning"?*):
Has it feet like Water lilies?
Has it feathers like a Bird?
Is it brought from famous countries
Of which I have never heard?

Weather Worn Way

From Dickinson poem 1484 (*Before you thought of Spring*):
A Fellow in the Skies
Of independent Hues
A little weather worn
Inspiriting habiliments
Of Indigo and Brown -

Yellow Bonnet Place

From Dickinson poem 92:
Perhaps you'd like to buy a flower,
But I could never sell -
If you would like to borrow,
Until the Daffodil

Unties her yellow Bonnet
Beneath the village door,

Huntington

The neighborhood name is from Huntington Quarter, an original land grant patented to Henry Ridgely Sr. and Henry Ridgely Jr. in 1696 for 259 acres.[64]

The street names in Huntington are drawn primarily from the work of Carl Sandburg, a 20th century American author. Some names come from the works of two 19th century poets, Emily Dickinson and Walt Whitman, which are also found in other Columbia neighborhoods.

Huntington neighborhood sign, 2007.

Andiron Lane
From Whitman poem *Song of Myself:*
Where the cheese-cloth hangs in the kitchen,
*   where andirons straddle the hearth-slab,*
*   where cobwebs fall in festoons from the*
*   rafters;*

Black Velvet Lane
Found twice in Sandburg poem *Chords*, the second being:
Yes, riding horseback on hills by the sea
*   . . . sitting at the ivory keys in black*
*   velvet, a rope of pearls on white shoulders.*

Book Row
Variation of "row of books" found in Sandburg poem *Love Is a Deep and a Dark and a Lonely:*
like a book read over and over again
like one book being a long row of books
like leaves of windflowers bending low
and bending to be never broken

Camerado Court
From poem title and found twice in Whitman poem *As I Lay with My Head in Your Lap Camerado*, the first being:
As I lay with my head in your lap camerado,
The confession I made I resume, what I said
*   to you and the open air I resume,*

Cipher Row
From Whitman poem title *Shakspere-Bacon's Cipher* and in verse:
In every object, mountain, tree, and star—
*   in every birth and life,*
As part of each—evolv'd from each—
*   meaning, behind the ostent,*
A mystic cipher waits infolded.

Clocktower Lane
Found twice in Sandburg poem *The Windy City*, the first being:
At the white clock-tower
lighted in night purples
over the boulevard link bridge
only the blind get by without
*   acknowledgments.*

Cold Star Court
From Sandburg poem *Slabs of the Sunburnt West:*
The worn tired stars say
you shall die early and die dirty.
The clean cold stars say
you shall die late and die clean.

Corn Tassel Court
Found twice in Sandburg poem *Haze*, the first being:
I don't care who you are, man:
I know a woman is looking for you
and her soul is a corn-tassel kissing a
*   south-west wind.*

Neighborhood poster by Gail Holliday.

Deep Smoke

From Sandburg poem *Honey and Salt*:
a slow blinking of two red lanterns in
*   river mist*
or a deep smoke winding one hump of a
*   mountain*
and the smoke becomes a smoke known to
*   your own twisted individual garments:*
the winding of it gets into your walk, your
*   hands, your face and eyes.*

Deerfoot Way

From Sandburg poem *The Windy City*:
It is easy to sit listening to a boy babbling
*   of the Pottawatomie moccasins in Illinois,*
*   how now the roofs and smokestacks cover*
*   miles*
*   where the deerfoot left its writing*
*   and the foxpaw put his initials*
*   in the snow. . . for the early moccasins . . .*
*   to read.*

Dragonclaw

Variation of "Claw of Dragon" found in
Dickinson poem 1032 (*Far from Love the*
Heavenly Father):
Oftener by the Claw of Dragon
Than the Hand of Friend
Guides the Little One predestined
To the Native Land -

Drumbeat Place

From Whitman poem *A Song of Joys*:
To go to battle—to hear the bugles play and
*   the drums beat!*

Early April Way

From Sandburg poem *Lesson*:
In early April the trees
end their winter waiting
with a creep of green on branches.

Early Spring Way

From Sandburg poem *Child Face*:
Once a child face lay in the moonlight
Of an early spring night.

Flagwalk Terrace

Variation of "flagg'd walks" found in
Whitman poem *Song of the Open Road*:
You flagg'd walks of the cities! you strong
*   curbs at the edges!*
You ferries! you planks and posts of wharves!
*   you timber-lined sides! you distant ships!*

Footprint Place

From Sandburg poem title *Bird Footprint*
and found twice in verse, the first being:
The footprint of a bird in sand brought
*   your face.*
I said, "What of it?"

Golden Rod Path

From Dickinson poem 123 (*Besides the*
Autumn poets sing):
A few incisive mornings -
A few Ascetic eves -
Gone - Mr Bryant's "Golden Rod" -
And Mr Thomson's "sheaves."

Gray Mouse Way
Found four times in Sandburg poem
Slabs of the Sunburnt West, the first
being:
A bluejay blue
and a gray mouse gray
ran up the canyon walls.

Green Moon Path
From Sandburg poem *Slabs of the*
Sunburnt West:
"Away and away on some green moon
a blind blue horse eats white grass
    And the blind blue horse knows more than
       I do
    because he saw more than I have seen
    and remembered it after he went blind."

Half Dollar Court
From Sandburg poem *Fame If Not*
Fortune:
A half-dollar in the hand of a gypsy
    tells me this and more:
You shall go broken on the wheel,
    lashed to the bars and fates of steel,
    a nickel's worth of nothing,
    a vaudeville gag,

Hundred Drums Row
From Dickinson poem 157 (*I have a King,*
who does not speak -):
And if I do - when morning comes -
It is as if a hundred drums
Did round my pillow roll,

Indigo Court
From Dickinson poem 1484 (*Before you*
thought of Spring):
Inspiriting habiliments
Of Indigo and Brown -
With Specimens of Song
As if for you to choose -

Keepsake Way
From Dickinson poem 591 (*I heard a Fly*
buzz - when I died -):
I willed my Keepsakes - Signed away
What portion of me be
Assignable - and then it was
There interposed a Fly -

Lady Bug Row
From Sandburg poem *Without Notice*
Beforehand:
all without notice beforehand, came down,
the same as the far hiding out of lady bugs,
woggle bugs spotted black polka dots
on box car red, on banana yellow,

Many Flower Lane
From Sandburg poem *Love Is a Deep and a*
Dark and a Lonely:
then may come the windflowers
and the breath of wind over many flowers
winding its way out of many lonely flowers
waiting in rainleaf whispers

Many Mile Mews
From Sandburg poem *Child Face:*
There are lips as strange and soft
As a rim of moon many miles off,
White on a fading purple sea.

Moonrider Lane
Sandburg poem title *Moon Riders* and in
verse:
A hayfield mist of evening saw him
Watching moon riders lose the moon
For new shooting stars— . . .

Morning Leap Terrace
From Dickinson poem 140 (*Bring me the*
sunset in a cup -):
Tell me how far the morning leaps -
Tell me what time the weaver sleeps
Who spun the breadths of blue!

Security Development Company developed an outparcel, known as Huntington South, in the middle of Huntington in 1986. In an effort to keep with the Huntington street naming theme the company solicited the help of the Kings Contrivance Village Board and The Rouse Company. The recommendations were pulled from a list of names taken from Carl Sandburg poems. Thus Lumberjack Row, Red Rain Way and Windbeat Way sound like Columbia even though the green street signs hint at the outparcel status.[65]

The gravestone of Conrad Vollmerhousen lies not far from Vollmerhausen Road on Columbia Association open space near Black Velvet Path and Keepsake Way. The difference in spelling is apparently just a "typo" carved in stone according to family members. This small family cemetery is one of several that dot the area.

Vollmerhausen Drive and Vollmerhausen Road ✳

When Howard County recorded street names in 1961, the road was locally known as Vollmerhausen's or Vollmerhausen Road referring to the Vollmerhausen family who lived there. Conrad Vollmerhausen, Sr. sold almost 143 acres of his farm to HRD in 1963 as part of the original Columbia land acquisition.[68]

West Window Way

From Sandburg poem *Panels*:
The west window is a panel of marching onions.
Five new lilacs nod to the wind and fence boards.

White Spring Way

From Sandburg poem *The Windy City*:
White spring winds, come off the bag wool clouds,
come off the running melted snow, come white
as the arms of snow-born children.

Wild Grass Court ☐1

From Sandburg poem *The Evening Sunsets Witness and Pass On*:
Passion may be a wind child
transient and made of air—
Passion may be a wild grass
where a great wind came and went.

Woodpark Lane

A mystery . . .

Macgill's Common

The neighborhood is named for the Reverend James Macgill who was appointed in 1730 to be the first rector of Christ Episcopal Church. The church is located on Oakland Mills Road but the over 800 acres that Macgill acquired is located near today's intersection of Routes 32 and 29. The home that he built, Athol, still stands, now overlooking Route 29 on Martin Road.[69]

The street names in Macgill's Common are drawn from folk songs that appear in *The Folk Songs of North America* compiled by Alan Lomax, an American folklorist.

Macgill's Common neighborhood sign, 2007.

Bushranger Path
From folk song *Bold Jack Donahue:*
Come all you gallant bushrangers and
outlaws of disdain,
Who scorn to live in slavery or wear the
brands of chains,

Cambric Court
From folk song *Strawberry Lane:*
'You'll have for to make me a cambric shirt,
And every stitch must be finicle work.'

Cape Ann Drive
From folk song title *Cape Ann* and in verse:
So we hunted and we halloed,
And the next thing we did find
Was the lighthouse in Cape Ann
And that we left behind.

Cotton Mill Lane
From folk song title *Cotton Mill Colic* and in chorus:
I'm a-gonna starve, ev'rybody will,
You can't make a livin' at a cotton mill.

Deer Chase
From folk song title *The Deer Chase.*

Fair Beauty
From folk song title *A Fair Beauty Bride* and in verse:
Once I courted a fair beauty bride,
I courted her by day and I courted her
by night,
Her parents found out I was courting her
for love,
They locked her in her sitting-room and
threw the keys away.

Flapjack Lane
From folk song *Lousy Miner:*
I've lived on swine till I grunt and squeal,
No one can tell how my bowels feel
With flapjacks a-swimming round in grease,
I'm a lousy miner,
I'm a lousy miner, when will my troubles
cease?

Goodin Circle
From folk song title *Sally Goodin* and found three times in verse, the first being:
Had a piece of pie an' I had a piece of
puddin',
An' I give it all away just to see my
Sally Goodin.

Neighborhood poster by Gail Holliday.

Quantrell Row

From folk song title *Charlie Quantrell* and found several times in verse, the first being:

It is of a fearless highwayman, a story I will tell,
His name was Charlie Quantrell and in Kansas he did dwell;
It was on the Nebraska prairies he commenced his wild career,
And many wealthy gentlemen before him stood with fear.

Rawhide Ridge

From folk song *My Love Is a Rider:*
Now all you young maidens where'er you reside,
Beware of the cowboy who swings the rawhide,
He'll court you and pet you and leave you and go
In the spring up the trail on his bucking bronco.

Roveout Lane

Variation of "Roved Out" found in folk song title *As I Roved Out* and in verse:
As I roved out one fine summer's evening
To view the flowers and take the air,
'Twas there I spied a tender mother
Talking to her daughter dear.

Shaker Drive

From folk song title *Come, Life, Shaker Life* and in verse:
Come, life, Shaker life! come, life eternal!
Shake, shake out of me all that is carnal!

Silver Twine

From folk song *Love Is Pleasin':*
If I'd a-knowed before I courted,
That love had a-been such a killin' crime,
I'd a-locked my heart in a box of gold,
And tied it up with a silver twine.

Hatbrim Terrace

From folk song *Talking Columbia:*
Filled up my hat-brim, drunk a little taste,
Thought about a river, just goin' to waste,
I thought about the dust, 'n thought about the sand,
I thought about the people, 'n thought about the land . . .
Ev'rybody runnin' around a-all over creation,
Just lookin' for some kind of a little place.

Herding Row

From folk song title *Night Herding Song* and variation of "herded" found in verse:
I have circle-herded, trail-herded, cross-herded, too,
But to keep you together that's what I can't do,
My horse is leg-weary and I'm awful tired,
But if I let you get away, I'm sure to get fired,
Bunch up, little dogies, bunch up.

South Carlinda Avenue

During development of the Macgill's Common neighborhood there was a plan to connect it to Carlinda Avenue in Allview Estates which was developed in the late 1950s. Financial estimates for constructing a bridge across the stream separating the neighborhoods were high enough to quash the plan. In 1977, "South" was added to the Macgill's Common street name to differentiate it from its namesake.[70]

Strawturkey Court

Variation of folk song title *Turkey in the Straw* and in chorus:

Turkey in the straw, haw, haw, haw,
Turkey in the hay, hay, hay, hay,
Roll 'em up and twist 'em up—a high
*   tuck a-haw,*
And hit 'em up a tune called Turkey in the
*   Straw.*

Turtle Dove Place

Found twice in folk song *Old Smokey*, the first being:

On top of old Smokey
On the mountain so high
Where the wild birds and turtle doves
Can hear my sad cry.

Wayover Way

From folk song title *Way Over in the Heavens* and in chorus:

Way over in the heavens,
To sit on the seat by Jesus.

ABOVE
Reverend James Macgill named his property and his home Athol after his ancestral home in Scotland. Atholton appeared on maps as a geographical designation as recently as the early 1970s. The reference survives in the name of the nearby schools, shopping center and park.
Photograph on file at Maryland Historical Trust Library.

LEFT
The stone marker designates a property boundary of the land granted to the Reverend James Macgill in 1730. It is inscribed "Athol Begins Here." The marker is located close to a pathway off Sixpence Circle in the neighborhood of Clemens Crossing in Hickory Ridge.

The Kings Contrivance

A Spirited Place to Wine & Dine

Country dining
in the manner and mood
of America's earliest inns.
Lunch and dinner
Tuesday through Sunday.
Dinner only Saturday.
Closed Monday. All major
credit cards. Facilities
for private parties.

**Where Routes 29 and 32 meet.
Columbia, Maryland**

KEystone 1-5131

This ad ran in 1968 in Columbia Today, a magazine produced by The Rouse Company in the early days of Columbia. The ad proclaimed "country dining" and it was. The village of Kings Contrivance did not grow around it until a decade later.

HAPPY HOUR DEFINED.

Join us for Happy Hour on the
Lakefront from 4:00 – 7:00 pm
each Wednesday all summer long
(weather permitting, of course)
featuring live music, drink specials
and fun on the deck.

10221 Wincopin Circle • Columbia, MD 21044 • 410.730.2829 • www.clydes.com

Clydes, the popular Columbia restaurant in Town Center, apparently was intrigued with naming in Columbia. It ran this ad featuring the definition of Kittamaqundi. Courtesy of Clyde's Restaurant Group. Reprinted with permission.

Long Reach was the name of an original land grant patented to Major Edward Dorsey in 1695 for 448 acres.[71]

Stonehouse

The name of the village community center comes from the Robinson Jeffers poem *"The polar ice-caps are melting"* or *Star-Swirls:*

And this place, where I have planted trees
  and built a stone house, . . .

Jeffers's own house, called Tor House, is built of stone and overlooks the Northern California coastline.

Old Dobbin Lane

Dobbin Road was rerouted in 1998 when the Columbia Crossing Shopping Center was built. At that time, the original segment connecting to Tamar Drive was renamed Old Dobbin Lane. See Dobbin Road.

Tamar Drive

From Jeffers poem title *Tamar* and found many times in verse. The character, Tamar, is also mentioned in Jeffers poem, *Apology for Bad Dreams:*

Someone flamelike passed me, saying, "I am
  Tamar Cauldwell, I have my desire,"

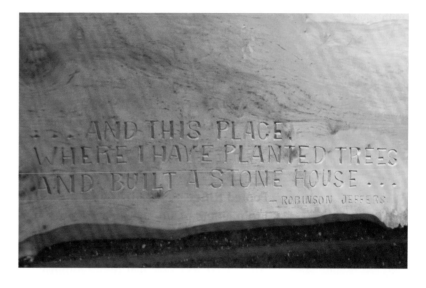

This plaque, with the Jeffers quote that inspired the name, hangs on the wall of Stonehouse, the Long Reach community center.

Jeffers Hill

The neighborhood name is derived from the last name of Robinson Jeffers, a 20th century poet whose work is the source of street names throughout the Village of Long Reach.

Bellfall Court

From Jeffers poem *In the Hill at Newgrange:*

"The holy men scream in their praying, the
  golden reliquaries are melted, the bell falls
  clanging."

Campfire

From Jeffers poem *The Inquisitors:*

They were more like Red Indians around a
  campfire, grave and dark, mountain-high,
  hams on heels
Squatting around a little fire of hundred-foot
  logs. . . .

Carriage House Lane

What was an unnamed lane leading to the historic house Linden Grove became a street in 1991 when Thomas and Valerie Nelson divided the large land tract and developed the community of townhouses.

Kendall Ridge

Kendall's Delight and Kendall's Enlargement were original land grants patented to Daniel Kendall in 1701 for 500 acres and 400 acres, respectively.[74]

The street names in Kendall Ridge are derived from the work of Robinson Jeffers, a 20th century poet.

Airybrink Lane ☐1
From Jeffers poem *Give Your Heart to the Hawks*:
. . . They met at Fraser's
And crossed the ridge; and were picketing
*   the horses*
Where they could ride no farther, on the
*   airy brink*
Above the great slides of the thousand-foot
*   cliff.*

April Brook Circle
Found three times in Jeffers poem *Roan Stallion*, the first being:
. . . Then one might hear the
*   hush of the wind in the tall redwoods,*
The tinkle of the April brook, deep in its
*   hollow.*

Autumn Ridge Drive
A mystery . . .

Bird Race
Variation of "race of birds" found in Jeffers poem *Their Beauty Has More Meaning*:
. . . And I say this: their beauty has more
*   meaning*
Than the whole human race and the race
*   of birds.*

Black Star Circle
From Jeffers poem *The Inhumanist*:
*   The old man heard*
An angry screaming in heaven and squinted
*   upward, where two black stars*
Hunted each other in the high blue; . . .

Breaking Wave Drive
From Jeffers poem *Cawdor*:
Like the blade of a breaking wave reaped
*   by the wind, or flame rising from fire, or*
*   cloud-coiled lightning*

Broken Wing Court
Variation of "wing broken" found in Jeffers poem *Prelude*:
On the breast of Palo Corona mountain
*   looking northward,*
Watches his brother Vidal and Julio the
*   youngest*
Play with a hawk they shot from the
*   mountain cloud,*
The wing broken. . . .

Burnt Mountain Path
From Jeffers poem *The Inhumanist*:
. . . it was thus Bull Gore's
And Daniel Larson's were borne down the
*   burnt mountain; . . .*

Canyon Head Lane
Found twice in Jeffers poem *The Love and the Hate*, the first being:
Riding the fence-trail across the canyon-head
*   to reach the gate; . . .*

Cliffside Trail
From Jeffers poem *The Deer Lay Down Their Bones*:
I followed the narrow cliffside trail half way
*   up the mountain*
Above the deep river-canyon. . . .

Cobblefield Drive
A mystery . . .

Cooperhawk Court

From Jeffers poem *Give Your Heart to the Hawks:*

. . . *A little Cooper's-hawk was tethered in front of Lance to a driven peg,*
One wing bloodily trailing; . . .

Dark Hawk Circle

From Jeffers poem *The Loving Shepherdess:*

. . . *A heavy dark hawk balanced in the storm*
And suddenly darted; . . .

Dawn Whistle

From Jeffers poem *The Love and the Hate:*

. . . *I can hardly wait*
To hear the hawks of dawn whistle on the mountain. . . .

Deep Earth Lane

From Jeffers poem *The Inhumanist:*

. . . *the house danced and bobbled, lightning flashed from the ground, the deep earth roared, yellow dust*

Deep River Canyon

From Jeffers poem *The Deer Lay Down Their Bones:*

I followed the narrow cliffside trail half way up the mountain
Above the deep river-canyon. . . .

Deer Season Run

From Jeffers poem *The Love and the Hate:*

" . . . *to-morrow is Monday the thirty-first; Tuesday*
Is the first day of deer-season." . . .

Distant Rock Path

From Jeffers poem *The Women at Point Sur:*

And heard what she supposed was the surf running
Under the distant rock of the lighthouse, it sounded
Like horses running. . . .

Dried Earth Boulevard

Variation of "earth dried" found in Jeffers poem *The Love and the Hate:*

Summer came on, earth dried, grass whitened,

Dry Barley Lane

From Jeffers poem *Roan Stallion:*

. . . *She found a box,*
Filled it with sweet dry barley and took it down to the old corral. . . .

Dry Stone Gate

From Jeffers poem *The Love and the Hate:*

. . . *and he led her captive*
Toward the foot of the house-yard, where a dry-stone fence
Edges the fall of the gorge. . . .

Each Leaf Court

From Jeffers poem *Prelude:*

All in a moment each leaf a distinct fire
Reflect the sharp flash over them: . . .

Endless Ocean Way

From Jeffers poem *Carmel Point:*

. . . *Meanwhile the image of the pristine beauty*
Lives in the very grain of the granite,
Safe as the endless ocean that climbs our cliff. . . .

of *The Counties of Maryland*, part of the Big Patuxent River was known as Snowdens River in the 17th and early 18th centuries.[76]

Soft Thunder Trail
From Jeffers poem *Roan Stallion*:
He drew away from it, the hooves making
    soft thunder in the trodden soil.

Starburn Path
From Jeffers poem *The Treasure*:
Stars burn, grass grows, men breathe: as a
    man finding treasure says "Ah!"

Steel Flower Path
Variation of "flower of steel" found in Jeffers poem *The Inhumanist*:
. . . Bird with two beaks, two-petalled
    flower of steel, . . .

Stonecutter Road
From poem title *To the Stone-Cutters* and in verse:
Stone-cutters fighting time with marble,
    you foredefeated
Challengers of oblivion

Summer Cloud Way
From Jeffers poem *The Love and the Hate*:
Her thin shift fallen from one shoulder,
    looking for Hoult, but summer cloud
Covered the mountain; . . .

Three Apple Downs
From Jeffers poem *The Loving Shepherdess*:
. . . There were three apples
From Fogler's trees, and a little jar of honey

Tide Rock Square
From Jeffers poem *Night*:
The ebb slips from the rock, the sunken
Tide-rocks lift streaming shoulders
Out of the slack, . . .

Treetop Circle
From Jeffers poem *The Love and the Hate*:
. . . flapping sheets of clear flame flew from
    the tree-tops to farther trees or into the air

Twenty Year Chase
From Jeffers poem *Their Beauty Has More Meaning*:
. . . I honestly do not know which day is
    more beautiful.
I know that to-morrow or next year or in
    twenty years
I shall not see these things:—and it does not
    matter, it does not hurt;
They will be here. . . .

Vast Rose Drive
From Jeffers poem *Oysters*:
. . . A vast rose and gold
    sunset, very beautiful, made in April,
Moved overhead. . . .

Warm Granite Drive
Variation of "worn granite" found in Jeffers poem *Gray Weather*:
It is true that, older than man and ages to
    outlast him, the Pacific surf
Still cheerfully pounds the worn granite
    drum;

Warm Waves Way
From Jeffers poem *"The unformed volcanic earth"* or *The Beginning and the End*:
. . . Meanwhile they had invented
Chlorophyll and ate sunlight, cradled
    in peace
On the warm waves; . . .

Wild Swan Way
From Jeffers poem title *Love the Wild Swan* and found three times in verse, the first being:
"Unlucky hunter, Oh bullets of wax,
The lion beauty, the wild-swan wings, the
    storm of the wings."

Wild Wing Way

From Jeffers poem *Give Your Heart to the Hawks:*

. . .   *Then noises like the cries of a woman*
    screaming, bird after bird of sharp-colored
    sound
Flew on the face of the cliff, tattered wild
    wings against jagged rock. . . .

Wind Dance Way

From Jeffers poem *Birds:*

The old gray sea-going gulls are gathered
    together, the northwest wind wakening
Their wings to the wild spirals of the
    wind-dance.

Wind Rider Way

From Jeffers poem *The Coast-Road:*

A world that is feverishly preparing new
    wars, peculiarly vicious ones, and
    heavier tyrannies, a strangely
Missionary world, road-builder, wind-rider,
    educator, printer and picture-maker and
    broad-caster

Window Latch Way

From Jeffers poem *Prelude:*

"The strange lover never breaks the window-
    latches again
When Joseph's at synagogue."

Winter Pasture Way

From Jeffers poem *Tamar:*

Lee Cauldwell rode across the roaring
    southwind to the winter pasture up
    in the hills.

Woodstaff Way

From Jeffers poem *The Loving Shepherdess:*

She lifted up the madrone-wood staff and
    called them.
"Fay, Fern, Oh Frannie. Come Saul.
Leader and Tiny and Nosie, we have to go on."

Warm Waves intersects Warm Granite in Snowden Overlook. What's wrong with this picture? Snowden Overlook is part of new town Columbia and under the Columbia Association assessment. This would normally mean blue street signs. Green signs have started to pop up in Columbia as less attention is paid to details like assuring that streets in the new town zoning get blue signs.

Worn Mountain Way

From Jeffers poem *Joy:*

Over the mountain; not for joy the
    worn mountain
Stands, while years like water
Trench his long sides. . . .

Yellow Dawn Court

From Jeffers poem *Animals:*

. . .   *Then, yellow dawn*
Colors the south, I think about the rapid and
    furious lives in the sun:
They have little to do with ours; . . .

Young Buck Circle

From Jeffers poem *The Love and the Hate:*

". . . by God, I can hardly wait
To kill a buck, a young buck."

Madrone—(Spanish in origin, listed as "madrona.") An evergreen plant or shrub of the Pacific Coast of North America that has smooth bark and thick shiny leaves.

Jackson Pond

Volunteers bring life to Columbia. They helped bring into being the community sports organizations, arts and cultural opportunities, religious groups and human services agencies. Names of countless individuals could be carved onto plaques and building and street signs to commemorate their contributions to Columbia—but very few are. One who was singled out was Howard Jackson for whom the pond in Phelps Luck is named. Jackson was a dedicated volunteer in Long Reach serving on several open space committees and in groups that lobbied for a left-hand turn signal at the intersection of Tamar Drive and Route 175, and street lighting along Tamar Drive. Long Reach was still in development stage in 1978 when the active village resident died. The Village Board voted to officially rename Hittman Pond in Jackson's memory. The pond had been built by Hittman Engineering as part of a study of the effect of urbanization on water quality during development. A commemorative plaque can be found on the island.

Phelps Luck

Phelps his Luck was an original land grant patented to Walter Phelps in 1695 for 238 acres.[78]

The street names in Phelps Luck are derived from the work of Robinson Jeffers, a 20th century poet.

Alderleaf Place
From Jeffers poem *Return:*
I will find my accounting where the alder leaf quivers
In the ocean wind over the river boulders.

Antrim Court
From Jeffers poem title *Antrim.*

Besthold Garth
Variation of "best told" found in Jeffers poem *"What's the best life"* or *The Silent Shepherds:*
. . . And I'll have lunatics
For my poets, strolling from farm to farm, wild liars distorting
The country news into supernaturalism—
For all men to such minds are devils or gods—and that increases
Man's dignity, man's importance, necessary lies
Best told by fools.

Billow Row
From Jeffers poem *On an Anthology of Chinese Poems:*
Beautiful the fantastically
Small farmhouse and ribbon of rice-fields a mile below; and billows of mist
Blow through the gorge. . . .

Blade Green Lane
Variation of "bladed green" found in Jeffers poem *Natural Music:*
(Winter has given them gold for silver
To stain their water and bladed green for brown to line their banks)

Blitheaire Garth
From Jeffers poem *"The unformed volcanic earth"* or *The Beginning and the End:*
. . . her atmosphere
Was the breath of her passion: not the blithe air
Men breathe and live, but marsh-gas, ammonia, sulphured hydrogen,

Buckskin Court
From Jeffers poem *Roan Stallion:*
The buckskin mare, leaning against the breastpiece, plodded into sight round the wet bank.

Chatterbird Place
Variation of "bird-chatter" found in Jeffers poem *Natural Music:*
The old voice of the ocean, the bird-chatter of little rivers,

Coltsfoot Court
From Jeffers poem *The Loving Shepherdess:*
The darkness under the trees in spring is starry with flowers, with redwood sorrel, colt's foot, wakerobin,
The slender-stemmed pale yellow violets,

Drystraw Drive
From Jeffers poem *The Loving Shepherdess:*
And finding sacks of dry straw with a worn blanket
In one of the cabins, slept well and awoke refreshed

Eaglebeak Row
Variation of Jeffers poem title *The Beaks of Eagles* and in verse:
. . . and it is good for him
To know that his needs and nature are no more changed in fact in ten thousand years than the beaks of eagles.

Enberend Terrace [1]

Variation of "ember ends" found in
Jeffers poem *Oh Lovely Rock:*
> *. . . I laid a clutch of dead bay-leaves*
> *On the ember ends and felted dry sticks*
> *   across them and lay down again.*

Flagflower Place

From Jeffers poem *Original Sin:*
> *. . .   Wet rocks were shining, a*
> *   little wind*
> *Stirred the leaves of the forest and the marsh*
> *   flag-flowers; . . .*

Flight Feather

From Jeffers poem *Vulture:*
> *. . .   I saw through half-shut eyelids a*
> *   vulture wheeling high up in heaven,*
> *And presently it passed again, but lower*
> *   and nearer, its orbit narrowing, I*
> *   understood then*
> *That I was under inspection. I lay death-still*
> *   and heard the flight-feathers*
> *Whistle above me and make their circle and*
> *   come nearer.   . . .*

Freelark Place

From Jeffers poem *The Loving Shepherdess:*
> *". . . All young, all gay, all moving, free*
> *   larks and foolery*
> *By gipsy fires." . . .*

Graywing Court

From Jeffers poem *"The storm blowing up"*
or *Storm Dance of the Sea Gulls:*
> *Gray wings and white, floating over*
> *   the storm,*

Greathead Court

From Jeffers poem *Passenger Pigeons:*
> *   And the American bison: their hordes*
> *Would hide a prairie from horizon to horizon,*
> *   great heads and storm-cloud shoulders,*
> *   a torrent of life—*

Tor House and Hawk Tower, Carmel, California. Robinson Jeffers lived and worked in these stone buildings overlooking the Pacific Coast from 1916 to his death in 1962. Courtesy of Tor House Foundation.

Halflight Garth

From Jeffers poem *Birds and Fishes:*
> *And dive from the high air, the cormorants*
> *Slip their long black bodies under the water*
> *   and hunt like wolves*
> *Through the green half-light.   . . .*

High Tor Hill

From Jeffers poem title *Tor House.*

Hillfall Court

From Jeffers poem *The Loving Shepherdess:*
> *. . .   We lived a long way south,*
> *   where the hills fall straight to the sea,*

Lightspun Lane

From Jeffers poem *The Loving Shepherdess:*
> *. . .   The land-wind lifted the light-spun*
> *   manes of the waves, a drift of sea-lions*
> *Swung in the surf and looked at the shore, . . .*

Luckpenny Place

From Jeffers poem *The Loving Shepherdess:*
> *A coin in shape, a mere coin, a flipped*
> *   luck-penny: . . .*

Tor—A heap, mound or a craggy hill. (Celtic origin)

Neighborhood poster
by Gail Holliday.

Wildwind Place
From Jeffers poem *"What's the best life"* or
The Silent Shepherds:
*And eat and sleep. He will live in the wild
     wind and quick rain, he will not ruin his
     eyes with reading,
Nor think too much.*

Windysun Court
From Jeffers poem *The Loving Shepherdess*:
*" . . .   I'll lie down here on the
     little grass in the windy sun
And think whether I can live. I have you,
     dear stragglers. . . ."*

Wingborne Court
From Jeffers poem *"The storm blowing up"*
or *Storm Dance of the Sea Gulls*:
*They feel the beauty of things—as we do—
     they give their flying hearts to it—their
     wing-borne hungers . . .*

White Mane
From Jeffers poem *The Wind-Struck
Music*:
*That flashy palamino he rode—cream-color,
     heavy white mane, white tail, his pride—. . .*

Wild Lilac ☐1
From Jeffers poem *Give Your Heart to
     the Hawks*:
*A rabbit with blazing fur broke through
     the back-fire,
Bounding and falling, it passed by Lance
     and ran
Straight into the stem of a wild lilac bush,*

Yellowrose Court
From Jeffers poem *Their Beauty Has
More Meaning*:
*Yesterday morning enormous the moon hung
     low on the ocean,
Round and yellow-rose in the glow of dawn;
The night-herons flapping home wore dawn
     on their wings. . . .*

Youngsea Place
From Jeffers poem *"The unformed volcanic
earth"* or *The Beginning and the End*:
*Water from the cloud and salts from the
     young seas,*

Oakland Mills was a 19th century flour and saw mill that was part of the historic Oakland estate. A village by the same name arose around the mill, filled with skilled laborers who provided services to the surrounding farms. A few structures of this bygone village remain along the east side of Route 29, across from Town Center.[80]

The Other Barn

The name of the village community center was dictated by its unique design. Two dairy barns sat on the land designated as the site for the Oakland Mills Village Center. Rather than demolishing them, The Rouse Company and the architect Louis Sauer proposed remodeling. Sauer said, "One of the problems in producing a new center is to have it belong to a place. Having the barns gives the center an historical basis." When the village center opened in 1969, one barn was used for meeting space and offices and one barn housed The Orange Propeller, a teen center. A colorful graphic unified the barns and identified them as The Other Barn and The Orange Propeller. The Orange Propeller had a short life and after it closed that building became known as The Barn. A plaque hanging in The Other Barn explains that the Dorsey Owings family built the barn in 1947 as part of their dairy farm that housed 50 cows.[81]

The Other Barn, 1969.

Steven's Forest

The neighborhood name is a variation of Stevens' Forest, an original land grant patented to Charles Stevens in 1709 for 702 acres. Later, Stevens' Forest Resurveyed was patented to Philip Hammond in 1746 for 1,283 acres.[82]

The street names in Steven's Forest are pulled from the works of 20th century writers John Dos Passos, Ernest Hemingway, and F. Scott Fitzgerald.

African Hill
Variation of Hemingway book title *Green Hills of Africa*.

Afternoon Lane
From Hemingway book title *Death in the Afternoon*.

Agail Place
Found several times in Dos Passos book *The Best Times*, the first being:
Jassem belonged to the Agail, which I understood to be a confederation of tribes that made a business of running caravans across the desert.

THE MOON IS A GONG

Part I

1.

(The hallway of an old house in an eastern coast city, a house th
that has penned into its high gloomy rooms the righteousness of two generations. Left is the front door which has opened a little before nine every
morning for fifty years to let out the men of the tribe on their way to
courtrooms and lawoffices where, in cold hard voices that never trembled
with a moment's doubt of the rightness of what was right in their eyes,
they inflicted the law on democracy . Opposite , running up across the wall
to a landing with a white colonial rail above the front door, are the
stairs where the women ran up and down in the mornings seeing to the clean
ing of the house and the cooking of meals , or down which they
rustled slowly in the evenings in stiff wide dresses to receive the company that waited for them on gilt spindlelegged chairs in the parlor. The
parlor door is very wide . Velvet curtains are drawn over it; on one side
is a bench and hatrack , on the other a grandfather clock. The wall is
covered with a blotchy paper of which the general effect is black and
purple. The carpet on the stairs is a very dull crimson. On the landing
above the parlor door is the door to a bedroom, beside it a telephone.

Jane Carroll has a strong well-muscled figure. She sits on the
bottom step of the stairs, hugging her knees. Tom , a skinny brownfaced
young man with restless eyes , lies flat on his belly on the little
space where the stairs turn , his face on the level with hers, his chin
in his hands.)

Jane(dreamily)   Thomas the Rhymer... Thomas the Rhymer.
Tom   You know what happened to him dont you? He was

First page of the original manuscript. The Moon is a Gong was the original name of John Dos Passos's first play which he wrote in 1923.
Reprinted with permission of Lucy Dos Passos Coggin. Papers of John Dos Passos, MSS 5950, Special Collections, University of Virginia Library.

Merryrest Road ☐1
Variation of "Rest You Merry" found in Hemingway short story title *God Rest You Merry, Gentlemen.*

Moongong Court
Variation of "Moon is a Gong" found in Dos Passos book T*he Best Times:*
My name for it when I designed the settings for Ed Massey's production at the Cambridge Dramatic Club many months before, was "The Garbage Man" but the lights across the front of the Greenwich Village Theatre spelled out "The Moon is a Gong."

New Leaf Court
From Fitzgerald short story title *A New Leaf.*

Night Street Hill
Variation of Dos Passos novel title *Streets of Night.*

Offshore Green
From Fitzgerald short story title *The Offshore Pirate.*

Old Man Court
From Hemingway short novel title *The Old Man and the Sea* and found several times in text referring to Santiago, the main character.

Orient Lane
From Dos Passos book title *Orient Express.*

Ourtime Lane
From Hemingway short story collection title *In Our Time.*

Owen Brown Road ✱
When Howard County recorded road names in 1961, the road was commonly referred to as Owen Brown Road, for Owen Brown, a onetime resident of the road. What is unusual about this family-based county road name is the inclusion of the first name. Most of the other roads named for county residents contain only the surname. Owen, however, appears to have been included to differentiate it from another county road, Lark Brown Road, named for past county resident Larkin Brown.[84]

Pamplona Road
Found several times in Hemingway book *The Sun Also Rises*, the first being:
. . . He was coming back in three weeks and we would leave for Spain to get in some fishing and go to the fiesta at Pamplona. . . .

Parallel Lane
From Dos Passos novel title *The 42nd Parallel* found in the *U.S.A.* trilogy

Pastora Place
From Dos Passos book *The Best Times:*
We ate and drank a great deal for supper and afterward I took them to see Pastora Império. I had seen her before. I thought her the greatest dancer ever.

Patchin Court
Found several times in Dos Passos book *The Best Times,* the first being:
Cummings already had his room on Patchin Place.

Pilar Court
Pilar is a main character in Hemingway book *For Whom the Bell Tolls.*

Pursuit Court
From the titles of the four parts of the Hemingway book *Green Hills of Africa: Part I. Pursuit and Conversation; Part II. Pursuit Remembered; Part III. Pursuit and Failure;* and *Part IV. Pursuit as Happiness.*

Pushcart Way
From the Dos Passos poem collection title *A Pushcart at the Curb* and found twice in opening poem, the first being:
No swift and shining modern limousine, But a pushcart, rather.

Reader Lane [1]
From Hemingway short story title *One Reader Writes.*

River Meadows Drive ✱
The road is part of and named for the subdivision River Meadows, owned and developed in the late 1950s by the Gales family. The subdivision lies just east of Route 29, across from Town Center.[85]

Robert Oliver Place
Robert Oliver (1757?-1834) was a successful Baltimore merchant, a director of the B&O Railroad, and a director of the Maryland Insurance Company. Using the wealth he accrued from these ventures, Oliver purchased Historic Oakland and surrounding rural land in what would become Howard County. The Historic Oakland property, often called Oakland Manor, included Oakland Mills and what is now called Oliver's Carriage House among its many structures. The namesake Carriage House is home today to the Kittamaqundi Community congregation and is located in Town Center.[86]

Rocksparkle Row
From Dos Passos book *The Best Times:*
. . . the sky is a crushing blue overhead and the rocks sparkle in the sun with their edgings of snow and you can see from Segovia to Toledo . . .

Rosinante Run
From Dos Passos book title *Rosinante to the Road Again.*

Saddlebag Row
From Dos Passos book *The Best Times:*
Finally, one early dawn Fahad and I packed my gear and my tent into an enormous pair of tasseled saddlebags and Fahad handed me up onto the back of a riding camel.

Santiago Road
A character named Santiago is found in two Hemingway books: *For Whom the Bell Tolls* (where he is better known as El Sordo), and *The Old Man and the Sea.*

Sinbad Place
From Dos Passos book *The Best Times* as a chapter title and in text:
*Oh Sinbad was in bad
    In Tokyo and Rome
In bad in Trinidad
    And twice as bad at home.*

Neighborhood Parade, 1977.
Photo by James Ferry.

Upwoods Lane
From Wyeth painting *Up in the Woods*, watercolor, 1960.

Weatherside Run
From Wyeth painting *Weather Side*, tempera, 1965.

Wild Bees Lane
From Wyeth painting *Wild Bees*, pencil drawing, 1958.

Wintercorn Lane
From Wyeth painting *Winter Corn*, dry brush drawing, 1948.

Winterfield Lane
From Wyeth painting *Winter Fields*, tempera, 1942.

Wolf River Lane
From Wyeth painting *Wolf Rivers*, tempera, 1959.

Wood Stove Lane
From Wyeth painting *Wood Stove*, dry brush, 1962.

OWEN BROWN

The village is named for Owen Brown, a onetime Howard County resident, postmaster and shopkeeper. The name was initially just a working title for the development because of its location near the existing Owen Brown Road but the name stuck. Street namer Kay Sarfaty reportedly said, "we wanted to name something for an ordinary guy." Brown was the postmaster of the Elioak Post Office which was located at the junction of Manor Lane and Clarksville Pike. It opened in 1893 on the first floor of a two-story frame building that also housed a country store. Brown served as the postmaster and kept the store at Elioak until it closed. His home was on Owen Brown Road.[93]

Owen Brown Community Center
See village name.

Broken Land Parkway
Broken Land was an original land grant patented to Thomas Worthington and Henry Ridgely in 1722 for 660 acres of land along the Middle Patuxent River.[94]

Snowden River Parkway
Richard Snowden and his sons held several original land grants in what is now Howard County, six of which included the Snowden name. Most of these were patented in the early to mid-1700's and were located along the Patuxent River in the southern portion of the county. According to Edward B. Mathews, author of *The Counties of Maryland*, part of the Big Patuxent River was known as Snowdens River in the 17th and early 18th centuries.[95]

Dasher Green

Dasher Green neighborhood sign, 2007.

The neighborhood is named for the Dasher family. George and Irvin Dasher owned close to 700 acres along Oakland Mills Road which was within the boundaries Rouse had outlined for the Columbia project. Purchase of a large portion of that land was key to the land acquisition plan. In 1963 the Dashers sold 670 acres to The Rouse Company but retained enough land to continue their beef and grain operation. The Dasher Green neighborhood grew up around the farm which continued until the late 1970s when the Dasher brothers sold the land except for two homesteads. Irvin died in 1984 and George in 1991, but their wives, Grace and Marie, remained in their respective homes until 1993. Grace sold her home and the property was soon developed as a townhouse development with streets named Cradle Rock Farm Court and Dasher Farm Court. Marie sold her parcel to Patriot Homes which built single family residences and named the street Dasher Court.[96]

Sea Change
Variation of "sea of change" found in Whittier poem *My Playmate:*
> Are moaning like the sea,—
> The moaning of the sea of change
>   Between myself and thee!

Second Morning Court
From Whittier poem *Snow-Bound:*
> And, when the second morning shone,
> We looked upon a world unknown,
> On nothing we could call our own.

Setting Star
From Whittier poem *Gone:*
> The light of her young life went down,
>   As sinks behind the hill
> The glory of a setting star,
>   Clear, suddenly, and still.

Street of the week

Sweet Fern

"I climbed a hill path strange and new/ With slow feet, pausing at each turn;/ A sudden waft of west wind blew/ The breath of the sweet fern," John Greenleaf Whit- tier wrote. Sweet Fern in the Owen Brown neighborhood of Dasher Green takes its name from his poem.

In 1977 The Columbia Times ran a series called "Street of the Week." Columbia artists Sue Anne Bottomley and Mary Jo Tydlacka were among those who provided original artwork to illustrate the featured street. Pictured here is Bottomley's interpretation for Sweet Fern.

Shadowshape Place
From Whittier poem *To My Old Schoolmaster:*
> Time is hastening on, and we
> What our fathers are shall be,—
> Shadow-shapes of memory!

Soft Shade Way
Variation of "softer shades" found in Whittier poem *Proem:*
> Unskilled the subtle lines to trace,
>   Or softer shades of Nature's face,
> I view her common forms with unanointed
>   eyes.

Sunset Light
From Whittier poem *The Last Walk in Autumn:*
> Around me all things, stark and dumb,
>   Seem praying for the snows to come,
> And, for the summer bloom and greenness
>   gone,
> With winter's sunset lights and dazzling
>   morn atone.

Sweet Clover
From Whittier poem *Telling the Bees:*
> There's the same sweet clover-smell in the
>   breeze;
>   And the June sun warm

Sweet Fern
From Whittier poem title *Sweet Fern* and in verse:
> I climbed a hill path strange and new
>   With slow feet, pausing at each turn;
> A sudden waft of west wind blew
>   The breath of the sweet fern.

Tauler Court
From Whittier poem title *Tauler* and found four times in verse, the first being:
> TAULER, the preacher, walked, one autumn
>   day,
> Without the walls of Strasburg, by the Rhine,

Tawney Bloom
Variation of "tawny bloom" found in
Whittier poem *The First Flowers:*
For ages, on our river borders,
These tassels in their tawny bloom,
And willowy studs of downy silver,
Have prophesied of Spring to come.

Tinted Hill
From Whittier poem *Mountain Pictures:*
And the warm sky, the sundown-tinted hill,
The forest and the lake, seemed dwarfed
and dim
Before the saintly soul, . . .

Tufted Moss
From Whittier poem *The Last Walk in*
Autumn:
Then ask not why to these bleak hills
I cling, as clings the tufted moss,
To bear the winter's lingering chills,
The mocking spring's perpetual loss.

Waning Moon Way
The phrase "waning moon" is found in
two Whittier poems: *Snow-Bound* and
The Christmas of 1888.

Windharp Way
From Whittier poem *Overruled:*
The wind-harp chooses not the tone
That through its trembling threads is blown;
The patient organ cannot guess
What hand its passive keys shall press.

Wishing Bridge
From Whittier poem title *The Wishing*
Bridge and found twice in verse, the first
being:
Among the legends sung or said
Along our rocky shore,
The Wishing Bridge of Marblehead
May well be sung once more.

George Dasher sat down
with students from Steven's
Forest Elementary School
in 1990 to help them understand what life was like in
Howard County when he
was growing up. Dasher
told the children that Owen
Brown Road was a dirt road
when he was a child.

Woven Moonbeam
From Whittier poem *To _____, with a Copy*
of Woolman's Journal:
O'er that mother's rugged features
Thou art throwing Fancy's veil,
Light and soft as woven moonbeams,
Beautiful and frail!

Youngheart Lane
From Whittier poem *The Bridal of*
Pennacook:
His commentaries, articles and creeds,
For the fair page of human loveliness,
The missal of young hearts, whose sacred text
Is music, its illumining, sweet smiles.

Neighborhood poster
by Gail Holliday.

Honeyladen Place

From Dunbar poem *The Lily of the Valley:*
But alike her ideal flower,
    With its honey-laden breath,
Still her heart blooms forth its beauty
    In the valley shades of death.

Kerry Hill Court 2

Kerry Hill Road appears on a list of street names based on farm animal breeds that street namer Kay Sarfaty compiled early on for consideration in Dorsey's Search. Kerry Hill is a breed of sheep. So even though "Kerry" appears in the Dunbar poem, *Deacon Jones' Grievance*, it is unlikely to be the source for the street name.[99]

Lacelike Row

From Dunbar poem *Dinah Kneading Dough:*
Lofty mountains, bold and proud,
Veiled beneath the lacelike cloud;
But no lovely sight I know
Equals Dinah kneading dough.

Lasting Light Way

From Dunbar poem *Behind the Arras:*
Still deeming that behind the arras lies
The lambent way that leads to lasting light.

Latchkey Row 1

From Dos Passos book *The Best Times:*
The French farce aspects of Mr. and Mrs. Smith registering in a hotel, or the tiptoe climbing of celestial stairs, the latchkey quietly turning in the lock.

Little Boots

From Dunbar poem title *Two Little Boots* and found in verse:
Two little boots all rough an' wo',
    Two little boots!
Law, I's kissed 'em times befo',
    Dese little boots!

Lookinglass Lane

From Dunbar poem title *The Looking-Glass* and found three times in verse, the first being:
Smilin' den an' poutin' now,
An' de lookin'-glass, I 'low
    Say: "Now, ain't she sweet?"

Madrigal Terrace

From Dunbar poem title *A Madrigal.*

Malindy Circle

From Dunbar poem title *When Malindy Sings* and found eight times in verse, the first being:
You cain't sta't no notes a-flyin'
    Lak de ones dat rants and rings
F'om de kitchen to be big woods
    When Malindy sings.

Many Days

From Dunbar poem title *After Many Days* and in verse:
The story of the generous bread
    He sent upon the waters,
Which after many days returns
    To trusting sons and daughters,

Mossy Brink Court

From Dunbar poem *A Boy's Summer Song:*
    To pause and drink,
    At a mossy brink;
Ah, that is the best of joy,
    And so I say
    On a summer's day,
What's so fine as being a boy?

Pigeonwing Place

From Dunbar poem *Angelina:*
Case de time is mighty temptin' when de
    chune is in de swing,
Fu' a darky, saint or sinner man, to cut de
    pigeon-wing.

Possum Court
From Dunbar poem title *Possum* and
found five times in verse, the first being:
W'en he want to cook a possum
  Tekin' off de possum's skin.

Quilting Way
From Dunbar poem title *The Quilting*
and in verse:
Dolly sits a-quilting by her mother, stitch
  by stitch,
Gracious, how my pulses throb, how my
  fingers itch,

Ripplestir Place
From Dunbar poem *A Lazy Day:*
No ripple stirs the placid pool,
  When my adventurous line is cast,

Robin Song
Variation of "robin sung his song" found
in Dunbar poem *Retrospection:*
And when the robin sung his song
The verdant woodland ways along,
  We whistled louder than he sung.

Seapearl Lane
From Dunbar poem *The Rising of
the Storm:*
  While a water-sprite,
  In sea-pearls dight,
Hums a sea-hymn's solemn bars.

Seedling Lane
From Dunbar poem title *The Seedling* and
found four times in verse, the first being:
As a quiet little seedling
  Lay within its darksome bed,
To itself it fell a-talking,
  And this is what it said:

Skyward Court
From Dunbar poem *One Life:*
The lark sings to me at the morn,
  And near me wings her skyward-soaring
    flight;
But pleasure dies as soon as born,

*Neighborhood poster
by Gail Holliday.*

Smooth Path
Variation of "path . . . Smooth" found in
Dunbar poem *The Path:*
Each for himself must cleave a path alone,
And press his own way forward in the fight.
Smooth is the way to ease and calm delight,
And soft the road Sloth chooseth for her own;

Dight—To put in order,
appoint or repair.

Snowman Court 2
From Dunbar poem *The Plantation
Child's Lullaby:*
Suppah done an' ovah,
  Evah t'ing is still;
Listen to de snowman
  Slippin' down de hill.

Spelling Bee
Variation of "Spellin'-Bee" found in
Dunbar poem title *The Spellin'-Bee* and
twice in verse, the first being:
But where that night a spellin'-bee was
  callin' us together.

Catwing Court

Two variations found in Lindsay poem *Shantung, or The Empire of China Is Crumbling Down*, the first is "fire-winged cats":

"His Town of Cheese the mouse affrights
With fire-winged cats that light the nights."

Constant Course ☐1

From Pope poem *Essay on Man, Epistle I, Part V*:

Then nature deviates; and can man do less?
As much that end a constant course requires
Of showers and sunshine, as of man's
*   desires;*

Cornshock Court

Variation of "shocks of corn" found in Lindsay poem *From "So Much the Worse for Boston"*:

Their clothes are but their bark and hide, and
*   sod and binding for their sheaves.*
Men are as the shocks of corn, as natural as
*   alfalfa fields.*

Crazyquilt Court

From Lindsay poem *Three Poems about Mark Twain: I. The Raft*:

The river-bank is one bright crazy-quilt
Of patch-work dream, of wrath more red
*   than lust,*

Curtis Drive

A mystery . . .

Deepage Drive

Variation of "Deep in the ages" found in Lindsay poem *The Chinese Nightingale*:

"Have you forgotten . . .
Deep in the ages, long, long ago,
I was your sweetheart, there on the sand—"

Deer Pasture

From Lindsay poem *In Praise of Johnny Appleseed: I. Over the Appalachian Barricade*:

Crossed the Appalachians,
Found the glades of rotting leaves, the soft
*   deer-pastures,*
The farms of the far-off future
In the forest.

Feathered Head

From Lindsay poem *Our Mother Pocahontas*:

Because, through drowsy Springfield sped
This redskin queen, with feathered head,

Flintfeet Lane

From Lindsay poem *The Ghost of the Buffaloes*:

Cows with their calves, bulls big and vain,
Goring the laggards, shaking the mane,
Stamping flint feet, flashing moon eyes.

Folded Palm

From Lindsay poem *The Prairie Battlements*:

Here lived gray Queen Silver Dreams,
Always singing psalms,
And haughty Grandma Silver Dreams,
Throned with folded palms.

Gentle Folk

From Lindsay poem *The Jingo and the Minstrel*:

"And you will find but gardens sweet
*   Prepared beyond the seas,*
And you will find but gentlefolk
*   Beneath the cherry-trees."*

Gentle Shade ☐2

From Pope poem *Epitaph Intended for Mr. Rowe in Westminster Abbey*:

To which thy tomb shall guide inquiring eyes,
Peace to thy gentle shade, and endless rest!

Gracious End Court [1]

From Pope poem *Essay on Man, Epistle I, Part V*:

But errs not Nature from this gracious end,
From burning suns when livid deaths
   descend,

Harp String

Found twice in Lindsay poem *I Heard Immanuel Singing*, the first being:

I watched his wandering hands
Lost amid the harp-strings;
Sweet, sweet I heard him play.

Hickory Limb

From Lindsay poem *The Statue of Old Andrew Jackson*:

Andrew Jackson was eight feet tall.
His arm was a hickory limb and a maul.

Hourglass Place

Found four times in Lindsay poem *Shantung, or The Empire of China Is Crumbling Down*, the first being:

Now let the generations pass—
Like sand through Heaven's blue hourglass.

Ivory Hand Place

From Lindsay poem *The Fairy from the Apple-seed*:

And a tiny dryad came, from out the
   doll tree,
And held the boughs in ivory hands,
And waved her black hair round,

Kilrain Court

Found four times in Lindsay poem *John L. Sullivan, The Strong Boy of Boston*, the first being:

John L. Sullivan
The strong boy
Of Boston
Fought seventy-five red rounds with
   Jake Kilrain.

Life Quest Lane

From Lindsay poem *Doctor Mohawk: III. One Brief Hour of Grown-up Glory on the Gulf of Mexico*:

Wherever I wander, beggar or guest,
The soul of the U.S.A.:—that is my
   life-quest.

Minstrel Way

From Lindsay poem *Prologue to "Rhymes to Be Traded for Bread"*:

These were their gifts to him,
To the minstrel chanting, begging,
As the sunset-fire grew dim.

Moonfire Place

From Lindsay poem *The Chinese Nightingale*:

"Do you remember
The little doll-faced children
With their lanterns full of moon-fire,"

Morning Walk [2]

The phrase "morning walks" is found in two Pope poems: *Epistle To The Same [Miss Teresa Blount], on her leaving the Town after the Coronation* and *Epitaph to Mr. C., St. James's Place.*

Nature's Road [1]

Found twice in Pope poem *Essay on Man, Epistle II, Part III*, the first being:

Suffice that reason keep to Nature's road,
Subject, compound them, follow her and God.

Opal Chain

From Lindsay poem *Niagara*:

Within the town of Buffalo
Are stores with garnets, sapphires, pearls,
Rubies, emeralds aglow,—
Opal chains in Buffalo,
Cherished symbols of success.

Street of the Week

Quick Fox Quick Fox is located in the Owen Brown neighborhood of Hopewell.

In 1977 The Columbia Times ran a series called "Street of the Week." Columbia artists Sue Anne Bottomley and Mary Jo Tydlacka were among those who provided original artwork to illustrate the featured street. Pictured here is Tydlacka's interpretation for Quick Fox.

Peace Chimes Court
Variation of "chimes of peace" found in Whittier poem *The Old Burying-Ground:*
And harebells swung as if they rung
*   The chimes of peace beneath.*

Perfect Hour
From Lindsay poem *Johnny Appleseed's Wife from the Palace of Eve:*
O Mother Eve in your deathless power,
*   By Adam's throne in the crumbling years,*
Send her one murmuring perfect hour
*   Of fear and passionate tears!*

Quick Fox
From Lindsay poem *Roosevelt:*
A peacock of peacocks! An eagle of eagles!
Defeating, within himself, the quick fox.

Riding Hood Circle
From Lindsay poem *The Lame Boy and the Fairy:*
"A hundred years
And
A day,
There we will fly
And play
I-spy and cross-tag.
And meet on the highway,
And call to the game
Little Red Riding Hood,"

Rustling Leaf
From Lindsay poem *Our Mother Pocahontas:*
Her step was like a rustling leaf:
Her heart a nest, untouched of grief.

Sharp Antler
From Lindsay poem *Roosevelt:*
Oh a moose with sharp antlers!
Oh a panther of panthers—Oh a fox of foxes
Often caught in tight boxes!

Silver Sod
From Lindsay poem *The Lame Boy and the Fairy:*
"Where is our house to be?
Far in the ether sea.
There where the North Star
Is moored in the deep.
Sleepy old comets nod
There on the silver sod."

Sleepsoft Circle
Found twice in Lindsay poem *The Eagle That Is Forgotten*, the first being:
Sleep softly . . . eagle forgotten . . . under the stone.
Time has its way with you there, and the clay has its own.

Solar Walk 2
From Pope poem *Essay on Man, Epistle I, Part III:*
*   Lo, the poor Indian! whose untutor'd mind*
Sees God in clouds, or hears Him in the wind;
His soul, proud Science never taught to stray
Far as the solar-walk, or the milky-way;

Spinning Seed
From Lindsay poem *In Praise of Johnny Appleseed: II. The Indians Worship Him, but He Hurries On:*
The maples, shedding their spinning seeds,
Called to his appleseeds in the ground,

Staghorn Path

From Whittier poem *The Old Burying-Ground*:

Without the wall a birch-tree shows
*   Its drooped and tasselled head;*
Within, a stag-horn sumach grows,
*   Fern-leafed, with spikes of red.*

Steamerbell Row 1

From Lindsay poem *Three Poems About Mark Twain: I. The Raft*:

No solace on the lazy shore excels
The Duke's blue castle with its steamer-bells.

Tunemaker Terrace

From Lindsay poem *The Kallyope Yell*:

I am the Gutter Dream,
Tune-maker, born of steam,
Tooting joy, tooting hope.

Wedding Ring Way 1

From Lindsay poem *The Sea Serpent Chantey*:

Oh, the totem poles . . . the skulls . . .
The altars cold . . .
The wedding rings, the dice . . .
The buoy bells old.

Wheatsheaf Way

From Lindsay poem *In Praise of Johnny Appleseed: II. The Indians Worship Him, but He Hurries On*:

And as though his heart were a wind-blown
*   wheat-sheaf,*
As though his heart were a new built nest,

Windbell Way

From Lindsay poem *The Chinese Nightingale*:

"There were golden lilies by the bay
*   and river,*
And silver lilies and tiger-lilies,
And tinkling wind-bells in the gardens of
*   the town."*

Rustling Leaf was cast into the national spotlight when Aaron McGruder mentioned it in his Boondocks *cartoon strip. For more about McGruder's treatment of street names see the* Introduction.

Bright graphic "poster trees" designed by Gail Holliday were planted in front of The Exhibit Center located on Wincopin Circle in Town Center from 1967 to1989. "Tree maintenance" included adding neighborhood posters as Columbia grew. This photograph, circa 1978, included Clemens Crossing, Jeffers Hill, Hawthorn, Locust Park, Steven's Forest and Hopewell.

RIVER HILL

The village is named for the River Hill Farm, a 450-acre game preserve developed by The Rouse Company in 1964 and operated from October 1964 through the 1970s. It was located on the north side of old Maryland Route 32 just west of W.R. Grace and Co. The land was originally part of the land grant White Wine and Claret (see Claret Hall). When The Rouse Company purchased the land, it was the Gallagher farm. Jim Rouse was an avid duck hunter and believed that "in an era of increasing demand for shooting area and declining game lands, these preserves have provided a worthwhile means of conservation as well as first-class gunning for hunters." The Rouse Company entertained business clients and numerous public figures at the preserve, including General Omar Bradley, Admiral E.S. Land and Oriole pitcher Dave McNally.[101]

Claret Hall

The name of the village community center is derived from the original land grant White Wine and Claret which was patented to John Dorsey in 1702 for 1400 acres. By 1735, Charles and William Ridgely had expanded the land tract to 2,145 acres.[102]

Trotter Road ✴

The road name has a bucolic equestrian sound to it. Yet the name, like most of the county road names recorded in 1961, comes from the family who lived there. Emma and John Trotter purchased an historic house from one of the Warfields and lived there during the 1930s-1940s. The road became known as Trotter Road. The Historic Sites Inventory refers to the house as the John L. Due House (Henry

Warfield House, Trotter House). Mr. Due recalls that Mrs. Trotter, who was living in a house on another piece of the original property, was in her 90s and of clear mind when he became the owner of the historic house circa 1965.[103]

ABOVE
John L. Due House, 1977. It is also known as the Henry Warfield House and the Trotter House reflecting some of the former owners. The property remains in private ownership. Photograph on file at Maryland Historical Trust Library.

LEFT
In 1972 the house at River Hill Farm served as the residence of the game preserve manager. The property dated to the mid-1800s and was demolished to make way for development in Pointer's Run. Photograph on file at Maryland Historical Trust Library.

Distant Thunder Trail
From Whitman poem *The Mystic Trumpeter*:
Swift to thy spell a shuddering hum like distant thunder rolls,
Lo, where the arm'd men hasten— . . .

Drum Taps Court ☐1
Whitman poetry section title, *Drum-Taps*, and found twice in Whitman poem *First O Songs for a Prelude*, the first being:
How you led to the war, (that shall serve for our prelude, song of soldiers,)
How Manhattan drum-taps led.

Early Lilacs Path
From Whitman poem *There Was a Child Went Forth*:
The early lilacs became part of this child,
And grass and white and red morning-glories, and white and red clover, and the song of the phœbe-bird,

Eternal Ocean Place
From Whitman poem *Two Rivulets*:
Two Rivulets side by side,
Two blended, parallel, strolling tides,
Companions, travelers, gossiping as they journey.
For the Eternal Ocean bound,

Every Sail Path
From Whitman poem *Passage to India*:
Away O soul! hoist instantly the anchor!
Cut the hawsers—haul out—shake out every sail.

Fall Moon Ride
Variation of "full moon" found twice in Whitman poem *Song of Myself*, the first being:
Earth of the vitreous pour of the full moon just tinged with blue!

Few Star Court
From Whitman poem *Song of Myself*:
Night of the south winds—night of the large few stars!
Still nodding night—mad naked summer night.

Fleets of Time Court ☐1
From Whitman poem *A Thought of Columbus*:
The restless armies and the fleets of time following their leader—the old camps of ages pitch'd in newer, larger areas,

Floating Clouds Path
From Whitman poem *Respondez* (Poem of Propositions of Nakedness):
Let a floating cloud in the sky—let a wave of the sea—let growing mint, spinach, onions, tomatoes—let these be exhibited as shows, at a great price for admission!

Flowing Water Trail
From Whitman poem *Of the Terrible Doubt of Appearances*:
May-be the things I perceive, the animals, plants, men, hills, shining and flowing waters,
The skies of day and night, colors, densities, forms, may-be these are (as doubtless they are) only apparitions, . . .

Gate Keeper Lane ☐1
From Whitman poem *Song of Myself*:
The machinist rolls up his sleeves, the policeman travels his beat, the gate-keeper marks who pass,
The young fellow drives the express-wagon, (I love him, though I do not know him;)

Gentle Call ☐1
From Whitman poem *Out of the Cradle Endlessly Rocking*:
With this just-sustain'd note I announce myself to you,
This gentle call is for you my love, for you.

Phœbe Bird—Any of several American fly-catchers of the genus Sayornis.

Hawser—a large rope for towing or mooring a ship or securing it to a dock.

Golden Star Place
Variation of "stars both silvery and golden" found in Whitman poem *On the Beach at Night:*
They are immortal, all those stars both silvery
*   and golden shall shine out again,*

Hay Boat Court
From Whitman poem *Crossing Brooklyn Ferry:*
On the river the shadowy group, the big
*   steam-tug closely flank'd on each side*
*   by the barges, the hay-boat, the belated*
*   lighter,*

Helmsman Way
The word "helmsman" is found in four Whitman poems: *O Star of France, Thou Mother with Thy Equal Brood, Fancies at Navesink: 1. The Pilot in the Mist,* and *While Behind All Firm and Erect.*

Hidden Waters Way
From Whitman poem *Nay, Tell Me Not Today the Publish'd Shame:*
(Plunging to these as a determin'd diver
*   down the deep hidden waters,)*

Indian Summer Drive
From Whitman poem *Supplement Hours:*
Sane, random, negligent hours,
Sane, easy, culminating hours,
After the flush, the Indian summer, of my
*   life,*
Away from Books—away from Art— . . .

Laurel Leaves Lane
From Whitman poem *These I Singing in Spring:*
Here, some pinks and laurel leaves, and a
*   handful of sage,*

Leaves Of Grass Court
Whitman poetry collection title *Leaves of Grass.*

Pheasant Ridge neighborhood sign, 2007.

Linden Linthicum Lane ✽
The street takes its name from the Linden Linthicum United Methodist Church, a 1959 union of Linden Church and Linthicum Chapel, which relocated to Clarksville Pike in 1964. When an access road was constructed on the south side of the church to connect to the newly constructed River Hill Village Center around 1977, the new road assumed the name of the long standing church. Linthicum Chapel was named for the Reverend Hezekiah Linthicum, founder and first minister of the chapel. The origin of Linden is unknown, but still being researched by the historian at Linden Linthicum United Methodist Church.[105]

Little Bells Row
From Whitman poem *I Heard You Solemn-Sweet Pipes of the Organ:*
Heart of my love! you too I heard murmuring
*   low through one of the wrists around*
*   my head,*
Heard the pulse of you when all was still
*   ringing little bells last night under my ear.*

Majestic Days Way [1]
From Whitman poem title *As I Walk These Broad Majestic Days* and in verse:
As I walk these broad majestic days of peace,
(For the war, the struggle of blood finish'd,
*   wherein, O terrific Ideal,*
Against vast odds erewhile having gloriously
*   won,*
Now thou stridest on, yet perhaps in time
*   toward denser wars,*

Misty Top Path
Variation of "misty-topt" found in Whitman poem *Song of Myself:*
Earth of departed sunset—earth of the
*   mountains misty-topt!*

Moonsails Lane
From Whitman poem *The Ship Starting:*
Lo, the unbounded sea,
On its breast a ship starting, spreading all
*   sails, carrying even her moonsails,*

Mystic Ocean Lane
The phrase "mystic ocean" is found in two very similar Whitman poems; one is *As Consequent, Etc.:*
In you whoe'er you are my book perusing,
In I myself, in all the world, these currents
*   flowing,*
All, all toward the mystic ocean tending.
—the other is *Two Rivulets:*
In You, whoe'er you are, my book perusing,
In I myself—in all the World—these ripples
*   flow,*
All, all toward the mystic Ocean tending.

Nodding Night Court
From Whitman poem *Song of Myself:*
Night of south winds—night of the large
*   few stars!*
Still nodding night—mad naked summer
*   night.*

Old Sea Place
From Riley poem *What the Wind Said:*
And the grand old sea invited me
*   With a million beckoning hands,*
And I spread my wings for a flight as free
*   As ever a sailor plans*

Perfect Calm Court [1]
From Whitman poem *Pictures:*
In the height of the roar and carnage of the
*   battle, all of a sudden, from some*
*   unaccountable cause, the whole fury of the*
*   opposing armies subsided—there was a*
*   perfect calm,*

Pioneers Court [1]
From Whitman poem title *Pioneers! O Pioneers!* and found several times in verse, the first being:
*   Come my tan-faced children,*
Follow well in order, get your weapons ready,
Have you your pistols? have you your sharp-
*   edged axes?*
*   Pioneers! O pioneers!*

Pouring Glories Lane
The phrase "pouring glories" is found in two very similar Whitman poems; one is *Apostroph:*
O prophetic! O vision staggered with weight
*   of light! with pouring glories!*
O copious! O hitherto unequalled!
—the other is *O Sun of Real Peace:*
O vision prophetic, stagger'd with weight of
*   light! with pouring glories!*
O lips of my soul, already becoming
*   powerless!*

Pure Sky Place
From Whitman poem *Passage to India:*
I mark from on deck the strange landscape,
*   the pure sky, the level sand in the*
*   distance,*

Quiet Ways Court
From Whitman poem *Nay, Tell Me Not Today the Publish'd Shame:*
Through all your quiet ways, or North or
*   South, you Equal States, you honest farms,*
Your million untold manly healthy lives, . . .

Red Clover Lane
From Whitman poem *There Was a Child Went Forth:*
The early lilacs became part of this child,
And grass and white and red morning-
*   glories, and white and red clover,*
*   and the song of the phœbe-bird,*

Rippling Tides Terrace
From Whitman poem *Death's Valley:*
Of the broad blessed light and perfect air,
*   with meadows, rippling tides, and trees*
*   and flowers and grass,*
And the low hum of living breeze—and in
*   the midst God's beautiful eternal right*
*   hand,*

Rippling Water Walk
From Whitman poem *After the Argument:*
A group of little children with their ways
*   and chatter flow in,*
Like welcome, rippling water o'er my heated
*   nerves and flesh.*

Same Voyage Way ⬚1
From Whitman poem *One Thought Ever at the Fore:*
One thought ever at the fore—
That in the Divine Ship, the World, breasting
Time and Space,
All Peoples of the globe together sail, sail the
*   same voyage, are bound to the same*
*   destination.*

Shining Stars Lane
From Whitman poem *From Pent-up Aching Rivers:*
From the hour of shining stars and
*   dropping dews,*

Signal Bell Lane ⬚1
From Whitman poem *Pictures:*
And this, out at sea, is a signal-bell—
*   see you, where it is built on a reef, and*
*   ever dolefully keeps tolling, to warn*
*   mariners;*

Signal Flame Court ⬚1
From Whitman poem *As the Greek's Signal Flame [For Whittier's eightieth birthday, December 17, 1887]:*
As the Greek's signal flame, by antique
*   records told,*
Rose from the hill-top, like applause and
*   glory,*
Welcoming in fame some special veteran, hero,

Silent Sun Place
From Whitman poem title *Give Me the Splendid Silent Sun* and found twice in verse, the first being:
Give me the splendid silent sun with all his
*   beams full-dazzling,*

Silvery Star Path
Variation of "stars both silvery" found in Whitman poem *On the Beach at Night:*
They are immortal, all those stars both
*   silvery and golden shall shine out again,*

South Wind Circle
From Whitman poem *Song of Myself:*
Night of south winds—night of the large
*   few stars!*
Still nodding night—mad naked summer
*   night.*

Summer Sky Path
From Whitman poem *Crossing Brooklyn Ferry:*
Saw the reflection of the summer sky in
*   the water,*
Had my eyes dazzled by the shimmering
*   track of beams,*

Sunlit Water Way

From Whitman poem *Crossing Brooklyn Ferry*:

*Look'd at the fine centrifugal spokes of light
round the shape of my head in the sunlit
water,*

Swift Current Way

From Whitman poem *Crossing Brooklyn Ferry*:

*Just as you stand and lean on the rail, yet
hurry with the swift current, I stood yet
was hurried,*

Tall Branches Pass

From Whitman poem *Roots and Leaves Themselves Alone*:

*If you become the aliment and the wet they
will become flowers, fruits, tall branches
and trees.*

Trackless Sea Court

From Whitman poem *Passage to India*:

*O we can wait no longer,
We too take ship O soul,
Joyous we too launch out on trackless seas,*

Trailing Moss Gate

From Whitman poem *O Magnet-South*:

*The range afar, the richness and barrenness,
the old woods charged with mistletoe
and trailing moss,*

Trumpet Sound Court ☐1

From Whitman poem *One Song, America, Before I Go*:

*One song, America, before I go,
I'd sing, o'er all the rest, with trumpet sound,
For thee—the Future.*

Western Sea Run

From Whitman poem *Facing West from California's Shores*:

*Look off the shores of my Western sea, the
circle almost circled;*

Whaleboat Drive ☐1

From Whitman poem *Song of Myself*:

*The pilot seizes the king-pin, he heaves down
with a strong arm,
The mate stands braced in the whale-boat,
lance and harpoon are ready,
The duck-shooter walks by silent and
cautious stretches,*

Whistling Winds Walk

From Whitman poem *After the Sea-Ship*:

*After the sea-ship, after the whistling winds,
After the white-gray sails taut to their spars
and ropes,*

White Marble Court ☐1

From Whitman poem *Pictures*:

*There is an old Egyptian temple—and again,
a Greek temple, of white marble;*

White Pebble Path

From Whitman poem *Debris*:

*You shall see how I stump clergymen, and
confound them,
You shall see me showing a scarlet tomato,
and a white pebble from the beach.*

Wild Orange Gate

From Whitman poem *These I Singing in Spring*:

*And twigs of maple and a bunch of wild
orange and chestnut,*

Winter Grain Path

From Whitman poem *There Was a Child Went Forth*:

*The field-sprouts of Fourth-month and
Fifth-month became part of him,
Winter-grain sprouts and those of the
light-yellow corn, and the esculent roots
of the garden,*

Pointer's Run

The neighborhood was named to convey the hunting theme suggested by the village name.

The street names in Pointer's Run are derived from the works of two 19th century American poets, James Whitcomb Riley and Walt Whitman.

Pointer's Run neighborhood sign, 2007

Angel Rose Court
From Riley poem *The Rose:*
That an Angel-rose in the world to be
Will hide in the leaves in wait for me.

Autumn Wind Circle
From Riley poem *A Country Pathway:*
Like blooms of lorn primroses blowing loose
*   When autumn winds arise.*

Best Times Path
From Riley poem title *The Best Times* and found in verse:
When Old Folks they wuz young like us
*   An' little as you an' me,—*
Them wuz the best times ever wuz
*   Er ever goin' ter be!*

Bright Memory Drive
From Riley poem *A Country Pathway:*
*   The more determined on my wayward*
*   quest,*
As some bright memory a moment dawns
*   A morning in my breast—*

Daring Prince Way
From Riley poem *A Session with Uncle Sidney: VII. And Makes Nursery Rhymes,* sub-section title *5. The Daring Prince* and in verse:
A Daring prince, of the realm Rangg Dhune,
Once went up in a big balloon
That caught and stuck on the horns of
*   the moon,*

Distant Melody Place
From Riley poem *Dead Leaves,* section *Dawn:*
. . . As one who wades, alone,
*   Deep in the dusk, and hears the minor talk*
Of distant melody, and finds the tone,
*   In some weird way compelling him to stalk*
The paths of childhood over,— . . .

Drifting Cloud Mews
From Riley poem *I Smoke My Pipe:*
And wrapped in shrouds of drifting clouds
*   I watch the phantom's flight,*
Till alien eyes from Paradise
*   Smile on me as I write:*

Early Lily Row
From Whitman poem *When Lilacs Last in the Dooryard Bloom'd:*
All over bouquets of roses,
O death, I cover you over with roses and
*   early lilies,*

Eastern Star Way
"Star" found many times and "Eastern sea" found once in Whitman poem *When Lilacs Last in the Dooryard Bloom'd:*
Sea-winds blown from east and west,
Blown from the Eastern sea and blown from
*   the Western sea, . . .*

Empty Song Road
From Riley poem title *The Empty Song*
and in verse:
"What have we but an empty song?"
  Said the minstrel, as he bent
To stay the fingers that trailed along
  The strings of her instrument.

Enchanted Key Gate
From Riley poem *To a Boy Whistling:*
The smiling face of a happy boy
  With its enchanted key
  Is now unlocking in memory
My store of heartiest joy.

Enchanted Solitude Place
From Riley poem *A Wraith of Summer-Time:*
'Twas a summer such as broods
O'er enchanted solitudes,
Where the hand of Fancy leads us
  through voluptuary moods,

Evening Company Circle
From Riley poem title *The Evening Company.*

Evening Shadows Court
From Riley poem title *When Evening Shadows Fall* and found four times in verse, the first being:
When evening shadows fall,
  She hangs her cares away
Like empty garments on the wall
  That hides her from the day;

Evensong Mews
From Riley poem title *Evensong.*

Fairest Dream Lane
From Riley poem *If I Knew What Poets Know:*
If I knew what poets know,
  I would find a theme
Sweeter than the placid flow
  Of the fairest dream:

Folded Leaf Square
From Riley poem *A Dream Unfinished:*
The idle book lies open, and the folded leaf
  is pressed
Over the half-told story while death relates
  the rest.

Forest Shade Trail
From Riley poem *What the Wind Said:*
Adown deep glades where the forest shades
  Are dim as the dusk of day—
Where only the foot of the wild beast wades,

Garden Walk
The phrase "garden walk" is found in two Riley poems; one is *Dusk Song—The Beetle:*
The shadows on the garden walk
  Are frayed with rifts of silver light;
And, trickling down the poppy-stalk,
  The dewdrop streaks the night.
—the other is *The Rose:*
I dream to-day, o'er a purple stain
  Of bloom on a withered stalk,
Pelted down by the autumn rain
  In the dust of the garden-walk,

Gentle Light Lane
Variation of "gentle soft-born measure-less light" found in Whitman poem *When Lilacs Last in the Dooryard Bloom'd:*
The gentle soft-born measureless light,
The miracle spreading bathing all, the
  fulfill'd noon,
The coming eve delicious, the welcome night
  and the stars,

Gleaming Sand Chase
From Riley poem *A Summer Sunrise:*
The tamarind on gleaming sands
  Droops drowsily beneath the heat;

Glittering Light Lane
A mystery . . .

Glorious Light Place

From Riley poem *Oh, Her Beauty:*
Indescribable luster of glorious light,
Swooning into the moon of a mid-summer
*   night.*

Golden Seeds Row

From Riley poem *Dusk Song—The Beetle:*
*   And lavishly to left and right*
The fireflies, like golden seeds,
*   Are sown about the night.*

Grateful Heart Gate

From Riley poem *When Evening Shadows*
Fall:
And while old memories throng,
*   And vanished voices call,*
She lifts her grateful heart in song
*   When evening shadows fall.*

Great Drum Circle

From Whitman poem *Dirge for Two*
Veterans:
*   I hear the great drums pounding,*
And the small drums steady whirring,
And every blow of the great convulsive
*   drums,*
*   Strikes me through and through.*

Great Star Drive

Found twice in Whitman poem *When*
Lilacs Last in the Dooryard Bloom'd, the
first being:
When lilacs last in the dooryard bloom'd,
And the great star early droop'd in the
*   western sky in the night,*
I mourn'd, and yet shall mourn with ever-
*   returning spring.*

Hazel Thicket Terrace

From Riley poem *The Lost Path:*
And from the covert of the hazel-thicket
*   The squirrel peeped and laughed at them*
*   again.*

Gail Holliday designed this
poster for the game preserve.

Jeweled Hand Circle

From Riley poem *What the Wind Said:*
I joyed to stand where the jeweled hand
*   Of the maiden-morning lies*
On the tawny brow of the mountain-land.

Last Sunbeam Place

From Whitman poem *Dirge for Two*
Veterans:
*   The last sunbeam*
Lightly falls from the finish'd Sabbath,
On the pavement here, and there beyond it
*   is looking,*
*   Down a new-made double grave.*

Lilac Bush Path

From Whitman poem *When Lilacs Last in*
the Dooryard Bloom'd:
In the dooryard fronting an old farm-house
*   near the white-wash'd palings,*
Stands the lilac-bush tall-growing with heart-
*   shaped leaves of rich green,*

Liquid Laughter Lane
From Riley poem *August*:
A melody of wrangling voices blent
*   With liquid laughter, and with rippling calls*
Of piping lips and thrilling echoes sent
*   To mimic waterfalls.*

Mellow Twilight Court
From Riley poem *A Dream of Long Ago*:
In staccato notes that mingle
Musically with the jingle-
*   Haunted winds that lightly fan*
Mellow twilights, crimson-tinted
By the sun, . . .

Mellow Wine Way
From Riley poem *An Old Sweetheart of Mine*:
For I find an extra flavor in Memory's
*   mellow wine*
That makes me drink the deeper to that old
*   sweetheart of mine.*

Morning Light Trail
From Riley poem *Liberty*:
And the dawn that springs from the
*   darkness there*
Is the morning light of an answered prayer.

Morning Time Lane
From Riley poem *When Early March Seems Middle May*:
When morning-time is bright with sun
*   And keen with wind, and both confuse*
The dancing, glancing eyes of one

Ocean Shore Lane
From Whitman poem *When Lilacs Last in the Dooryard Bloom'd*:
The night in silence under many a star,
The ocean shore and the husky whisper-
    ing wave whose voice I know,

Old Romance Row
From Riley poem *What the Wind Said*:
And the trader sails where the mist unveils
*   The glory of old romance.*

Onward Trail
From Riley poem title *The Onward Trail* and in verse:
We feel, with him, that by and by
Our onward trails will meet and then
Merge and be ever one again.

Phantom Moon Walk
From Whitman poem *Dirge for Two Veterans*:
*   Lo, the moon ascending,*
Up from the east the silvery round moon,
Beautiful over the house-tops, ghastly,
*   phantom moon,*

Quiet Night Ride
Variation of "nights perfectly quiet" found in Whitman poem *Give Me the Splendid Silent Sun*:
Give me nights perfectly quiet as on high
*   plateaus west of the Mississippi,*
*   and I looking up at the stars,*

Radiant Gleam Way
From Riley poem *"Dream"*:
Were dazzled with a radiant gleam—
Because of this I called her "Dream."

Ranging Hills Gate
From Whitman poem *When Lilacs Last in the Dooryard Bloom'd*:
With ranging hills on the banks, with many
*   a line against the sky, and shadows,*
And the city at hand with dwellings so
*   dense, . . .*

Reedy Song Knoll
From Whitman poem *When Lilacs Last in the Dooryard Bloom'd*:
Sing on dearest brother, warble your
*   reedy song,*
Loud human song, with voice of uttermost woe.

Ripe Apple Lane
From Riley poem *What Smith Knew about Farming*:
And hundreds o' kinds

Of all sorts o' vines,
To tickle the most horticultural minds;
And little dwarf trees not as thick as
    your wrist
With ripe apples on 'em as big as your fist:

Rising Waves Way
Variation of "rising and sinking waves"
found in Whitman poem *When Lilacs*
Last in the Dooryard Bloom'd:
Over the tree-tops I float thee a song,
Over the rising and sinking waves, over
    the myriad fields and the prairies wide,

River Run
From Riley poem *Liberty:*
Days at last when the smiling sun
    Glanced down from a summer sky,
And a music rang where the rivers run,
    And the waves went laughing by;

Silent Moon Run
From Whitman poem *Dirge for Two*
Veterans:
    Lo, the moon ascending,
Up from the east the silvery round moon,
Beautiful over the house-tops, ghastly,
        phantom moon,
    Immense and silent moon.

South Trotter Road ✳
The southern portion of Trotter Road was
renamed in 1995. See Trotter Road.

Summer Sunrise Drive
From Riley poem title *A Summer Sunrise.*

Sundown Trail
From Whitman poem *I Hear America*
Singing:
The shoemaker singing as he sits on his
    bench, the hatter singing as he stands,
The wood-cutter's song, the ploughboy's on
    his way in the morning, or at noon
    intermission or at sundown,
The delicious singing of the mother, or of
    the young wife at work, . . .

Tender Mist Mews
From Riley poem *"Dream":*
Because the looks, whose ripples kissed
The trembling lids through tender mist,
Were dazzled with a radiant gleam—
Because of this I called her "Dream."

Towering Elm Terrace
Variation of "towering oak and elm"
found in Riley poem *A Country Pathway:*
    To where the pathway enters in a realm
Of lordly woodland, under sovereign reign
    Of towering oak and elm.

Towering Oak Path
From Riley poem *A Country Pathway:*
    To where the pathway enters in a realm
Of lordly woodland, under sovereign reign
    Of towering oak and elm.

Velvet Path
From Riley poem *A Wraith of Summer-Time:*
And woos our feet o'er velvet paths and
    honeysuckle floors.

Victorious Song Lane
From Whitman poem *When Lilacs Last in*
the Dooryard Bloom'd:
Passing the song of the hermit bird and the
    tallying song of my soul,
Victorious song, death's outlet song, yet
    varying ever-altering song,

Waking Dreams Knoll
From Riley poem *The Song I Never Sing:*
It flavors all the atmosphere
    With harmony divine,—
        So, often in my waking dreams,
        I hear a melody that seems
        Like fairy voices whispering
        To me the song I never sing.

Warm Sunshine Path
From Riley poem *What the Wind Said:*
I drifted by where sea-groves lie
    Like brides in the fond caress
Of the warm sunshine and the tender sky—

You can name your game at Columbia

The name of your game could have been pheasant, quail or duck at the River Hill Farm. But this ad, which The Rouse Company ran in Washington and Baltimore newspapers in 1968, also mentioned the golf, tennis, hiking, horseback riding, swimming and sailing that was available in Columbia— "a sportsman's paradise with the convenience of city living close at hand." The copy also noted "40 model homes . . . with prices ranging from $19,800 to $67,000."

Waving Tree Court
From Riley poem *The Rose:*
>   And the sun, like a bashful swain,
> Beamed on it through the waving trees
>   With a passion all in vain,—

Waving Willow Path
Variation of "willows waving" found in Riley poem *Louella Wainie:*
> Water-lilies and oozy leaves—
>   Lazy bubbles that bulge and stare
> Up at the moon through the gloom it weaves
>   Out of the willows waving there!
>   Is it despair I am wading through?
>   Louella Wainie! where are you?

Welcome Night Path
From Whitman poem *When Lilacs Last in the Dooryard Bloom'd:*
> The coming eve delicious, the welcome night
>   and the stars,
> Over my cities shining all, enveloping man
>   and land.

Western Star Run
Variation of "western fallen star" found in Whitman poem *When Lilacs Last in the Dooryard Bloom'd:*
> O powerful western fallen star!
> O shades of night—O moody, tearful night!

The self-explanatory term Town Center is used and understood world-wide. Town Center was the term used in Columbia's initial presentation to Howard County officials and residents making it clear that Columbia was not a suburb but a place with a central area for commerce, recreation, education, business, housing and entertainment.

Historic Oakland

The Town Center community center is housed in Historic Oakland. It is believed that Charles Sterrett Ridgely had a Baltimore housewright named Abraham Lerew build the mansion between 1810 and 1811. The name is likely to have come from a large oak tree that had stood on the property at the time. The Rouse Company purchased the property during the initial land acquisition and preserved it to help give a sense of history to the new town. The Rouse Company used it for offices for a short time. Over time it served as a campus for Antioch College, the home of Dag Hammarskjöld College and then offices of the local Red Cross. In 1989 the Columbia Association restored the building and it became the setting for special events, monthly teas, home to the African Art Museum of Maryland and offices for the Town Center Community Association. The Town Center Community Association became managers of the historic site in May 2002. Although Historic Oakland is in Town Center, its setting off Vantage Point Road borders open space along the Little Patuxent River and gives visitors a taste of its rural beginnings.[106]

Broken Land Parkway

Broken Land was an original land grant patented to Thomas Worthington and Henry Ridgely in 1722 for 660 acres of land along the Middle Patuxent River.[107]

Governor Warfield Parkway

Edwin Warfield (1848-1920) served as governor of Maryland from 1904 to 1908. He was the only Maryland governor born in Howard County. Oakdale, built by Warfield's father Albert, in 1838, was the home in which Warfield was born and raised and which he later enlarged and made his residence. Warfield first

BELOW RIGHT
Edwin Warfield, was born in Howard County, served as governor of Maryland from 1904 to 1908 and was owner and editor of the Ellicott City Times. *This portrait was done while he was governor.* Courtesy of the Collection of the Maryland State Archives.

BELOW LEFT
Oakdale, the home of Governor Edwin Warfield, was built in 1838. In 1898 the future governor did extensive renovations and transformed the original modest structure into one of the grandest interiors in Howard County. The house, listed on the Maryland Historical Sites Inventory, is located on Edwin Warfield Road in Woodbine and is a private residence. Photograph by Cleora B. Thompson, 1980. Courtesy of Maryland Historical Trust.

entered public service in 1874 as the Register of Wills in Howard County. Prior to his term as Governor, he served as a Maryland State Senator from 1882 to 1886, and as the Senate President in 1886. After leaving public office, Warfield practiced law in Ellicott City, became the owner and editor of the *Ellicott City Times*, and established and/or oversaw several financial institutions.[108]

Little Patuxent Parkway
The name of this main thoroughfare through Town Center is from the Little Patuxent River that runs through Columbia.

South Entrance Road
The first entrance into Columbia from Route 29 was called North Entrance Road. When the second entrance was constructed slightly south of the first, it was called South Entrance Road. Later North Entrance Road became Vantage Point Road and access to Route 29 was removed, replaced by the newly constructed Route 175 entrance to Columbia. The name and alignment of South Entrance Road never changed.

Sterrett Place
Charles Sterrett Ridgley (c. 1781-1847) was born to Deborah (Ridgely) and John Sterrett, and given the name Charles Sterrett. Later, he added Ridgely to his name as a condition of inheriting land from the estate of captain Charles Ridgely of Baltimore County. He is believed to have had Oakland Manor built in 1811, and by at least 1823, Oakland Mills was part of Ridgely's property. Ridgely served in the Maryland House of Delegates (1834-1836, 1838-1841), and was elected as Speaker for the 1838, 1840 and 1841 Sessions.[109]

Symphony Woods Road
The road is named for Symphony Woods, a 40-acre park in Town Center that surrounds the Merriweather Post Pavilion. The outdoor amphitheater was built as the summer home of the National Symphony Orchestra (NSO). The music venue is named for Marjorie Merriweather Post, heiress to the Post Cereal fortune, who was serving as vice president of the NSO in 1967 and had been on the board of directors since 1942. Today, the Merriweather Post Pavilion serves as a venue for a variety of musical events.[110]

Wincopin Circle
Wincopin Neck was an original land grant patented to Benjamin and Richard Warfield in 1702 for 883 acres.[111]

Amesbury

The neighborhood name is from the Frost poem *A Blue Ribbon at Amesbury*.

Amesbury Drive
See neighborhood name.

Banneker

The neighborhood is named for Benjamin Banneker (1731-1806). Banneker is very close to being a true native son of Howard County having lived across the Patapsco River in Baltimore County, in the area that is now known as Oella. He was born a free black with a strong acumen in mathematics and astronomy which he pursued throughout his life. His interests led him to a friendship with George Ellicott, who shared these talents. His Ellicott association positioned him to assist Andrew Ellicott in surveying the boundaries of Washington, D.C. in 1791. Some of his other notable accomplishments include creating almanacs (one cover can be viewed at America's Story website, http://www.americaslibrary. gov/jb/colonial/jb_colonial_banneker_1 _e.html), engaging in correspondence with Thomas Jefferson over the issue of slavery (view exhibit website, American Treasures of the Library of Congress, http://www.loc.gov/exhibits/treasures /trr022.html; and University of Virginia's digital resource, http://etext.virginia. edu /readex/24073.html), and writing math puzzles (paper by John Mahoney, http: //web.mit.edu/qmahoney/www/nctm /NCTM2004atalk.doc).[112]

Banneker Road
See neighborhood name.

Banneker neighborhood sign, 2007.

Cloudy April Way
A mystery . . .

Laurel Wreath Way
A mystery . . .

Same Song Square
A mystery . . .

Shepherd Square 2
Shepherd's Lawn Golf Club was one of the twelve names proposed in 1966 for what became Hobbit's Glen Golf Club. A follow-up memo stated that the origin of the name was "self-explanatory" being "descriptive of the area around the golf course."[113]

Thoroughbred Way 2
Thoroughbred Drive was first suggested as a street name in the area that became Dorsey Hall when TRC was exploring the use of animal breed names. Thoroughbred is a horse breed.[114]

Weekend Way
A mystery . . .

Wyndham Circle
A mystery . . .

Warfield Triangle

The residential area adjacent to The Mall in Columbia and bounded by Governor Warfield Parkway and Little Patuxent Parkway is named Warfield Triangle, drawing its name from the Parkway. (See Governor Warfield Parkway.) Several of the street names in this development were pulled from lists of street names compiled for earlier villages and follow no theme.

Ashton Ridge Place
Ashton first appeared on a street name list as Ashton Park Ridge when TRC was naming the roads of what would become Creighton's Run. The origin of Ashton was given as being the "[s]eat in England of [the] Lawrence family of Howard C[ou]nty." The name was not used at that time but later the name would be varied to Ashton Hills and proposed for Long Reach, then to Ashton Park Court and used for a street in Hickory Ridge. Ashton Ridge Place is another variation.[118]

Brighton Ridge Way
A mystery . . .

Bristol Park Place
A mystery . . .

Chestnut Park Lane
Chestnut Hill was first proposed by local historian Celia Holland as a possible name for the tract that became Dorsey Hall, stating that it "has a pleasant sound and is definitely associated with the Hammonds, builders of many magnificent homes . . ." Later, it would appear on lists of names for what would become the Village of Kings Contrivance, a neighborhood in Kings Contrivance, and as the variation, Chestnut Circle, for a street in Creighton's Run. Chestnut Hill was an original land grant patented to Nathan Hammond in 1754 for 1246 acres.[119]

Gramercy Place
A mystery . . .

Pembroke Green Place
Pembroke Green found its way to lists for Kings Contrivance neighborhood names, Creighton's Run road names, a Hickory Ridge street name, and then finally one for Warfield Triangle street names, all without indication of the origin. A mystery . . .[120]

Rutland Round Lane
Rutland Round Circle first appeared on a memo listing possible names for the roads that became Creighton's Run with the origin of the name given as an original land grant, Rutland's Purchase Enlarged, which was patented to Thomas Rutland in 1759 for 991 acres.[121]

Sherman Heights Place
Sherman Heights was first proposed as a possible street name for the roads that became Creighton's Run; however, no information was given as to the origin of the name. A mystery . . .[122]

Swiftstream Place
Swift Stream Golf Club was one of the twelve names proposed in 1966 for what became Hobbit's Glen Golf Club. A follow-up memo stated that the origin of the name was "self-explanatory" being "descriptive of the area around the golf course."[123]

Symphony Way ☐1
The street name was likely inspired by Symphony Woods.

Town Center Avenue
See Town Center.

Warfield Place
See Governor Warfield Parkway.

The village name honors Frazar B. Wilde, chairman of the board of Connecticut General Life Insurance in the early 1960s when James Rouse approached him and his company for the initial financing of the development of Columbia. Wilde was among the first and most ardent backers of the dream Rouse envisioned for Columbia. He is the only person involved in the creation of Columbia for whom a village is named.

Columbia Road/Columbia Pike ✳

On January 6, 1810, Maryland's General Assembly passed "an act to incorporate a Company to make a Turnpike Road from near Ellicott's lower Mills towards George-Town, in the District of Columbia." It would be several years before construction was completed on the Columbia Turnpike Road, the commonly used name derived from the southern terminus, the District of Columbia. During the early part of the 20th century, advances in railroad lines and the inception of the State Highway Commission were making companies like The Columbia Turnpike Road Company obsolete. Over the years, the State assumed maintenance of the road, the turnpike apparatus was removed, and the name became Columbia Road—although some still refer to it as Columbia Pike, a remnant of its historical past.[124]

Harper's Farm Road
See Village of Harper's Choice name.

Lynx Lane
From two Audubon paintings: *Lynx rufus, Common American Wild Cat*, and *Lynx canadensis, Canada Lynx.*

James Rouse, left, and Frazar Wilde flank the plaque affixed to a large rock near the dock at Wilde Lake after dedication of the lake that marked the beginning of Columbia on June 21, 1967. The plaque can be easily found along the path between the dock and the dam.

John (Jack) Slayton, right, and Columbia's project director William Finley study the Columbia model.

FROM AN ORIGINAL COLUMBIA POSTER SCREEN PRINT BY GAIL HOLLIDAY • PRODUCED BY GENERAL GROWTH PROPERTIES INC. • ALL PROCEEDS BENEFIT THE COLUMBIA FOUNDATION

For Wilde Lake Gail Holliday designed both a village poster and neighborhood posters. Wilde Lake is the only village that received that treatment.

Slayton House

The village community center is named for John (Jack) Slayton who, in 1966, was named the first manager of the Columbia Association. He and his wife, Barbara, became Columbia's first residents when they moved into a 19th century stone house on what would become lakefront property on the shore of Wilde Lake. When they moved in, the lake was little more than a mud pit and the recreational facilities and community centers of the Columbia Association were just plans. The former chief administrative officer of Vancouver, Washington died about six months after coming to Columbia, never seeing the town he was to manage. Barbara stayed in Columbia becoming an active member of the community including one of the first board members of the Wilde Lake Community Association, an executive with the original Columbia Bank and Trust and a founding board member of the Columbia Archives.

Trumpeter Road

From two Audubon paintings, both titled *Trumpeter Swan*, watercolors, ca. 1836 and ca. 1821, New York Historical Society.

Twin Rivers Road

The Twin Rivers name was inspired by the two river branches located in the vicinity.

Bryant Woods

The neighborhood is named for William Cullen Bryant, a 19th century American poet whose work is the source of most of the neighborhood street names.

Barcan Circle
From Bryant poem *Thanatopsis:*
. . . —Take the wings
Of morning, pierce the Barcan wilderness,
Or lose thyself in the continuous woods

Blue Heron Lane
From two Audubon paintings: *Great Blue Heron*, watercolor, ca. 1821, and *Little Blue Heron*, watercolor, ca. 1832, New York Historical Society.

Catterskill Court
From Bryant poem title *Catterskill Falls* and in verse:
Midst greens and shades the Catterskill leaps,
*   From cliffs where the wood-flower clings;*

Crimson Tree Court
From Bryant poem *Autumn Woods:*
*   But 'neath you crimson tree,*
Lover to listening maid might breathe his
*   flame,*
Nor mark, within its roseate canopy,
*   Her blush of maiden shame.*

Cullen Terrace
Named for the poet William Cullen Bryant.

Daystar Court
From Bryant poem *A Walk at Sunset:*
*   And blessed is thy radiance, whether thou*
*   Colorest the eastern heaven and night-*
*   mist cool,*
Till the bright day-star vanish, . . .

Evening Wind Court
From Bryant poem title *The Evening Wind.*

Gray Owl Garth
From Audubon painting *Great Gray Owl*, watercolor, ca. 1834, New York Historical Society.

Greek Boy Place
From Bryant poem title *The Greek Boy.*

Green Mountain Circle
From Bryant poem title *The Green Mountain Boys.*

May Wind Court [1]
From Bryant poem *The Planting of the Apple-Tree:*
*   What plant we in this apple-tree?*
Sweets for a hundred flowery springs
To load the May-wind's restless wings,

Mid Summer Lane
From Bryant poem title *Midsummer.*

Morning Wind Lane [1]
From Bryant poem *An Indian Story:*
The boughs in the morning wind are stirred,
*   And the woods their song renew,*
With the early carol of many a bird,

New Moon Place
From Bryant poem title *The New Moon*
and in verse:
Amid that flush of crimson light,
The new moon's modest bow grow bright,
  As earth and sky grow dark.

Nightmist Court
From Bryant poem *A Walk at Sunset:*
And blessed is thy radiance, whether thou
  Colorest the eastern heaven and night-
    mist cool,
Till the bright day-star vanish, . . .

Open Sky
From Bryant poem *Thanatopsis:*
And breathless darkness, and the narrow
  house,
Make thee to shudder, and grow sick at
  heart;—
Go forth, under the open sky, and list
To Nature's teachings, . . .

Painted Cup
From Bryant poem title *The Painted Cup*
and in verse:
The wanderers of the prairie know them well,
And call that brilliant flower the Painted
  Cup.

Placid Lake Court
A mystery . . .

Rain Dream Hill
From Bryant poem title *A Rain-Dream.*

Rivulet Row
From Bryant poem title *The Rivulet* and
in verse:
Thou, ever-joyous rivulet,
Dost dimple, leap, and prattle yet;

Thicket Lane
From Bryant poem *Green River:*
Lonely—save when, by thy rippling tides,
From thicket to thicket the angler glides;

Waterfowl Terrace
From Bryant poem title *To a Waterfowl.*

Wild Turkey Lane
From two Audubon paintings, both titled
Wild Turkey, watercolors, ca. 1825 and ca.
1820, New York Historical Society.

Wilde Lake Terrace
See village name.

William Tell Lane
From Bryant poem title *William Tell.*

Windstream Drive
Variation of "Wind and Stream" found in
Bryant poem title *The Wind and Stream.*

Faulkner Ridge

The neighborhood is named for William Faulkner, a 20th century author whose prose is the source of all the neighborhood street names.

August Light
Variation of Faulkner novel title *Light in August*.

Big Woods Court
From Faulkner novel title *Big Woods: The Hunting Stories*.

Cross Fox Lane
From Audubon painting *Vulpes Fulvus, American Cross Fox*.

Fable Row
From Faulkner novel title *A Fable*.

Faulkner Ridge Circle
See neighborhood name.

Green Bough Court
From Faulkner poetry book title *A Green Bough*.

Jason Court
See Jason Lane.

Jason Lane
Jason Compson, a main character, is found many times in Faulkner novel *The Sound and the Fury*, one being:

"I know you wont come." Mother said. I'd feel safer if you would."

"Safe from what." Jason said. "Father and Quentin cant hurt you."

Marble Faun Lane
From Faulkner poetry book title *The Marble Faun*.

Faulkner Ridge neighborhood sign, 2007.

Spotted Horse Lane
From Faulkner short novel title *Spotted Horses*.

Tolling Clock Way
The tolling clock is a symbol used throughout Faulkner's novel *The Sound and the Fury*. Each of the four main characters has a radically different concept of time and of how time affects their lives. A selection of six clock- and watch-related quotes are included below:

I don't suppose anybody ever deliberately listens to a watch or a clock.

The watch ticked on.

While I was eating I heard a clock strike the hour.

I wouldn't begin counting until the clock struck three.

And after a while I had been hearing my watch for some time . . .

. . . a cabinet clock ticked, then with a preliminary sound as if it had cleared its throat, struck five times.

Running Brook

The neighborhood name comes from the poem title *West-Running Brook* by Robert Frost and is found three times in verse, the first two being:

   "West-Running Brook then call it."
(West-Running Brook men call it to this day.)

The street names in Running Brook are derived primarily from the work of Robert Frost, a 20th century poet.

Brook Way
   A mystery . . . [the word "brook" is found many times in Frost poems]

Cloudburst Hill
From Frost poem title *In Time of Cloudburst.*

Darlington Road ✱
A mystery . . .

Darting Bird Lane
From Frost poem *A Prayer in Spring:*
And make us happy in the darting bird
That suddenly above the bees is heard,

Downwest Ride
Variation of "down the west" found in Frost poem *The Death of the Hired Man:*
Part of a moon was falling down the west,
Dragging the whole sky with it to the hills.

Flowertuft Court
Variation of "tuft of flowers" found in poem title and in Frost poem *The Tuft of Flowers:*
But he turned first, and led my eye to look
At a tall tuft of flowers beside a brook,

Fox Grape Terrace
From Frost poem *Wild Grapes:*
"Now you know how it feels," my brother said,
"To be a bunch of fox grapes, as they call them,"

Good Hours Place
From Frost poem title *Good Hours.*

Goodbody Court
From Tolkien book *The Return of the King,* under "Family Trees, Baggins of Hobbiton," which lists Togo Goodbody as the ancestor marrying into the Baggins family. The family name is mentioned several times, as well, at Bilbo's farewell party in Tolkien book *The Fellowship of the Ring,* such as the listing of attendees:
. . . and a selection of Burrowses, Bolgers, Bracegirdles, Brockhouses, Goodbodies, Hornblowers and Proudfoots.

Hayload Court
Variation of "load of hay" found in Frost poem *The Death of the Hired Man:*
"He thinks if he could have another chance
To teach him how to build a load of hay—"

Hermit Path
From Frost poem *To the Thawing Wind:*
Melt the glass and leave the sticks
Like a hermit's crucifix;
Burst into my narrow stall;

Homecoming Lane
Variation of "come home" found in Frost poem *The Death of the Hired Man:*
"Warren," she said, "he has come home
   to die:
You needn't be afraid he'll leave you this
   time."

Hyla Brook Road
From Frost poem title *Hyla Brook.*

Moonfall Way
Variation of "moon was falling" found in Frost poem *The Death of the Hired Man:*
Part of the moon was falling down the west,
Dragging the whole sky with it to the hills.

Oven Bird Green
From Frost poem title *The Oven Bird.*

Pale Orchis Court
From Frost poem *Mowing:*
Not without feeble-pointed spikes of flowers
(Pale orchises), and scared a bright green
snake.

Pasture Gate Lane
Variation of "pasture bars" found in Frost poem *The Peaceful Shepherd:*
And on the pasture bars

Reedy Brook Lane
From Frost poem *The Tuft of Flowers:*
A leaping tongue of bloom the scythe had
spared
Beside a reedy brook the scythe had bared.

Silas Choice
Silas, the hired man, is found eleven times in Frost poem *The Death of the Hired Man*, the first being:
To meet him in the doorway with the news
And put him on his guard. "Silas is back."

Snowy Reach
From Frost poem title *Stopping by Woods on a Snowy Evening.*

Spring Pools Lane
From Frost poem title *Spring Pools.*

Starsplit Lane
Variation of "Star-Splitter" found in Frost poem title *The Star-Splitter* and twice in verse, the first being:

That telescope was christened the Star-
Splitter,
Because it didn't do a thing but split
A star in two or three . . .

Still Corners
From Frost poem *New Hampshire:*
. . . Still Corners (so called not because
The place is silent all day long, nor yet
Because it boasts a whisky still—because
It set out once to be a city and still
Is only corners, crossroads in a wood).

Stoneboat Row
From Frost poem title *A Star in a Stone-boat* and in verse:
He loaded an old stoneboat with the star

Ten Mills Road
From Frost poem section title *Ten Mills.*

The Mending Wall
From Frost poem title *Mending Wall.*

West Running Brook Road
From Frost poem title *West-Running Brook* and found three times in verse, the first two being:
"West-Running Brook then call it."
(West-Running Brook men call it to this day.)

Whetstone Road
From Frost poem *The Tuft of Flowers:*
I looked for him behind an isle of trees;
I listened for his whetstone on the breeze.

Wildflower Terrace
Variation of "tumultuous flowers" and "go wild in" found in Frost poem *The Last Mowing:*
For you, O tumultuous flowers,
To go to waste and go wild in,

Woodward Gardens
From Frost poem title *At Woodward's Gardens.*

The Birches is a section of Running Brook comprised of Goodbody Court,
Hyla Brook Road, Pasture Gate Lane, Spring Pools Lane and The Mending Wall.
The name is from Frost poem title Birches. Birch trees appropriately framed the
sign until late 2007. Dia Pascault, James Rouse's sister, was responsible for much
of the early landscaping including several clumps of birch trees planted in
Wilde Lake Park. Some of those other clumps still thrive.

Columbia Crossing Shopping Center

Columbia Crossing Circle
The name is from the shopping center name.

Columbia Gateway Center

The Rouse Company's brochure heralding "Columbia's 20!" included "Columbia Opens a Busy New 'Gateway,'" an article describing their newest venture—developing a 584-acre business park. Vice president Jerry Brock stated, "We really see it as a 'Gateway' type of project. It is located at Columbia's front door, and we're making every effort to create not just a quality location but also the kind of quality environment that is attractive to high technology firms, major national corporations and others. It will be a true corporate Community." The streets all bear the names of inventors carrying through the technology theme.[125]

Albert Einstein Drive
Albert Einstein (1879-1955). Physicist whose work included quantum theory, theory of relativity, and the well-known equation relating mass and energy, $E = mc^2$. Einstein was awarded the 1921 Nobel Prize in Physics.[126]

Alexander Bell Drive
Alexander Graham Bell (1847-1922). Inventor of the telephone.[127]

Columbia Gateway Drive
See business park name.

Eli Whitney Drive
Eli Whitney (1765-1825). Inventor who perfected the cotton gin.[128]

John McAdam Drive
John Loudon McAdam (1756-1836). Engineer who created "macadamized" roads.[129]

Robert Fulton Drive
Robert Fulton (1765-1815). Inventor and engineer who invented the first operational steamboat, Clermont, which was launched in 1803.[130]

Samuel Morse Drive
Samuel F. B. Morse (1791-1872). Inventor of telegraphy and creator of the Morse code.[131]

Thomas Edison Drive
Thomas Alva Edison (1847-1931). Inventor extraordinaire, holding over 1000 patents, including the phonograph, the incandescent electric lamp and the motion picture projector.[132]

Columbia Restaurant Park

Benson Drive 1
Benson Park was proposed as a possible name for a business park in 1971 with the name attributed to Benson's Park, an original land grant patented to Daniel Benson in 1696 for 250 acres.[133]

Lark Brown Road ✽
Larkin Brown was a onetime resident of this road. When the County recorded official road names in 1961, they used the full name that the street was known by, Lark Brown Road, to differentiate it from Owen Brown Road.[134]

Gateway Overlook

Perched on a hillside overlooking the Columbia Gateway Center that sits across Route 175, the Gateway Overlook shopping center opened for business in Summer 2007. The name is descriptive of the location.

Gateway Overlook Drive
See shopping center name.

Marie Curie Drive
Marie Sklodowska Curie (1867-1934). Polish-French scientist whose lifelong research in radiation and X-ray technology led to two Nobel Prizes awarded to her in different disciplines—in physics in 1903 for radiation research and then in chemistry in 1911 for the discovery of radium.[135]

Robinson Jeffers Drive
Robinson Jeffers is the poet whose works are the source of street names in the neighboring village of Long Reach.

Guilford Industrial Park

Berger Road ✱
Alexander X. Berger was Rector at Christ Church, the Mother Church of Trinity Chapel when it was first consecrated in 1857 and became Trinity's first Rector. Trinity Chapel, known as Trinity Church since its independence from Christ Church in 1866, is located on Route 1 near Waterloo. Berger resigned his duties at Christ Church in 1861.[136]

Gerwig Lane
The road is named for Charles Lee Gerwig. Gerwig was a member of the Stromberg family, owners of Stromberg Publications which published the *Howard County Times*. Gerwig, his wife

Lodona, his sister Doris Stromberg Thompson, and Thompson's husband, Phillip all had positions at the family-run paper. The Strombergs and the Thompsons both had strong ties to Columbia. The Strombergs were consistent supporters of Columbia and the Thompson family sold considerable land, located near Oakland Mills Road, to The Rouse Company during the initial land acquisition. When Gerwig died in 1966, it is likely that his sister asked Rouse to name a road after him.[137]

Hillcroft Executive Park

Hillside Court
The street name was likely inspired by area topography.

Woodside Court
The street name was likely inspired by area topography.

Oakland Ridge Industrial Center

Red Branch Road
The Red Hill Branch of the Little Patuxent River was the inspiration for the street name.

Rumsey Road
James Rumsey (1743-1792). Inventor of world's first jet-propelled boat.[138]

Patuxent Woods Business Park

Patuxent Woods Drive
Topographically inspired name from the nearby Little Patuxent River and the wooded acres it runs through.

Rivers Corporate Park

Riverwood Drive
Dave Forester, a development director of HRD at the time, wrote that the road is named "after salient features of the park."[139]

Sieling Industrial Center

Henry Sieling sold approximately 870 acres of land to The Rouse Company in August 1963, as part of the initial land acquisition for Columbia.

Dobbin Road
George W. Dobbin's (1809-1891) role as the first person appointed Visitor from Howard County to the Maryland Hospital by Act, Chapter 364 may have been what caught the eye of one of Columbia's namers; however, he meant so much more to the history of Howard County and Maryland at large. Dobbin, son of an immigrant, was born and raised in Baltimore and chose law for his studies and future profession. Dobbin began his law practice in Baltimore, but like many other city dwellers he acquired land in the outlying county as an escape from the summer heat. He chose land in Elkridge, and started building The Lawn around 1835. Eventually, he would make this his permanent residence, but the impact would be far greater for Elkridge as other lawyers joined their colleague in building homes along the hill banking the Patapsco River. The migration earned

this section of Elkridge the moniker "Lawyers' Hill" which still is used today. Dobbin's law career evolved, leading him to a judicial position on the Supreme Bench of Baltimore City from 1867-1882. His stature in the community at large earned Judge Dobbin positions on boards ranging from such varied fields as health care, education, agriculture and transportation. He was also the co-founder of the Maryland Historical Society. The Lawn was the 2007 decorator show house for Historic Ellicott City, Inc.[140]

Herrmann Drive
Charles A. Herrmann wore many hats in Ellicott City at the turn of the 20th century. He was an insurance broker, a member of Emory Methodist Church, an office building owner, a member of the City Council, and an engineer for Volunteer Fire Company No. 1. It is perhaps the latter that caught the eye of the street namer whose notes read: "Mr. Herrmann—only man able to get old gas powered pumper started." Later, after watching a demonstration of a motorized fire engine in 1920, Herrmann became an advocate for the need to improve Ellicott City's fire fighting equipment. He passed away in 1936.[141]

George Dobbin, a prominent Baltimore lawyer, built a summer home in Elkridge and led the migration of other colleagues. The area became known as "Lawyer's Hill." Courtesy of the Collection of Maryland State Archives.

McGaw Court/McGaw Road

Northwestern University Archives holds the papers of Foster G. McGaw (1897-1986) and the records of the American Hospital Supply Corporation (AHSC), the company he founded in 1922. McGaw was an exceedingly accomplished individual, and AHSC was very successful under his tenure. AHSC, an Illinois based company, located its Scientific Products Division in Columbia on McGaw Road in the early 1970s. The AHSC name no longer exists as a result of mergers, and the Columbia-based operations have moved from McGaw Road, yet the name of the man who started it all remains.[142]

Mendenhall Road

Thomas Mendenhall bought a mill from the Ellicott's in 1794 for the purposes of making paper. Later the mill was bought by Edward Gray who turned it into a cotton mill in 1812. The mill was located on the Patapsco down river from Ellicott's Mills.[143]

Oak Hall was built by Richard Dorsey in 1809. The house and outbuildings were demolished in November 1985. Photo by Cleora Barnes Thompson, 1977. Courtesy of Maryland Historical Trust.

Oak Hall Lane

Home to Columbia's Main U.S. Post Office, the road takes its name from Oak Hall, an historic house that used to stand along it. The house and outbuildings were demolished in November 1985. When the historic inventory was conducted in 1977, the archivist wrote: "In perfect condition and lovingly cared for by Mr. and Mrs. William Dorsey, Oak Hall remains one of Howard County's most valuable landmarks." The inventory identifies this house to have been the sister house of Waveland (still standing in Sewell's Orchards), built by Larkin Dorsey, brother of Richard Dorsey who built Oak Hall in 1809. Continuously owned by Dorsey's until 1882, it was then sold to John Sieling whose family maintained it until 1969 when the Dorsey family name returned to ownership through marriage (Elise Sieling married Hammond Dorsey III and their son, William Dorsey was owner at time of the 1977 inventory).[144]

Stanford Boulevard

A mystery . . .

Snowden Square Shopping Center

Commerce Center Drive

The street name likely reflects the area's commercial activity.

Snowden Square Drive

The street name is from the shopping center name. See Snowden River Parkway.

- **Endnotes**
- **Enhanced Bibliography**
- **Index**

Endnotes

Most of the documents needed to research the place names of Columbia, Maryland can be found in the Columbia Archives. When Columbia was being planned, built and named, many memoranda, letters, maps, and other printed materials passed between the hands of James Rouse and the various department heads of Howard Research and Development Corporation (HRD) documenting the process and the decisions made. It is not surprising, therefore, that many of the endnotes for this book come from two collections in the Columbia Archives: the James W. Rouse Papers (1914-1996), and the Howard Research and Development Corpora-

tion Records (1959-2000). Several of the Archives' vertical files (vfs) were used fairly heavily during the research process as well. Vfs are files arranged by subject matter and primarily contain clippings, photocopies of secondary source materials, and in some instances, correspondence and other printed materials. The titles of the vfs collections are descriptive of the subjects covered. To keep the endnotes brief, the frequently cited materials appear in the endnotes in an abbreviated format. A key listing the abbreviated formats and the full collection titles follows. All uses of C. A. stand for the Columbia Archives.

Abbreviated format	Refers to
Names folder, Rouse Papers, C. A.	folder titled "Names" found in the James W. Rouse Papers (RG I), Series 3 Columbia, box 56, C. A.
Rouse Papers [following a folder title]	material from the James W. Rouse Papers (RG I), Series 3 Columbia (unless other series noted)
Forester folder, HRD Records, C. A.	folder titled "David E. Forester 1973-1997" found in HRD Records (RG II), Series 10.1 Development Directors, box 1, C. A.
Columbia Names [date specified] folder, HRD Records, C. A.	one of nine folders arranged chronologically from 1966-2000 and one undated folder found in HRD Records (RG II), Series 14 Marketing, box 1, C. A.
Biographical File, C. A.	vfs titled Biographical File, C. A.
Columbia Articles, C. A.	vfs titled Articles About Columbia, C. A.
Columbia Builders, C. A.	vfs titled Columbia Builders and Developers, C. A.
Columbia Place Names, C. A.	vfs titled Columbia Place Names, C. A.
Howard County History, C. A.	vfs titled Howard County History, C. A.

Introduction

1 Michael Chabon, "Maps and Legends," *Architectural Digest,* April 2001, 46. Columbia Articles, C. A.

2 James Rouse to Richard Anderson, memorandum, 17 June 1970, Names folder, Rouse Papers, C. A.

3 James Rouse to Scott Ditch, memorandum, 11 October 1965, Names folder, Rouse Papers, C. A.

4 Robert Keller, "What's In A Name? On Columbia's Streets, Almost Anything," *Baltimore Sun,* September 18, 1968. Columbia Articles, C. A.

5 Scott Ditch, "The Naming of Columbia," in *Creating a New City,* ed. Robert Tennenbaum (Columbia, MD: Partners in Community Building and Perry Publishing, 1996), 77.

6 Evelyn Menzies, in discussion with Barbara Kellner and Missy Burke, November 25, 2003.

7 Ibid.

8 William Finley to James Rouse, memorandum, 4 January 1966, Names folder, Rouse Papers, C. A.

9 Eleanor Lewis to James Rouse, 26 January 1966, Names folder, Rouse Papers, C. A.

10 Ralph DeGroff to James Rouse, 28 January 1966, Names folder, Rouse Papers, C. A.

11 Nancy Allison to James Rouse, note, 6 February 1967, Names folder, Rouse Papers, C. A.

12 Ditch, *Creating a New City,* 77.

13 Rouse to Anderson, memorandum, 17 June 1970, Names folder, Rouse Papers, C. A.

14 Menzies, in discussion with Kellner and Burke, November 25, 2003.

15 Michael Chabon, interview by Patrick Farrell and Josef Sawyer, December 2005. Audio-Visual, C. A.

16 Douglas Butcher, "Columbia's Street Name Process Banks On Artists," *The Columbia Times,* May 20, 1971. Columbia Place Names, C. A.

17 Kay Sarfaty to Don Brunner, 3 January 1973, Columbia Names 1973 folder, HRD Records, C. A.

18 Jackie Ball, "Answers From Alice," *Columbia Magazine,* November 1985, 15. Columbia Place Names, C. A.

19 Nancy Miller, in discussion with Barbara Kellner, March 26, 2007.

20 Ibid.

21 Aaron McGruder, "The Boondocks," *Baltimore Sun,* October 20, 1999. Columbia Place Names, C. A.

22 Ben McGrath, "The Radical: Why do editors keep throwing 'The Boondocks' off the funnies page?" *The New Yorker,* April 19 & 26, 2004, 153-161. Biographical File, C. A.

23 Paige Murphy, in discussion with Barbara Kellner, January 10, 2005.

24 James Rouse, "It Can Happen Here," speech, Conference on The Metropolitan Future, University of California at Berkeley, 26 September 1963, Rouse Papers, Series 5 Speeches, box 4, C. A.

How Did Columbia Get Its Name?

25 Wallace Hamilton to James Rouse, William Finley, and Morton Hoppenfeld, "Naming the New Town," memorandum, 17 June 1964, folder "HRD: Columbia History (3 of 3)," HRD Records, Series 2 Work Group, box 1, C. A.

26 Ibid.

27 James Rouse to Samuel Neel, 5 November 1963, folder "August – November 1963," Rouse Papers, Series 4 Mail-By-Month, box 3, C. A.

28 Hamilton to Rouse, Finley, and Hoppenfeld, "Naming the New Town," memorandum, 17 June 1964, folder "HRD: Columbia History (3 of 3)," HRD Records, Series 2 Work Group, box 1, C. A.

29 Ibid.

30 Ditch, *Creating a New City,* 77.

Dorsey's Search

31 Caleb Dorsey, *Original Land Grants of Howard County, Maryland,* map, 1968; and [Caleb Dorsey], *Index to Dorsey Map,* 4.

32 *Archives of Maryland Online,* vol. 570, "Session Laws, 1809," Chapter 128, 77-85; vol. 628, "Session Laws, 1823," Chapter 163, 102-3; and vol. 547, "Session Laws, 1832," Chapter 108, 113 (Maryland State Archives (MSA), 2003) http://aomol.net/html/index.html (accessed January 25, 2007).

33 Cleora Barnes Thompson, *HO-28 Dorsey Hall,* Howard County Historic Sites Inventory (Maryland Historical Trust, 1978-1979); National Park Service, National Register Information System (NRIS), http://www.nps.gov (accessed November 3, 2004); and folder "Dorsey Hall," Howard County History, C. A.

34 Thompson, *HO-412 Gray Rock,* Historic Sites Inventory, 1977; and folder "Gray Rock," Howard County History, C. A.

35 G. M. Hopkins, *Atlas of Fifteen Miles Around Baltimore including Howard County, Maryland, 1878* (Ellicott City, MD: Howard County Bicentennial Commission, 1975), 9; and Simon J. Martenet, *Martenet's Map of Howard County, Maryland* (Baltimore, 1860).

36 Ogden Nash to Mr. Rouse, 24 January 1969, folder "VCK: Complaints 1969-1972," Rouse Papers, Series 1.5 The Rouse Company, box 64, C. A.; and Ogden Nash, "A Plaintive Plaintiff," *Keynotes* [newsletter], February 1970, p. 1, folder "VCK: General 1969-1973," Rouse Papers, Series 1.5 The Rouse Company, box 65, C. A.

Harper's Choice

37 James Rouse to Mrs. R.G.H. Carroll, 22 March 1966, Names folder, Rouse Papers, C. A.

38 Granville Wehland, in discussion with Barbara Kellner and Robin Emrich, February 28, 2007.

39 John Shallcross to Scott Ditch, memorandum, 3 and 4 March 1969, folder "Correspondence – Scott Ditch 1967-1970," HRD Records, Series 15 Public Affairs, box 1, C. A.

40 Jean Moon to Barbara Kellner, e-mail, 31 October 2005.

41 James W. Rouse to Muriel Carroll, 22 March 1966, Names folder, Rouse Papers, C. A.

42 Gerald Brock to Douglas McGregor, memorandum with note, 27 February 1986; and Forester to Douglas McGregor, memorandum, 29 April 1993—both from Forester folder, HRD Records, C. A.

43 E. Menzies to William E. Finley, memorandum, 30 April 1966, Columbia Names 1966 folder, HRD Records, C. A.

44 Ingrid M. Hattendorf and Christian-Albrecht Gollub, "From Longfellow's Journal," *The Old Stone Mill* (online finding aid), Redwood Library & Anthenæum, http://www.redwoodlibrary.org (accessed February 15, 2007).

45 E. C. Menzies to Bernard Rodgers, memorandum, 7 July 1969, Columbia Names 1969 folder, HRD Records, C. A.

46 Ibid.

Hickory Ridge

47 Dorsey, *Original Land Grants,* map; and *Index,* 7; and Thompson, *HO-20 Hickory Ridge,* Historic Sites Inventory, 1976.

48 Dorsey, *Original Land Grants,* map; and *Index,* 3.

49 Pam Taylor [on behalf of Melvin Anders] to Missy Burke, e-mail, 4 August 2003.

50 Phillip Stevens, in discussion with Missy Burke, October 28, 2004.

51 Wehland, in discussion with Kellner and Emrich, February 28, 2007; and Howard County Planning Commission, *Road Index* (Howard County, MD: the Commission, 1961).

52 Paulina C. Moss and Levirn Hill, eds., *Seeking Freedom: A History of the Underground Railroad in Howard County, Maryland* (Columbia, MD: Howard County Center of African American Culture, 2002), 36; Barbara W. Feaga, et al., *Howard's Roads to the Past* (Ellicott City, MD: Howard County Sesquicentennial Celebration Committee, 2001), 85; and Howard County Sesquicentennial Committee, Religious Subcommittee, *Profiles of Faith: Histories of Religious Communities of Howard County* (Howard County, MD: the Committee, 1999), 188.

53 Wehland, in discussion with Kellner and Emrich, February 28, 2007; and Joetta M. Cramm, *Howard County: A Pictorial History* (Norfolk: The Donning Company, 1987), 216.

54 Forester to Office of Planning and Zoning, memorandum, 6 September 1977; Lesa Borg to Mickey Dunham, memorandum, 4 December 1978; and Forester to William Roberts, memorandum, 22 December 1989—all from Forester folder, HRD Records, C. A.

55 Richard Wilson to Missy Burke, e-mail, 23 September 2003.

56 Ibid.

57 Ibid.

Kings Contrivance

58 Anderson Barnes to Michael Spear, et al., memorandum, 4 October 1973, Forester folder, HRD Records, C. A.

59 Wehland, in discussion with Kellner and Emrich, February 28, 2007; and Hopkins, *Atlas,* 22.

60 Hamill Kenny, *Placenames of Maryland: Their Origin and Meaning* (Baltimore, MD: Maryland Historical Society, 1984), 105.

61 Richard Ackman, in discussion with Barbara Kellner, April 15, 2006.

62 Cramm, *Howard County: A Pictorial History,* 67; Thompson, *HO-39 Worthington's Quarter's (White Hall, Iris Hill),* Historic Sites Inventory, ca. 1977; and Wehland, in discussion with Kellner and Emrich, February 28, 2007.

63 Folder "Dunham, Mickey 1970-1971," Rouse Papers, box 29; Minutes, 23 May 1981, 5, folder "1980-1981," Kings Contrivance Community Association Records, Series 3 Minutes, box 1; and John Musselman to Mr. Woodford, 14 August 1981, Forester folder, HRD Records—all C. A.

64 "Ridgely, Henry," *Maryland Patents Index – Index 54* (MSA, 2005), http://www.msa.md.gov (accessed July 20, 2006).

65 Minutes, 25 September 1986, 2, folder "1986-1987," Kings Contrivance Community Association Records, Series 3 Minutes, box 1, C. A.

66 Wehland, in discussion with Kellner and Emrich, February 28, 2007.

67 Cramm, *Howard County: A Pictorial History,* 58 and 107.

68 Wehland, in discussion with Kellner and Emrich, February 28, 2007.

69 Howard County Sesquicentennial Religious Subcommittee, *Profiles of Faith,* 99; and Thompson, *HO-37 Athol,* Historic Sites Inventory, 1976.

70 Thomas G. Harris, Jr., in discussion with Barbara Kellner and Robin Emrich, March 6, 2007.

Long Reach

[71] Dorsey, *Original Land Grants*, map; and *Index*, 8.

[72] Dorsey, *Original Land Grants*, map; and *Index*, 8; untitled list, 14 May 1969, Columbia Names 1969 folder, HRD Records, C. A.; and Katherine Sarfaty to Ralph Everhart, memorandum, 19 January 1970, Columbia Names 1970 folder, HRD Records, C. A.

[73] Martenet, *Martenet's Map.*

[74] Dorsey, *Original Land Grants*, map; and *Index*, 8.

[75] Diane M. Howard to David E. Forester, 2 March 1989, includes Forester's handwritten reply, 3 March 1969, Forester folder, HRD Records, C. A.

[76] Dorsey, *Original Land Grants*, map; and *Index*, 11; and Edward B. Mathews, "The Counties of Maryland, Their Origin, Boundaries, and Election Districts," *Maryland Geological Survey* 6, part 5 (1906): 475 (article reprinted in *Archives of Maryland Online*, vol. 630, 59, (MSA, 2006), http://aomol.net/html/index.html (accessed May 19, 2005)).

[77] Dorsey, *Original Land Grants*, map; and *Index*, 8.

[78] Dorsey, *Original Land Grants*, map; and *Index*, 9.

[79] Dorsey, *Original Land Grants*, map; and *Index*, 9.

Oakland Mills

[80] Hopkins, *Atlas*, 19 and 23.

[81] Plaque hanging in The Other Barn, Oakland Mills Village Center; and press release, 19 November 1969, folder "Village Center, Opening Ceremonies 1969," Oakland Mills Community Association Records, Series 1 Histories, box 1, C. A.

[82] Dorsey, *Original Land Grants*, map; and *Index*, 12.

[83] Wehland, in discussion with Kellner and Emrich, February 28, 2007; and Howard County Planning Commission, *Road Index.*

[84] Wehland, in discussion with Kellner and Emrich, February 28, 2007; and Cramm, *Howard County: A Pictorial History*, 216.

[85] Wehland, in discussion with Kellner and Emrich, February 28, 2007; and Howard County Planning Commission, *Road Index.*

[86] "American Obituary – 1834-1835," *The American Almanac and Repository of Useful Knowledge*, 1830-1861, 297; "Reminiscences of Baltimore, or Baltimore Town in 1795," *The Bankers' Magazine and St. Financial*, July 1848, 9; and "Anecdote of the Late Robert Oliver," *The Baltimore Literary and Religious Magazine (1835-1841)*, February 1835, 59 (*APS Online*, database online, accessed via Howard County Public Library (HCPL), April 10, 2007).

[87] Dorsey, *Original Land Grants*, map; and *Index*, 12.

[88] Dorsey, *Original Land Grants*, map; and *Index*, 13.

[89] Wehland, in discussion with Kellner and Emrich, February 28, 2007; and Chesapeake Bay Program (Annapolis, MD), http://www.chesapeakebay.net (accessed March 2007).

[90] J. H. Clawson, Jr. to Ralph C. Everhart, 8 January 1970, Columbia Names 1970 folder, HRD Records, C. A.

[91] Wehland, in discussion with Kellner and Emrich, February 28, 2007; and Chesapeake Bay Program (Annapolis, MD), http://www.chesapeakebay.net (accessed March 2007).

[92] Wehland, in discussion with Kellner and Emrich, February 28, 2007.

Owen Brown

[93] Tom Horton, "A Poetic License Gives Columbia Arty Addresses," *Baltimore Sun*, August 5, 1973; Cramm, *Howard County: A Pictorial History*, 216; and Feaga, *Howard's Roads to the Past*, 60-61.

[94] Dorsey, *Original Land Grants*, map; and *Index*, 2.

[95] Dorsey, *Original Land Grants*, map; and *Index*, 11; and Edward B. Mathews, "The Counties of Maryland, Their Origin, Boundaries, and Election Districts," *Maryland Geological Survey* 6, part 5 (1906): 475 (article reprinted in *Archives of Maryland Online*, vol. 630, 59, (MSA, 2006), http://aomol.net/html/index.html (accessed May 19, 2005)).

[96] Susan Thornton, "Port in a Storm," *Howard County Times*, February 21, 1991.

[97] Mary Carter [Smith] to Mr. Rouse, 4 July 1974, folder "Smith, Mary C. 1968- 1970," Rouse Papers, Series 1.5 The Rouse Company, box 59, C. A.

[98] Dorsey, *Original Land Grants*, map; Wehland, in discussion with Kellner and Emrich, February 28, 2007; and Community Research & Development, "First Lake Named for Frazar Wilde," *Columbia*, Winter 1966, 3, C. A.

[99] Kay Sarfaty to Don Chorney, memorandum, 6 November 1973, Columbia Names 1973 folder, HRD Records, C. A.

[100] Dorsey, *Original Land Grants*, map; and *Index*, 8.

River Hill

[101] Folder "Game Preserve [River Hill Farm] 1964-1966," lists, and quote from James Rouse to Edwin Warfield III, 17 April 1964, Rouse Papers, box 36, C. A.; Community Research & Development, "River Hill in Second Season," *Columbia,* Winter 1966, 15 and Steven E. Ambrose, "Go Hunt Someplace Else," *Columbia Today,* October-November 1969, 8-10, C. A.; Scrapbook, October 1964-October 1965, HRD Records, Series 21 Scrapbooks, C. A.; and Thompson, *HO-158 River Hill Farm (Four Brothers Portion, Richard B. Owings House),* Historic Sites Inventory, 1977.

[102] Dorsey, *Original Land Grants,* map; and *Index,* 13.

[103] Wehland, in discussion with Kellner and Emrich, February 28, 2007; John L. Due, in discussion with Robin Emrich, May 22, 2007; and Thompson, *HO-161 John L. Due House (Henry Warfield House, Trotter House),* Historic Sites Inventory, 1977.

[104] Dorsey, *Original Land Grants,* map; and *Index,* 9.

[105] Howard County Sesquicentennial Religious Subcommittee, *Profiles of Faith,* 186.

Town Center

[106] Oakland Manor Research Collection, Howard County Historical Society; and folders "Oakland" and "Olivers," Howard County History, C. A.

[107] Dorsey, *Original Land Grants,* map; and *Index,* 2.

[108] Thompson, *HO-2 Oakdale,* Historic Sites Inventory, 1978-1979; Robert J. Brugger, *Maryland: A Middle Temperament, 1634-1980* (Baltimore, MD: The Johns Hopkins University Press, 1988), 406; and Frank F. White, Jr., *The Governors of Maryland 1777-1970* (Baltimore, MD: Twentieth Century Printing Company, 1970), 232-236.

[109] *Archives of Maryland Online,* vol. 204, "Laws of Maryland 1785-1795," 459; and vol. 628, "Session Laws, 1823," 18 (MSA, 2003) http://aomol.net/html/index.html (accessed May 23, 2007).

[110] The Rouse Company, "Symphony Pavilion Named to Honor Mrs. Merriweather Post, Exciting Season Scheduled," *Columbia,* Winter 1967, 6, C. A.

[111] Dorsey, *Original Land Grants,* map; and *Index,* 13.

[112] Silvio A. Bedini, *The Life of Benjamin Banneker: The First African-American Man of Science* (2nd ed, Baltimore, MD: Maryland Historical Society, 1999); and The Library of Congress, *America's Stories,* http://www.americaslibrary.gov (accessed May 3, 2007).

[113] Scott Ditch to William Finley, memorandum, 27 April 1966, and E. Menzies to William Finley, memorandum, 30 April 1966, Columbia Names 1966 folder, HRD Records, C. A.

[114] Kay Sarfaty to Don Chorney, memorandum, 6 November 1973, Columbia Names 1973 folder, HRD Records, C. A.; and Axel Loen to J. H. Clawson, 7 June 1974, Forester folder, HRD Records, C. A.

[115] Folder "Winchester Homes," Columbia Builders, C. A.; and "Shareholder Letters," *Weyerhaeuser 1997 Annual Report,* Weyerhaeuser Company, www.weyerhaeuser.com/annualreport/ar97/shareholder-creighton.htm (accessed July 20, 2006).

[116] "Governors under Proprietary and Parliamentary Government, 1634-1689," Special Collections, MSA SC 2685, Maryland State Archives, http://www.msa.md.gov (accessed July 25, 2006).

[117] Dorsey, *Original Land Grants,* map; and *Index,* 4; "Doddridge, John," *Maryland Patents Index – Index 54* (MSA, 2005), http://www.msa.md.gov (accessed July 12, 2006); and Charles Francis Stein, Jr., *Origin and History of Howard County, Maryland* (Baltimore, MD: the author in cooperation with The Howard County Historical Society, 1972), 344.

[118] Forester to Office of Planning and Zoning, memorandum, 6 September 1977; Lesa Borg to Mickey Dunham, memorandum, 4 December 1978; Forester to William Roberts, memorandum, 22 December 1989; and Forester to Alvis Hagelis, memorandum, 15 August 2000—all from Forester folder, HRD Records, C. A.

[119] Kay Sarfaty to Scott Ditch, memorandum, 29 June 1972, Columbia Names 1972 folder, HRD Records, C. A.; K. Sarfaty to A. Barnes and A. Scavo, memorandum, 28 September 1973; Lesa Borg to Forester, et al., memorandum, 29 August 1977; Lesa Borg to Forester, memorandum, February 27, 1978—previous three from Forester folder, HRD Records, C. A.; and Dorsey, *Original Land Grants,* map; and *Index,* 3.

[120] Lesa Borg to Forester, et al., memorandum, 29 August 1977; Lesa Borg to Forester, memorandum, 27 February 1978; and Forester to Alvis Hagelis, memorandum, 15 August 2000—all from Forester folder, HRD Records, C. A.

[121] Lesa Borg to Forester, et al., memorandum, 29 August 1977; Forester to Alvis Hagelis, memorandum, 15 August 2000—both from Forester folder, HRD Records, C. A.; and Dorsey, *Original Land Grants,* map; and *Index,* 11.

[122] Lesa Borg to Forester, et al., memorandum, 29 August 1977; Forester to Alvis Hagelis, memorandum, 15 August 2000—both from Forester folder, HRD Records, C. A.

[123] Scott Ditch to William Finley, memorandum, 27 April 1966, and E. Menzies to William Finley, memorandum, 30 April 1966, Columbia Names 1966 folder, HRD Records, C. A.

Wilde Lake

[124] *Archives of Maryland Online,* vol. 570, "Session Laws, 1809," Chapter 128, 77-85; vol. 628, "Session Laws, 1823," Chapter 163, 102-103; and vol. 547, "Session Laws, 1832," Chapter 108, 113 (MSA 2003) http://aomol.net/html/index.html (accessed January 25, 2007).

Business, Industrial and Shopping Centers

[125] The Rouse Company, "Columbia's 20!" folder "Marketing Publications 1980's," HRD Records, Series 14 Marketing, box 3, C. A.

[126] "Albert Einstein," *Science and Its Times 6: 1900-49,* (Detroit: Gale Group, 2000), (*Science Resource Center,* database online, accessed via Howard County Public Library (HCPL), May 1, 2007).

[127] "Alexander Graham Bell," *Science and Its Times 5: 1800-99,* (*Science Resource Center,* database online, accessed via HCPL, May 1, 2007).

[128] "Eli Whitney," *Science and Its Times 4: 1700-99,* (*Science Resource Center,* database online, accessed via HCPL, May 1, 2007).

[129] "John Loudon McAdam," *World of Invention,* ed. Kimberley A. McGrath, (Detroit: Thomson Gale, 2006), (*Science Resource Center,* database online, accessed via HCPL, May 1, 2007).

[130] "Robert Fulton," *Science and Its Times 5: 1800-99,* (*Science Resource Center,* database online, accessed via HCPL, May 1, 2007).

[131] "Samuel Finley Breese Morse," *Science and Its Times 5: 1800-99,* (*Science Resource Center,* database online, accessed via HCPL, May 1, 2007).

[132] "Thomas Alva Edison," *Science and Its Times 5: 1800-99,* (*Science Resource Center,* database online, accessed via HCPL, May 1, 2007).

[133] Kay Sarfaty to Rob Shuman, memorandum, 27 July 1971, Columbia Names 1971 folder, HRD Records, C. A.; and Dorsey, *Original Land Grants,* map; and *Index,* 2.

[134] Wehland, in discussion with Kellner and Emrich, February 28, 2007.

[135] "Marie Curie," *Science and Its Times 5: 1800-99,* (*Science Resource Center,* database online, accessed via HCPL, August 2, 2007).

[136] Wehland, in discussion with Kellner and Emrich, February 28, 2007; and Trinity Episcopal Church, "Trinity Episcopal Church 1857-Present," http://www.trinity-waterloo.ang-md.org/history.htm (accessed May 23, 2007).

[137] Wehland, in discussion with Kellner and Emrich, February 28, 2007; and James Rouse to Phillip Thompson, 21 February 1978, folder "Howard County Times," Rouse Papers, box 43, C. A.

[138] "James Rumsey," *World of Invention,* ed. McGrath (*Science Resource Center,* database online, accessed via HCPL, May 24, 2007).

[139] DEF [Forester] to Walt, memorandum, 25 August 1981, Forester folder, HRD Records, C. A.

[140] Thompson, *HO-141 The Lawn,* Historic Sites Inventory, 1978; and folder "The Lawn," Howard County History, C. A.

[141] Columbia Names undated folder, HRD Records, C. A.; B. H. Shipley, Jr., *Remembrances of Passing Days: A Pictorial History of Ellicott City and Its Fire Department* (Virginia Beach, VA: The Donning Company, 1997), 26, 38, and 58; and Celia M. Holland with updates from Janet P. Kusterer and Charlotte T. Holland, *Ellicott City, Maryland Mill Town, U. S. A.* (Ellicott City, MD: Historic Ellicott City Inc., 2003), 102, 115-116 and 126.

[142] Folder "AHSC," Rouse Papers, box 1, C. A.; "American Hospital Supply Corp.," *The Electronic Encyclopedia of Chicago,* Chicago Historical Society, http://www.encyclopedia.chicagohistory.org (accessed May 9, 2007); and "American Hospital Supply Corporation" and "Foster McGaw," online finding aids, www.library.northwestern.edu/archives/findingaids (accessed May 9, 2007), Northwestern University Archives, Evanston, IL.

[143] John W. McGrain, *From Pig Iron to Cotton Duck. A History of Manufacturing Villages in Baltimore County* (Towson, MD: Baltimore County Public Library, 1985), 285; Folder "Mills," Howard County Historical Society, vertical files; Dennis Griffith, *Map of the State of Maryland . . . June 20th, 1794* (Philadelphia: J. Vallance, 1795); and Martenet, *Martenet's Map,* (labeled as Gray's Mill).

[144] Thompson, *HO-36 Oak Hall site,* Historic Sites Inventory, 1977.

Enhanced Bibliography

Includes Page Citations for Place Name Entries

The search for and research on the over 1,000 Columbia, Maryland place names found in this book required many sources. The sources, like the place names themselves, tended to fall into two distinct groups. There were sources used for the names derived from literary and artistic works, and there were sources required to dig deeper into the local history of the area. The bibliographic entries were divided into two sections along this distinction. Section 1 covers the sources used to research the works of writers and artists chosen by The Rouse Company (TRC). For clarity, the word "source" is used to refer to the book or website used to find the "works" (i.e., poems, novels, folk songs, paintings, and etchings) that were chosen by TRC. So for poetry, the source is the book containing the individual work, the poem. For almost all of the literary and artistic entries, the source and the work differ. The only exceptions are the citations for novelists who typically have one work per source (e.g., Hemingway's *For Whom the Bell Tolls*). Section 2 covers the references of a more general nature, with an emphasis on local history.

Section 1 consists of 28 subsections headed by the names of the poets, authors and artists, arranged alphabetically. Under each heading is a list of sources used to write the place name entries. The sources within each subsection are listed alphabetically by author's last name. A truly unique aspect of the bibliography is the source-specific citations found in the two columns that follow the source listing. Titles of the works appear in the left column. TRC-derived place names lead the right column, followed by abbreviations of the corresponding Columbia locations in parentheses. The location abbreviations reveal patterns of where various artists and writers were used throughout Columbia. Questions like, "how many neighborhoods have streets inspired by Sandburg's works?" can be answered quickly with the location information. (FYI, the answer is 2.) The right column lines end with page citations specific to the source listed in the bibliographic entry. The page listed in the source is the same verse, prose, title, or image that appears for the place name entry in this book. If other sources are consulted, different titles and/or different verses for some of the works might be found. The adage about "poetic license" applies to some of the compilers and editors of the works as well. Some place name searches did not give *one* definitive source, but rather several possible poems, stories or works of art. For these place names, each possible title is cited using "see also"(SA) notes in parentheses at the end of the line. Many of the subsections close with additional information gained during the research process. Most of these list alternative sources to consult, but some go into stylistic issues of the writers, artists, compilers or editors, and a few even focus on a particular work.

In Section 2, entries follow a standard bibliographic format, arranged alphabetically. These are the sources used to find information on place names that were derived from historical figures or sites, from science and technology, and for those names that either existed prior to Columbia's development or were named by builders and developers other than TRC. Individual street names do not appear under the sources in this section; however, by using the endnotes found in the main text, you can locate all sources listed in Section 2 that were consulted to write the historical and general place name entries.

One of the underlying intentions of writing this book is to stimulate interest in the poems, stories, paintings, etchings, folk songs and local history that are the basis of the place names of Columbia. At most, the main text of the book includes a snippet of the work containing the inspirational words behind the place names—only enough, hopefully, to entice the reader to want more. To facilitate the quest to read or see the entire work, local library information is included, and, when not present in the local library, the means and/or place where the work can be found. Not all sources are carried in the Howard County Public Library system. It is also true that those found in the library today and cited in the bibliography may not be there in the future. In both sections of the bibliography, library specific information is enclosed in brackets directly following the traditional bibliographic information for each source. Unfortunately, the library specific information will have limited value to those residing outside Howard County, Maryland. Abbreviations for the repositories we cite are: HCPL for the Howard County Public Library system; Marina for the Maryland public libraries interlibrary loan system; UMCP for the University of Maryland Libraries, College Park; HCHS for the Howard County Historical Society; LC for Library of Congress; MSA for the Maryland State Archives; and MHS for the Maryland Historical Society. LitFinder is an electronic database available to HCPL card carrying members through the HCPL website. Even though it was not used to write the place name entries, it was particularly useful to search poetry in those relatively few cases where there were little to no clues. LitFinder is also an easy way to access many, if not most of the poems cited in this book.

Note: the 1, 2 and * notation found in the main text entries accompany the place names listed in the bibliography (see Navigating section for key to symbols).

Key to Columbia Location Information:
The format of the parenthetic location information is as follows: (village abbreviation:neighborhood abbreviation). The abbreviations used in the bibliographic entries are:

DS: Dorsey's Search
    DH: Dorsey Hall
    FH: Fairway Hills
HC: Harper's Choice
    HG: Hobbit's Glen
    Lo: Longfellow
    Sw: Swansfield
HR: Hickory Ridge
    CF: Clary's Forest
    CC: Clemens Crossing
    Ha: Hawthorn
KC: Kings Contrivance
    Di: Dickinson
    Hu: Huntington
    MC: Macgill's Common
LR: Long Reach
    JH: Jeffers Hill
    KR: Kendall Ridge
    LP: Locust Park
    PL: Phelps Luck
OM: Oakland Mills
    SF: Steven's Forest
    TS: Talbott Springs
    TH: Thunder Hill
OB: Owen Brown
    DG: Dasher Green
    El: Elkhorn
    Ho: Hopewell
RH: River Hill
    PhR: Pheasant Ridge
    PoR: Pointer's Run
TC: Town Center
    Am: Amesbury
    Ba: Banneker
    CR: Creighton's Run
    VP: Vantage Point
    WT: Warfield Triangle
WL: Wilde Lake
    BW: Bryant Woods
    FR: Faulkner Ridge
    RB: Running Brook

Section 1. Literary and Artistic Sources, including citations for place names entries.

John James Audubon (1785-1851), American artist and ornithologist.

Audubon, John James. *The Original Watercolor Paintings by John James Audubon for The Birds of America.* NY: American Heritage Publishing Company, [1966]; or Bonanza Books, distributed by Crown Publishers, Inc., 1985. [HCPL: 598A oversized]

BLUE HERON	Blue Heron Lane (WL: BW) Plate 326 and Plate 362
GREAT GRAY OWL	Gray Owl Garth (WL: BW) Plate 34
TRUMPETER SWAN	Trumpeter Road (WL) Plate 7 and Plate 334
WILD TURKEY	Wild Turkey Lane (WL: BW) Plate 1 and Plate 5

Audubon, John James and John Bachman. *The Quadrupeds of North America.* 3 vols. NY: Arno Press, 1974. [HCPL: R599.097A]

AMERICAN CROSS FOX	Cross Fox Lane (WL: FR) vol. 1, Plate 6, opposite page 44
LYNX RUFUS and LYNX CANADENSIS	Lynx Lane (WL) vol. 1, Plate 1, opposite page 2 and vol. 1, Plate 16, opposite page 136

Other Audubon sources consulted:

Audubon, John James. *The Birds of America.* 7 vols. Mineola, NY: Dover Publications, 1969. [HCPL: R598A]

Audubon, John James and George Dock. *Audubon's Birds of America.* New York: H. N. Abrams, 1979. [HCPL: 598.297A; book includes Havell colorplates for *Thirty Great Audubon Birds*]

Audubon, John James. *The Birds of America, from Drawings Made in the U. S. and their Territories.* New York: J. J. Audubon and Philadelphia: J. B. Chevalier, 1840-44. [New York Public Library Digital Gallery, http://digitalgallery.nypl.org/nypldigital/ (accessed June 6, 2006)]

Audubon, John James. *The Viviparous Quadrupeds of North America.* 3 vols. New York: J. J. Audubon, 1843, 1846, 1848. [New York Public Library Digital Gallery, http://digitalgallery.nypl.org/nypldigital/ (accessed June 6, 2006)]

William Cullen Bryant (1794-1878), American poet and editor.

Bryant, William Cullen. *The Poetical Works of William Cullen Bryant.* Roslyn Edition. New York: AMS Press, 1972. [UMCP: McK PS1150.F69]

A RAIN-DREAM	Rain Dream Hill (WL: BW) p. 226
A WALK AT SUNSET	Daystar Court (WL: BW) p. 37
	Nightmist Court (WL: BW) p. 37
AN INDIAN AT THE BURIAL-PLACE OF HIS FATHERS	Smooth Meadow Way (TC: VP) p. 58
AN INDIAN STORY	Morning Wind Lane 1 (WL: BW) p. 55
AUTUMN WOODS	Crimson Tree Court (WL: BW) p. 68
CATTERSKILL FALLS	Catterskill Court (WL: BW) p. 169
GREEN RIVER	Thicket Lane (WL: BW) p. 28
MIDSUMMER	Mid Summer Lane (WL: BW) p. 107
THANATOPSIS	Barcan Circle (WL: BW) p. 22
	Open Sky (WL: BW) p. 21
THE EVENING WIND	Evening Wind Court (WL: BW) p. 124
THE GREEK BOY	Greek Boy Place (WL: BW) p. 120
THE GREEN MOUNTAIN BOYS	Green Mountain Circle (WL: BW) p. 178
THE NEW MOON	New Moon Place (WL: BW) p. 98
THE PAINTED CUP	Painted Cup (WL: BW) p. 196
THE PLANTING OF THE APPLE-TREE	May Wind Court 1 (WL: BW) p. 223
THE RIVULET	Rivulet Row (WL: BW) p. 51
THE WEST WIND	Ring Dove Lane (TC: VP) p. 33
THE WIND AND STREAM	Windstream Drive (WL: BW) p. 235
TO A WATERFOWL	Waterfowl Terrace (WL: BW) p. 26
WILLIAM TELL	William Tell Lane (WL: BW) p. 118

On Bryant sources:
There are other volumes of Bryant's poetry at UMCP libraries and available through Marina loans.

Emily Elizabeth Dickinson (1830-1886), American poet.

Dickinson, Emily. *The Poems of Emily Dickinson.* Reading edition. Edited by R. W. Franklin. Cambridge, MA: The Belknap Press of Harvard University Press, 1999. [HCPL: 811.4D]

POEM 24 (FREQUENTLY THE WOODS ARE PINK -)	Pink Wood (KC: Di) p. 28
POEM 92 (PERHAPS YOU'D LIKE TO BUY A FLOWER,)	Yellow Bonnet Place (KC: Di) p. 52
POEM 123 (BESIDES THE AUTUMN POETS SING)	Golden Rod Path (KC: Hu) p. 63
POEM 140 (BRING ME THE SUNSET IN A CUP -)	Morning Leap Terrace (KC: Hu) p. 70
POEM 143 (EXULTATION IS THE GOING)	First League (KC: Di) p. 72
POEM 148 (WILL THERE REALLY BE A "MORNING"?)	Water Lily Way (KC: Di) p. 74
POEM 157 (I HAVE A KING, WHO DOES NOT SPEAK -)	Hundred Drums Row (KC: Hu) p. 76
POEM 210 (IF I SHOULD'NT BE ALIVE)	Red Cravat Court (KC: Di) p. 97
POEM 219 (MY RIVER RUNS TO THEE -)	Blue Sea Drive (KC: Di) p. 100
POEM 306 (A SHADY FRIEND - FOR TORRID DAYS -)	Broadcloth Way (KC: Di) p. 136
POEM 314 ("HOPE" IS THE THING WITH FEATHERS -)	Little Bird Path (KC: Di) p. 140
POEM 331 (THE ONLY GHOST I EVER SAW)	Sandalfoot Way (KC: Di) p. 148
POEM 368 (I ENVY SEAS, WHEREON HE RIDES -)	Summer Leave Lane (KC: Di) p. 168
POEM 370 (WITHIN MY GARDEN, RIDES A BIRD)	Single Wheel Path (KC: Di) p.169
POEM 378 (BETTER - THAN MUSIC!)	Cadence Court (KC: Di) p. 174
	Eden Brook Drive (KC: Di) p. 173
	Second Time Lane (KC: Di) p. 173
POEM 479 (BECAUSE I COULD NOT STOP FOR DEATH -)	Setting Sun Way (KC: Di) p. 219
POEM 591 (I HEARD A FLY BUZZ - WHEN I DIED -)	Keepsake Way (KC: Hu) p. 265
POEM 676 (YOU KNOW THAT PORTRAIT IN THE MOON -)	
POEM 706 (I CANNOT LIVE WITH YOU -)	Moon Portrait Way (KC: Di) p. 301
POEM 931 (AN EVERYWHERE OF SILVER)	New Grace Mews (KC: Di) p. 315
POEM 1032 (FAR FROM LOVE THE HEAVENLY FATHER)	Sandrope Court (KC: Di) p. 398
POEM 1099 (AT HALF PAST THREE)	Dragonclaw (KC: Hu) p. 423
POEM 1121 (THE SKY IS LOW - THE CLOUDS ARE MEAN.)	Single Bird Lane (KC: Hu) p. 444
POEM 1348 (THE WAY TO KNOW THE BOBOLINK)	Narrow Wind Way (KC: Di) p. 452
POEM 1368 (OPON A LILAC SEA)	Bobolink Court (KC: Di) p. 518
POEM 1484 (BEFORE YOU THOUGHT OF SPRING)	Lilac Sea (KC: Di) p. 525
	Indigo Court (KC: Hu) p. 557
	Weather Worn Way (KC: Di) p. 557
POEM 1488 (ONE OF THE ONES THAT MIDAS TOUCHED)	
POEM 1513 ('TIS WHITER THAN AN INDIAN PIPE -)	Midas Touch (KC: Di) p. 558
POEM 1665 (THE FARTHEST THUNDER THAT I HEARD)	Indian Pipe Court (KC: Di) p. 564
POEM 1741 (A LANE OF YELLOW LED THE EYE)	Farthest Thunder Court (KC: Di) p. 602
POEM 1785 (SWEET HOURS HAVE PERISHED HERE,)	Silent Bird Court (KC: Di) p. 622
	Sweet Hours Way (KC: Di) p. 634

Notes on using other Dickinson sources:
HCPL offers several Dickinson poetry books. Dickinson's works are difficult to cite universally across books, since more than one numbering system has arisen to address the absence of titles on her poems. Published editions of her poems usually include a first line index to help identify specific poems. The listing above includes the first line information in parentheses following the poem number. Besides not titling her poems, Dickinson also took great liberties with spelling and punctuation as a means of conveying her thoughts and feelings in verse. Some compilers of her works took additional liberties to alter her spelling, wording and punctuation. Thomas Johnson worked diligently to publish a comprehensive work of Dickinson's verse in 1955, returning to her original verse and developing a numbering system. This became the definitive system for scholars to use. The volume cited above is by a Dickinson scholar who uses Johnson's system. If a different Dickinson book is used, the verse might not appear exactly as printed here.

John Roderigo Dos Passos (1896-1970), American writer.

Dos Passos, John. *The Best Times: An Informal Memoir.* New York, NY: The New American Library, 1966. [UMCP: McK PS3507.O743Z49]

THE BEST TIMES . . .
    Agail Place (OM: SF) p. 110
    Cameldriver Court (OM: SF) p. 114
    Castile Court (OM: SF) p. 31
    Clear Smoke Court (OM: SF) p. 69
    Commitment Court (OM: SF) p. 161
    Commodore Court (OM: SF) p. 1 and p. 19
    Fallen Stone (OM: SF) p. 66
    Greco Garth (OM: SF) p. 31
    Landbreeze Row (OM: SF) p. 87
    Latchkey Row [1] (OB: El) p. 138
    Moongong Court (OM: SF) p. 163
    Pastora Place (OM: SF) p. 33
    Patchin Court (OM: SF) p. 82
    Rocksparkle Row (OM: SF) p. 31
    Saddlebag Row (OM: SF) p. 112
    Sinbad Place (OM: SF) p. 79 and p. 66
    Woodblock Row (OM: SF) p. 49

Dos Passos, John. *First Encounter.* New York, NY: Philosophical Library, 1945. [UMCP: McK PS3507.O743F5]

FIRST ENCOUNTER   Encounter Row (OM: SF)

Dos Passos, John. *The Ground We Stand On: Some Examples from the History of a Political Creed.* New York: Harcout, Brace and Company, 1941. [UMCP: HBK Maryland Room, Special Collections Stacks, E183.D7; and off-site shelving]

THE GROUND WE STAND ON . . .   Standon Place [1] (OM: SF)

Dos Passos, John. *Manhattan Transfer.* Boston: Houghton Mifflin Company, 1990. [UMCP: McK PS3507.O743M35 1990; other editions available]

MANHATTAN TRANSFER   Transfer Row [1] (OM: SF)

Dos Passos, John. *Streets of Night.* Edited by Michael Clark. Selinsgrove, PA: Susquehanna University Press, 1990. [UMCP: McK PS3507.O743S77 1990]

STREETS OF NIGHT   Night Street Hill (OM: SF)

Dos Passos, John. *Travel Books and Other Writings, 1916-1941.* New York, NY: The Library of America, 2003. [UMCP: McK PS3507.O743A62003; and Marina loan] This volume includes: Orient Express (1930): pp. 125-268, *A Pushcart at the Curb* (1922): pp. 489-586, and *Rosinante to the Road Again* (1922): pp. 1-124.

ORIENT EXPRESS   Orient Lane (OM: SF) p. 125
A PUSHCART AT THE CURB   Pushcart Way (OM: SF) p. 491
ROSINANTE TO THE ROAD AGAIN   Rosinante Run (OM: SF) p. 1

Dos Passos, John. *U.S.A. (The 42nd Parallel/ 1919 / The Big Money).* Boston: Houghton Mifflin Company, 1963 [c1960]. [HCPL: F Dos]

THE 42ND PARALLEL   Parallel Lane (OM: SF) p. 3

Other Dos Passos sources:

Dos Passos, John. *The Garbage Man, a Parade With Shouting.* New York, NY: Haper & Brothers, 1926. [UMCP HBK PS3507.O743G3 1926] This is the revised title to the play Dos Passos wrote and originally titled *The Moon Is a Gong* as is mentioned in Dos Passos's memoirs.

Paul Laurence Dunbar (1872-1906), American poet.

Dunbar, Paul Laurence. *The Collected Poetry of Paul Laurence Dunbar.* Edited and with an
      introduction by Joanne M. Braxton. Charlottesville: University Press of Virginia, 1993.
      [HCPL: 811.4D]

A BOY'S SUMMER SONG	Mossy Brink Court (OB: El) p. 235
A DROWSY DAY	Drowsy Day (OB: El) p. 65
A LAZY DAY	Ripplestir Place (OB: El) p. 249
A MADRIGAL	Madrigal Terrace (OB: El) p. 287
	Winter Rose Path [1] (OB: El) p. 288 (SA: ROSES)
A SAILOR'S SONG	Fairmead Lane [2] (OB: El) p. 92
AFTER MANY DAYS	Many Days (OB: El) p. 267
ALEXANDER CRUMMELL – DEAD	Westering Sun (OB: El) p. 113
ANGELINA	Angelina Circle (OB: El) p. 138
	Pigeonwing Place (OB: El) p. 138
AT LOAFING-HOLT	Weatherwise Way (OB: El) p. 264
BALLADE	Sylvan Dell (OB: El) p. 204
BEHIND THE ARRAS	Lasting Light Way (OB: El) p. 95
DAWN	Dawnblush Court (OB: El) p. 65
DINAH KNEADING DOUGH	Lacelike Row (OB: El) p. 188
HOW SHALL I WOO THEE	Star Path (OB: El) p. 289
IONE	Farbell Row (OB: El) p. 34, section 2
JUST WHISTLE A BIT	Talisman Lane (OB: El) p. 99
KIDNAPED	Wingflash Lane (OB: El) p. 255
LIZA MAY	Bendbough Court (OB: El) p. 267
ODE FOR MEMORIAL DAY	Bugledrum Way (OB: El) p. 22
ONE LIFE	Skyward Court (OB: El) p. 72
POSSUM	Possum Court (OB: El) p. 141
RETROSPECTION	Robin Song (OB: El) p. 24
ROSES	Winter Rose Path [1] (OB: El) p. 222 (SA: A MADRIGAL)
THE CHANGE	Downdale Place (OB: El) p. 258
THE DANCE	Curtsey Court (OB: El) p. 170
THE DISCOVERY	Dewlit Way (OB: El) p. 252
	Elffolk Terrace [2] (OB: El) p. 251
THE LILY OF THE VALLEY	Gentle Way (OB: El) p. 238
	Honeyladen Place (OB: El) p. 238
THE LOOKING-GLASS	Lookinglass Lane (OB: El) p. 206
THE MEADOW LARK	Happy Heart Lane [1] (OB: El) p. 71
THE OL' TUNES	Homespun Lane (OB: El) p. 54 (SA: THE PLANTATION CHILD'S LULLABY)
THE OLD HOMESTEAD	Barchink Place (OB: El) p. 283
THE PATH	Smooth Path (OB: El) p. 21
THE PLANTATION CHILD'S LULLABY	Hickory Log Circle [1] (OB: El) p. 241
	Homespun Lane (OB: El) p. 241 (SA: THE OL' TUNES)
	Snowman Court [2] (OB: El) p. 241
THE QUILTING	Quilting Way (OB: El) p. 240
THE RISING OF THE STORM	Deep Cup (OB: El) p. 9
	Seapearl Lane (OB: El) p. 9
THE SEEDLING	Seedling Lane (OB: El) p. 12
THE SPELLIN'-BEE	Spelling Bee (OB: El) p. 42
THE VOICE OF THE BANJO	Banjo Court (OB: El) p. 124
TIME TO TINKER 'ROUN'!	Tinker Round (OB: El) p. 135
TO DAN	Garland Lane (OB: El) p. 249
	Gayheart Court (OB: El) p. 248
TO HER	Spicewind Court (OB: El) p. 266
TO THE ROAD	Sunfleck Row (OB: El) p. 163
TWO LITTLE BOOTS	Little Boots (OB: El) p. 163
WHEN MALINDY SINGS	Malindy Circle (OB: El) p. 82

Other Dunbar sources consulted:
Dunbar, Paul Laurence. *The Complete Poems of Paul Laurence Dunbar.* Philadelphia: Hakim's
      Publications, 1980. [HCPL: 811.4D]

Ralph Waldo Emerson (1803-1882), American essayist and poet.

Emerson, Ralph Waldo. *Collected Poems and Translations.* New York, NY: The Library of America, 1994. [HCPL: 811.3E]

EACH AND ALL	Morningbird Lane (OM: TS) p. 10
GOOD-BYE	Riverark Road (OM: TS) p. 30
THE HUMBLE-BEE	Humblebee Road 1 (OM: TS) p. 31
THE RHODORA: ON BEING ASKED, WHENCE IS THE FLOWER?	Rhodora Court (OM: TS) p. 31

William Cuthbert Faulkner (1897-1962), American novelist.

Faulkner, William. *Big Woods: the Hunting Stories.* New York: Vintage Books, 1994. [HCPL: F Fa]

BIG WOODS: THE HUNTING STORIES	Big Woods Court (WL: FR)

Faulkner, William. *Light in August.* New York: Vintage International, 1990. [HCPL: F Fa]

LIGHT IN AUGUST	August Light (WL: FR)

Faulkner, William. *The Marble Faun and A Green Bough.* New York: Random House, 1965. [UMCP: McK PS3511.A86M3 1965]

A GREEN BOUGH	Green Bough Court (WL: FR)
THE MARBLE FAUN	Marble Faun Lane (WL: FR)

Faulkner, William. *Novels 1942-1954.* New York: The Library of America, 1994. [HCPL: F Fa; UMCP: McK PS3511.A86A6 1994]

A FABLE	Fable Row (WL: FR)

Faulkner, William. *The Sound and the Fury.* The Corrected Text with Faulkner's Appendix. The Modern Library edition. New York: Random House, Inc., 1992. [HCPL: F Fau; different editions at UMCP: McK PS3511.A86S7 1987]

THE SOUND AND THE FURY	Jason Court (WL: FR)
	Jason Lane (WL: FR) p. 11
	Tolling Clock Way (WL: FR) pp. 76, 80, 83, 88, 92 and 274
	respectively

Faulkner, William. *Three Famous Short Novels.* New York: Vintage Books, 1961. [HCPL: F Fau]

SPOTTED HORSES	Spotted Horse Lane (WL: FR)

Other Faulkner sources:
Spotted Horses is cited as being from: Faulkner, William. *The Hamlet.* New York, NY: Random House, 1964. [HCPL: F Fa] This book is the first volume of Faulkner's Snopes trilogy that also includes, *The Town* and *The Mansion.*

Faulkner, William. *The Faulkner Reader, Selections from the Works of William Faulkner.* New York, NY: Random House, 1954. [Marina loan; also 1959 and 1961 editions] Besides being able to read *The Sound and The Fury, Spotted Horses* and a selection from *Light in August* all in one volume, this book reprints Faulkner's Nobel Prize address.

Faulkner, William. *The Portable Faulkner.* Edited by Malcolm Cowley. New York, NY: Penguin Books, 2003. [HCPL: 813.52F]

Frances Scott Key Fitzgerald (1896-1940), American writer.

Fitzgerald, F. Scott. *Before Gatsby: the First Twenty-Six Stories.* Columbia: University of South Carolina Press, 2001. [HCPL: F Fit]

THE CAMEL'S BACK	Camelback Lane (OM: SF) p. 212
THE CUT-GLASS BOWL	The Bowl (OM: SF) p. 111 (SA: The Bowl)

Fitzgerald, F. Scott. *The Great Gatsby*. New York: Simon and Schuster, 2003. [HCPL: F Fit (pbk)] or *F. Scott Fitzgerald's The Great Gatsby*. Edited by Harold Bloom. New York: Chelsea House Publishers, c1986. [HCPL: 813.509F]

    THE GREAT GATSBY   Gatsby Green (OM: SF)

Fitzgerald, F. Scott. *The Short Stories of F. Scott Fitzgerald: a New Collection*. New York: Charles Scribner's Sons, 1989. [HCPL: F Fit]

A NEW LEAF	New Leaf Court (OM: SF) p. 634
BABYLON REVISITED	Babylon Crest (OM: SF) p. 616
JACOB'S LADDER	Jacob's Ladder (OM: SF) p. 350
THE BOWL	The Bowl (OM: SF) p. 390 (SA: THE CUT-GLASS BOWL)
THE OFFSHORE PIRATE	Offshore Green (OM: SF) p. 70

Fitzgerald, F. Scott. *Six Tales of the Jazz Age and Other Stories*. New York: Charles Scribner's Sons, 1960. [UMCP: McK PZ3.F5754Si]

    GRETCHEN'S FORTY WINKS   Forty Winks Way (OM: SF) p. 175

Fitzgerald, F. Scott. *Tales of the Jazz Age*. Edited by James L. W. West III. Cambridge, UK: Cambridge University Press, 2002. [McK PS3511.I9T35 2002]

    JEMINA, THE MOUNTAIN GIRL   Jamina Downs (OM: SF) p. 269

Other Fitzgerald sources consulted:

Fitzgerald, F. Scott. *Babylon Revisited and Other Stories*. New York: Charles Scribner's Sons, 1971. [HCPL: F Fit] This book has *Babylon Revisited* but not the other stories cited above in the short stories collection.

The University of Adelaide Library. *eBooks @Adelaide*. [http://etext.library.adelaide.edu.au/f/fitzgerald/f_scott/ (accessed October 17, 2007)] This website has online versions of *The Great Gatsby* and *Tales of the Jazz Age*.

Robert Lee Frost (1874-1963), American poet.

Frost, Robert. *The Poetry of Robert Frost: the Collected Poems, Complete and Unabridged*. Edited by Edward Connery Lathem. New York: Henry Holt and Company, 1979. [HCPL: 811.5F]

A BLUE RIBBON AT AMESBURY	Amesbury Drive (TC: Amesbury) p. 279
	Amesbury (TC: neighborhood) p. 279
A LEAF-TREADER	Leaf Treader Way (TC: VP) p. 297
A PRAYER IN SPRING	Darting Bird Lane (WL: RB) p. 12
A STAR IN A STONEBOAT	Stoneboat Row (WL: RB) p. 173
AT WOODWARD'S GARDENS	Woodward Gardens (WL: RB) p. 293
GOOD HOURS	Good Hours Place (WL: RB) p. 102
HYLA BROOK	Hyla Brook Road (WL: RB) p. 119
IN TIME OF CLOUDBURST	Cloudburst Hill (WL: RB) p. 285
MENDING WALL	The Mending Wall (WL: RB) p. 33
MOWING	Pale Orchis Court (WL: RB) p. 17
NEW HAMPSHIRE	Still Corners (WL: RB) p. 165
SPRING POOLS	Spring Pools Lane (WL: RB) p. 245
STOPPING BY WOODS ON A SNOWY EVENING	Snowy Reach (WL: RB) p. 224
TEN MILLS	Ten Mills Road (WL: RB) p. 308
THE DEATH OF THE HIRED MAN	Downwest Ride (WL: RB) p. 38
	Hayload Court (WL: RB) p. 37
	Homecoming Lane (WL: RB) p. 38
	Moonfall Way (WL: RB) p. 38
	Silas Choice (WL: RB) p. 34
THE LAST MOWING	Wildflower Terrace (WL: RB) p. 264
THE OVEN BIRD	Oven Bird Green (WL: RB) p. 119
THE PEACEFUL SHEPHERD	Pasture Gate Lane (WL: RB) p. 252
THE STAR-SPLITTER	Starsplit Lane (WL: RB) p. 179
THE TUFT OF FLOWERS	Flowertuft Court (WL: RB) p. 22
	Reedy Brook Lane (WL: RB) p. 22
	Whetstone Road (WL: RB) p. 22

THE VANTAGE POINT	Vantage Point Road (TC: VP) p. 17
	Vantage Point (TC: neighborhood) p. 17
TO THE THAWING WIND	Hermit Path (WL: RB) p. 11
WEST-RUNNING BROOK	West Running Brook Road (WL: RB) p. 257
	Running Brook (WL: neighborhood) p. 257
WILD GRAPES	Fox Grape Terrace (WL: RB) p. 198

Other Frost sources:

Frost, Robert. *Frost: Collected Poems, Prose, and Plays.* New York: The Library of America, c1995. [HCPL: 811.5F]

Frost, Robert. *The Poetry of Robert Frost.* New York: Holt, c1969. [HCPL: 811.5F]

Ernest Miller Hemingway (1899-1961), American writer and journalist.

Hemingway, Ernest. *The Complete Short Stories of Ernest Hemingway.* New York: Charles Scribner's Sons, 1987. [HCPL: F He and F Hem]

A SIMPLE ENQUIRY	Enquiry Court (OM: SF) p. 250
BIG TWO-HEARTED RIVER: PART I AND PART II	Big River Run (OM: SF) p. 163 and p. 173
GOD REST YOU MERRY, GENTLEMEN	Merryrest Road 1 (OM: SF) p. 298
INDIAN CAMP	Indian Camp Road 1 (OM: SF) p. 67
ONE READER WRITES	Reader Lane 1 (OM: SF) p. 320
THE BATTLER	Battler Court (OM: SF) p. 97
THE GOOD LION	Good Lion Road (OM: SF) p. 482
THE SHORT HAPPY LIFE OF FRANCIS MACOMBER	Macomber Lane (OM: SF) p. 5
THE SNOWS OF KILIMANJARO	Kilimanjaro Road (OM: SF) p. 39

Hemingway, Ernest. *Death in the Afternoon.* New York: Simon & Schuster, 1996. [HCPL: 791.82H]

DEATH IN THE AFTERNOON	Afternoon Lane (OM: SF)
	Bullring Lane (OM: SF) (SA: THE SUN ALSO RISES)
	Maera Court (OM: SF) p. 77 (SA: IN OUR TIME)

Hemingway, Ernest. *A Farewell to Arms.* New York: Simon & Schuster, 1995. [HCPL: F Hem] or *Ernest Hemingway's A Farewell to Arms.* Edited by Harold Bloom. New York: Chelsea House Publishers, 1987. [HCPL: 813.5E]

| A FAREWELL TO ARMS | Farewell Road (OM: SF) |

Hemingway, Ernest. *For Whom the Bell Tolls.* New York: Scribner, 2003. [HCPL: F Hem (pbk)]

FOR WHOM THE BELL TOLLS	Matador Road (OM: SF) p. 26
	Pilar Court (OM: SF)
	Santiago Road (OM: SF) (SA: THE OLD MAN AND THE SEA)

Hemingway, Ernest. *Green Hills of Africa.* New York: Simon & Schuster, Inc., 1996. [HCPL: 967.6H]

| GREEN HILLS OF AFRICA | African Hill (OM: SF) |
| | Pursuit Court (OM: SF) pp. 1, 45, 175 and 215 |

Hemingway, Ernest. *In Our Time.* New York: Scribner, 1998. [HCPL: F Hem (pbk)]

| IN OUR TIME | Maera Court (OM: SF) p. 113 (SA: DEATH IN THE AFTERNOON) |
| | Ourtime Lane (OM: SF) |

Hemingway, Ernest. *The Old Man and the Sea.* New York: Scribner, 2003. [HCPL: F He or F Hem (pbk)]

| THE OLD MAN AND THE SEA | Old Man Court (OM: SF) |
| | Santiago Road (OM: SF) (SA: FOR WHOM THE BELL TOLLS) |

Hemingway, Ernest. *The Sun Also Rises.* New York: Scribner, 2003. [HCPL: F Hem (pbk)] or *Ernest Hemingway's The Sun Also Rises.* Edited by Harold Bloom. New York: Chelsea House Publishers, 1987. [HCPL: 813.509E]

THE SUN ALSO RISES	Brett Lane (OM: SF)
	Bullring Lane (OM: SF) (SA: DEATH IN THE AFTERNOON)
	Pamplona Road (OM: SF) p. 76

Hemingway, Ernest. *The Torrents of Spring: a Romantic Novel in Honor of the Passing of a Great Race.*
New York: Simon & Schuster, Inc., 1998. [HCPL: F Hem (pbk)]

THE TORRENTS OF SPRING . . .   Torrent Row (OM: SF)

Oliver Wendell Holmes (1809-1894), American physician and author.

Holmes, Oliver Wendell. *The Poetical Works of Oliver Wendell Holmes.* Boston: Houghton Mifflin
Company, 1975. [Marina loan, 1975 and other versions; UMCP: McK PS1955.A1 1905 edition]

A MODEST REQUEST, COMPLIED WITH AFTER THE DINNER AT PRESIDENT EVERETT'S INAUGURATION	Fragile Sail Way (DS: DH) p. 40
A RHYMED LESSON (URANIA)	Bright Bay Way (DS: DH) p. 53
	Red Bandana Way (DS: DH) p. 43
	Seabird Way (DS: DH) p. 47
	Sweet Bell Court (DS: DH) p. 46
A SONG FOR THE CENTENNIAL CELEBRATION OF HARVARD COLLEGE, 1836	Coattail Court (DS: DH) p. 31
	Ram's Horn Row (DS: DH) p. 31 (SA: TWO SONNETS: HARVARD. I. "CHRISTO ET ECCLESIAE," 1700)
A SONG OF OTHER DAYS	Alpine Rose Bend (DS: DH) p. 41
AFTER A LECTURE ON WORDSWORTH	Henhawk Court (DS: DH) p. 91
	Kingscup Court (DS: DH) p. 91
	Larkspring Row (DS: DH) p. 90
	Oxbow Court (DS: DH) p. 90
	Wildwood Way (DS: DH) p. 91
AN AFTER-DINNER POEM (TERPSICHORE)	Bright Rocket Way (DS: DH) p. 54
	Old Dragon Path (DS: DH) p. 55
FROM AN AFTER-DINNER SPEECH	White Star Way (DS: DH) p. 341
LES BOHÉMIENS	Chariot's Flight Way (DS: DH) p. 348
	Learned Sage (DS: DH) p. 348
LEXINGTON	Mustering Drum (DS: DH) p. 29
MUSA	Linden Hall [1] (DS: community center) p. 151
MY AVIARY	Sunlit Passage (DS: DH) p. 248
PENITENTIA	Firefly Way (DS: DH) p. 349
	Twilight Grove Court (DS: DH) p. 349
POETRY: A METRICAL ESSAY	Lilac Lane (DS: DH) p. 19, section I
PROGRAMME	Scarlet Sage Court (DS: DH) p. 185
ROBINSON OF LEYDEN	Leyden Way (DS: DH) p. 165
	Speedwell Court (DS: DH) p. 165
SONG AT THE HUNT	Eagles Wing Court (DS: DH) p. 345
SPRING HAS COME	Blue Barrow Ride (DS: DH) p. 153
	Maydew Mews Way (DS: DH) p. 153
	Morning Ride Court (DS: DH) p. 153
	Snowdrop Court (DS: DH) p. 153
	Wild Filly Court (DS: DH) p. 153
THE LAST READER	Purple Twilight Way [1] (DS: DH) p. 15
THE LAST SURVIVOR	Huckleberry Row [1] (DS: DH) p. 140
	Starwreath Way (DS: DH) p. 140
	Willow Bend (DS: DH) p. 141
THE NEW EDEN	Hemlock Cone Way (DS: DH) p. 95
THE STEAMBOAT	Smokey Wreath Way (DS: DH) p. 28
TO JULIA WARD HOWE	Hallowed Stream (DS: DH) p. 340
TWO SONNETS: HARVARD. I. "CHRISTO ET ECCLESIAE," 1700	Ram's Horn Row (DS: DH) p. 251 (SA: A SONG FOR THE CENTENNIAL CELEBRATION OF HARVARD COLLEGE, 1836)
VARIATIONS ON AN ARIA	Broken Lute Way (DS: DH) p. 347
VESTIGIA QUINQUE RETRORSUM	Dancing Sunbeam (DS: DH) p. 245

Winslow Homer (1836-1910), American artist.

Cikovsky, Nicolai, Jr. *Winslow Homer.* New York: Harry N. Abrams, Inc., 1990. [HCPL: 759.13C]

A GLOUCESTER FARM misnomer of	
A TEMPERANCE MEETING	Gloucester Road (HC: Sw) p. 61
EIGHT BELLS	Eight Bells Lane (HC: Sw) p. 90
FRESH AIR	Freshaire Lane (HC: Sw) p. 66
HIGH TIDE	High Tide Court (HC: Sw) p. 45
LOST ON THE GRAND BANKS	Grand Banks Road (HC: Sw) pp. 84 and 147
THE BERRY PICKERS	
(watercolor and gouache)	Berrypick Lane (HC: Sw) p. 55 (SA: THE BERRYPICKER
	(watercolor))
THE BRIDLE PATH, WHITE MOUNTAINS	The Bridle Path (HC: Sw) p. 44
THE GULF STREAM (oil)	Gulf Stream Row (HC: Sw) pp. 120-21 (SA: THE GULFSTREAM
	(watercolor))
THE WOODCUTTER	Woodcutter Way (HC: Sw) p. 109
WRECK OF THE IRON CROWN	Iron Crown Court (HC: Sw) p. 77

Cikovsky, Nicolai, Jr. and Franklin Kelly (with contributions by Judith Walsh and Charles Brock). *Winslow Homer.* Washington, DC: National Gallery of Art, 1995. [HCPL: 759.13C]

A GLOUCESTER FARM misnomer of	
A TEMPERANCE MEETING	Gloucester Road (HC: Sw) p. 114
EIGHT BELLS	Eight Bells Lane (HC: Sw) p. 237
HIGH TIDE	High Tide Court (HC: Sw) pp. 81, 85 and 86
LOST ON THE GRAND BANKS	Grand Banks Road (HC: Sw) p. 229
MORNING GLORIES (oil)	Morning Glory Court (HC: Sw) p. 125 (SA: MORNING
	GLORIES (watercolor))
OLD SETTLERS	Settler Place (HC: Sw) p. 292
RUM CAY	Rum Cay Court (HC: Sw) p. 347
THE BRIDLE PATH, WHITE MOUNTAINS	The Bridle Path (HC: Sw) p. 75
THE GULF STREAM (oil)	Gulf Stream Row (HC: Sw) p. 382
THE GULFSTREAM (watercolor)	Gulf Stream Row (HC: Sw) p. 382
THE WOODCUTTER	Woodcutter Way (HC: Sw) p. 279
WRECK OF THE IRON CROWN	Iron Crown Court (HC: Sw) p. 204

Smithsonian Institution Research Information System (SIRIS), Art Inventories Catalog. Smithsonian American Art Museum. [http://siris-artinventories.si.edu/ (accessed February 20, 2007)]

A GLOUCESTER FARM misnomer of	
A TEMPERANCE MEETING	Gloucester Road (HC: Sw)
EIGHT BELLS	Eight Bells Lane (HC: Sw)
FRESH AIR	Freshaire Lane (HC: Sw)
HARVEST SCENE	Harvest Scene (HC: Sw)
HIGH TIDE	High Tide Court (HC: Sw)
LOST ON THE GRAND BANKS	Grand Banks Road (HC: Sw)
MORNING GLORIES (oil)	Morning Glory Court (HC: Sw)
MORNING GLORIES (watercolor)	Morning Glory Court (HC: Sw)
OLD SETTLERS	Settler Place (HC: Sw)
ROCKY COAST (MAINE COAST)	Rock Coast Road (HC: Sw)
RUM CAY	Rum Cay Court (HC: Sw)
THE BERRY PICKERS	
(watercolor and gouache)	Berrypick Lane (HC: Sw)
THE BERRYPICKER (watercolor)	Berrypick Lane (HC: Sw)
THE BRIDLE PATH, WHITE MOUNTAINS	The Bridle Path (HC: Sw)
THE GREEN DORY	Green Dory Lane (HC: Sw)
THE GULF STREAM (oil)	Gulf Stream Row (HC: Sw)
THE GULFSTREAM (watercolor)	Gulf Stream Row (HC: Sw)
THE WOODCUTTER	Woodcutter Way (HC: Sw)
WRECK OF THE IRON CROWN	Iron Crown Court (HC: Sw)

Unger, Miles. The Watercolors of Winslow Homer. New York: W.W. Norton & Company, Inc., 2001.
[HCPL: 759.13U]

FRESH AIR	Freshaire Lane (HC: Sw) p. 60
OLD SETTLERS	Settler Place (HC: Sw) p. 148
THE BERRY PICKERS (watercolor and gouache)	Berrypick Lane (HC: Sw) pp. 30-31 (SA: THE BERRYPICKER (watercolor))
THE GULF STREAM (oil)	Gulf Stream Row (HC: Sw) p. 13 (SA: THE GULFSTREAM (watercolor))
THE WOODCUTTER	Woodcutter Way (HC: Sw) pp. 142-143
WRECK OF THE IRON CROWN	Iron Crown Court (HC: Sw) pp. 102-103

(John) Robinson Jeffers (1887-1962), American poet.

Jeffers, Robinson. *The Collected Poetry of Robinson Jeffers.* Edited by Tim Hunt. vol. 1. Stanford, CA: Stanford University Press, 1988. [UMCP: McK PS3519.E27A17 1988 v.1]

AN ARTIST	Shining Rock (LR: JH) p. 390
APOLOGY FOR BAD DREAMS	Tamar Drive (LR) p. 210, section 3 (SA: TAMAR)
BIRDS	Bright Hawk Court (OM: TH) p. 108
	Silver Arrows Way (LR: KR) p. 108
	Wind Dance Way (LR: KR) p. 108
CAWDOR	Breaking Wave Drive (LR: KR) p. 511, section 15
	Sea Water Path (LR: KR) p. 511, section 15
	Shining Oceans Way (LR: KR) p. 511, section 15
CONTINENT'S END	Waiting Spring (LR: JH) p. 16
JOY	Worn Mountain Way (LR: KR) p. 117
NATURAL MUSIC	Blade Green Lane (LR: PL) p. 6
	Chatterbird Place (LR: PL) p. 6
NIGHT	Prophecy Place (LR: JH) p. 115
	Tide Rock Square (LR: KR) p. 114
OCTOBER EVENING	Glad Rivers Row (LR: KR) p. 206
PRELUDE	Broken Wing Court (LR: KR) p. 242
	Each Leaf Court (LR: KR) p. 246
	Four Foot Trail (LR: KR) p. 247
	Window Latch Way (LR: KR) p. 242
ROAN STALLION	April Brook Circle (LR: KR) p. 189
	Buckskin Court (LR: PL) p. 179
	Dry Barley Lane (LR: KR) p. 181
	Moonglass Court (LR: KR) p. 192
	Old Buggy Court (LR: PL) p. 179
	Red Lake (LR: PL) p. 196
	Roan Stallion Lane (LR: KR) p. 179
	Soft Thunder Trail (LR: KR) p. 191
	Wetbanks Court (LR: PL) p. 179
SOLILOQUY	Tower Top (LR: JH) p. 215
SUMMER HOLIDAY	Kind Rain (LR: JH) p. 202
TAMAR	Gray Sea Way (LR: KR) p. 20, section 1
	Hobnail Court (LR: JH) p. 71
	Sheerock Court (LR: PL) p. 18, section 1
	Tamar Drive (LR) p. 18 (SA: APOLOGY FOR BAD DREAMS)
	Tame Bird Court (LR: LP) p. 40, section 5
	Winter Pasture Way (LR: KR) p. 22, section 2
THE BROKEN BALANCE	Good Hunters Ride 1 (LR: KR) p. 374, section 3
THE MAID'S THOUGHT	Bronze Bell Circle 1 (LR: LP) p. 3
THE TORCH-BEARERS' RACE	Gate Sill (LR: JH) p. 101
	Nest Side (LR: JH) p. 100
THE TREASURE	Starburn Path (LR: KR) p. 102
THE WOMEN AT POINT SUR	Distant Rock Path (LR: KR) p. 355, section 29
	Honeycomb Gate (LR: KR) p. 294, section 13
	Millrace Court (LR: KR) p. 350, section 28
	North Slope Path (LR: KR) p. 255, section 4
	Oak Bush Terrace (LR: KR) p. 265, section 6
	Silver Trumpet Drive (LR: KR) p. 293, section 13

TO THE STONE-CUTTERS	Stonecutter Road (LR: KR) p. 5
TOR HOUSE	Granite Knoll (LR: JH) p. 408
	High Tor Hill (LR: PL) p. 408
	Storm Drift (LR: PL) p. 408

Jeffers, Robinson. *The Collected Poetry of Robinson Jeffers.* Edited by Tim Hunt. vol. 2. Stanford, CA: Stanford University Press, 1989. [Marina loan]

ANTRIM	Antrim Court (LR: PL) p. 118
	Red Cart Court (LR: JH) p. 118 (SA: OSSIAN'S GRAVE)
DECAYING LAMBSKINS	Lambskin Lane (LR: LP) p. 604
FLIGHT OF SWANS	Flicker Place (LR: LP) p. 419
GHOSTS IN ENGLAND	Roll Right Court (LR: LP) p. 123
GIVE YOUR HEART TO THE HAWKS	Airybrink Lane [1] (LR: KR) p. 313, section 2
	Cooperhawk Court (LR: KR) p. 355, section 9
	Fire Cloud Court (LR: KR) p. 380, section 12
	Wild Lilac [1] (LR: PL) p. 343, section 7
	Wild Wing Way (LR: KR) p. 324, section 3
GRAY WEATHER	Warm Granite Drive (LR: KR) p. 485
HANDS	Sealed Message Road (LR: JH) p. 4
IN THE HILL AT NEWGRANGE	Bellfall Court (LR: JH) p. 115
	New Grange Garth (LR: PL) p. 114
	Spiral Cut (LR: LP) p. 116
LOVE THE WILD SWAN	Wild Swan Way (LR: KR) p. 410
MARGRAVE	Greenblade Garth (LR: JH) p. 168
	Margrave Mews (LR: PL) p. 161
OH LOVELY ROCK	Enberend Terrace [1] (LR: PL) p. 546
OSSIAN'S GRAVE	Red Cart Court (LR: JH) p. 109 (SA: ANTRIM)
RED MOUNTAIN	Sage Brush Way (LR: KR) p. 486
RETURN	Alderleaf Place (LR: PL) p. 409
ROCK AND HAWK	Crosshive Court (LR: LP) p. 416
SUBJECTED EARTH	Lapwing Court (LR: JH) p. 128
THE BEAKS OF EAGLES	Eaglebeak Row (LR: PL) p. 537
	Footed Ridge (LR: JH) p. 537
THE BED BY THE WINDOW	Twelvemonth Court (LR: PL) p. 131
THE COAST-ROAD	Wind Rider Way (LR: KR) p. 522
THE LOVING SHEPHERDESS	Coltsfoot Court (LR: PL) p. 103, section 11
	Dark Hawk Circle (LR: KR) p. 61, section 4
	Drystraw Drive (LR: PL) p. 104, section 12
	Foreland Garth (LR: LP) p. 104, section 12
	Freelark Place (LR: PL) p. 81, section 8
	Hayshed Lane (LR: KR) p. 67, section 6
	Hillfall Court (LR: PL) p. 83, section 8
	Lightspun Lane (LR: PL) p. 52, section 3
	Luckpenny Place (LR: PL) p. 97, section 11
	Millwheel Place (LR: PL) p. 71, section 6
	Shepherdess Court (LR: PL) p. 59, section 4
	Sidelong Place (LR: PL) p. 53, section 3
	Three Apple Downs (LR: KR) p. 62, section 5
	Tilted Stone [1] (LR: PL) p. 88, section 9
	Watercress Place (LR: PL) p. 63, section 5
	Windysun Court (LR: PL) p. 88, section 9
	Woodstaff Way (LR: KR) p. 49, section 2
THE PURSE-SEINE	Flamepool Way (LR: LP) p. 517
THE WIND-STRUCK MUSIC	White Mane (LR: PL) p. 520
THURSO'S LANDING	Flowerstock Row (LR: LP) p. 237
	Thurso Court (LR: PL) p. 175, section 2

Jeffers, Robinson. *The Collected Poetry of Robinson Jeffers.* Edited by Tim Hunt. vol. 3. Stanford, CA: Stanford University Press, 1991. [UMCP: McK PS3519.E27A17 1988 v.3]

ANIMALS	Yellow Dawn Court (LR: KR) p. 364
BIRDS AND FISHES	Halflight Garth (LR: PL) p. 426
CALM AND FULL THE OCEAN	Rainprint Row (LR: JH) p. 124
CARMEL POINT	Endless Ocean Way (LR: KR) p. 399

Jeffers, Robinson. *The Collected Poetry of Robinson Jeffers.* Edited by Tim Hunt. vol. 5. Stanford, CA: Stanford University Press, 2001. [UMCP: McK PS3519.E27A17 1988 v.5] and

Jeffers, Robinson. *The Beginning and the End.* New York: Random House, 1963. [UMCP: McK PS3519.E27B45]

THE MONSTROUS DROUGHT   Treefrog Place (LR: PL) p. 1087 and p. 43, respectively

Other Jeffers sources consulted:

Jeffers, Robinson. *The Collected Poetry of Robinson Jeffers.* Edited by Tim Hunt. vol. 4. Stanford, CA: Stanford University Press, 1998. [UMCP: McK PS3519.E27A17 1988 v.4]

Jeffers, Robinson. *Rock and Hawk: A Selection of Shorter Poems by Robinson Jeffers.* New York: Random House, 1987. [HCPL: 811.5J]

Jeffers, Robinson. *The Wild God of the World: an Anthology of Robinson Jeffers.* Selected and introduction by Albert Gelpi. Stanford, CA: Stanford University Press, 2003. [HCPL: 811.52J] This volume includes 64 of Jeffers poems, 26 of which were used for Columbia place names, and 10 of those poems are from the second volume of *The Collected Poetry . . .* that requires inter-library loan.

(Nicholas) Vachel Lindsay (1879-1931), American poet.

Lindsay, Vachel. *Selected Poems of Vachel Lindsay.* Edited by Mark Harris. New York: The Macmillan Company, 1967 [c1963]. [HCPL: 811.5L]

A GOSPEL OF BEAUTY: I. THE PROUD FARMER.	Knighthood Lane (OB: DG) p. 70
ALEXANDER CAMPBELL: III. A RHYMED ADDRESS TO ALL RENEGADE CAMPBELLITES, EXHORTING THEM TO RETURN	Brush Run (OB: Ho) p. 83, verse III.
DOCTOR MOHAWK: III. ONE BRIEF HOUR OF GROWN-UP GLORY ON THE GULF OF MEXICO	Life Quest Lane (OB: Ho) p. 65
FROM "SO MUCH THE WORSE FOR BOSTON"	Cornshock Court (OB: Ho) p. 53
I HEARD IMMANUEL SINGING	Harp String (OB: Ho) p. 87
IN PRAISE OF JOHNNY APPLESEED: I. OVER THE APPALACHIAN BARRICADE	Deer Pasture (OB: Ho) p. 22
IN PRAISE OF JOHNNY APPLESEED: II. THE INDIANS WORSHIP HIM, BUT HE HURRIES ON	Spinning Seed (OB: Ho) p. 26
	Wheatsheaf Way (OB: Ho) p. 25
JOHN L. SULLIVAN, THE STRONG BOY OF BOSTON	Kilrain Court (OB: Ho) p. 13
JOHNNY APPLESEED'S WIFE FROM THE PALACE OF EVE	Perfect Hour (OB: Ho) p. 181
NIAGARA	Opal Chain (OB: Ho) p. 55, section I
OUR MOTHER POCAHONTAS	Feathered Head (OB: Ho) p. 116, section II
	Rustling Leaf (OB: Ho) p. 115, section I
PROLOGUE TO "RHYMES TO BE TRADED FOR BREAD"	Minstrel Way (OB: Ho) p. 99
ROOSEVELT	Quick Fox (OB: Ho) p. 137
	Sharp Antler (OB: Ho) p. 137
SHANTUNG, OR THE EMPIRE OF CHINA IS CRUMBLING DOWN	Catwing Court (OB: Ho) p. 165, section III
	Hourglass Place (OB: Ho) p. 163
THE CHINESE NIGHTINGALE	Carved Stone (OB: Ho) p. 7
	Deepage Drive (OB: Ho) p. 7
	Moonfire Place (OB: Ho) p. 8
	Windbell Way (OB: Ho) p. 11
THE EAGLE THAT IS FORGOTTEN	Sleepsoft Circle (OB: Ho) p. 131
THE FAIRY FROM THE APPLE-SEED	Ivory Hand Place (OB: Ho) p. 183
THE GHOST OF THE BUFFALOES	Flintfeet Lane (OB: Ho) p. 175
THE JINGO AND THE MINSTREL	Gentle Folk (OB: Ho) p. 155
THE KALLYOPE YELL	Tunemaker Terrace (OB: Ho) p. 35, section II
THE LAME BOY AND THE FAIRY	Riding Hood Circle (OB: Ho) p. 189
	Silver Sod (OB: Ho) p. 188
THE PRAIRIE BATTLEMENTS	Folded Palm (OB: Ho) p. 90
THE SEA SERPENT CHANTEY	Wedding Ring Way [1] (OB: Ho) p. 184, section II
THE STATUE OF OLD ANDREW JACKSON	Hickory Limb (OB: Ho) p. 128
THREE POEMS ABOUT MARK TWAIN: I. THE RAFT	Candleshine Court (OB: Ho) p. 17
	Crazyquilt Court (OB: Ho) p. 18
	Steamerbell Row [1] (OB: Ho) p. 17

Other Lindsay sources consulted:
Lindsay, Vachel. *Collected Poems.* New York: The Macmillan Company, 1967. [HCPL: 811.5L]

Alan Lomax (1915 - 2002), American folklorist.

Lomax, Alan, ed. *The Folk Songs of North America, in the English Language.* Garden City, NY:
      Doubleday & Company, Inc., 1960. [Columbia Archives]

A FAIR BEAUTY BRIDE	Fair Beauty (KC: MC) p. 195, verse 1
AS I ROVED OUT	Roveout Lane (KC: MC) p. 30, verse 1
BOLD JACK DONAHUE	Bushranger Path (KC: MC) p. 117, verse 1
CAPE ANN	Cape Ann Drive (KC: MC) p. 13, verse 3
CHARLIE QUANTRELL	Quantrell Row (KC: MC) p. 347, verse 1
COME, LIFE, SHAKER LIFE	Shaker Drive (KC: MC) p. 73, verse 1
COTTON MILL COLIC	Cotton Mill Lane (KC: MC) p. 287, chorus
LOUSY MINER	Flapjack Lane (KC: MC) p. 338, verse 2
LOVE IS PLEASIN'	Silver Twine (KC: MC) p. 136, verse 3
MY LOVE IS A RIDER	Rawhide Ridge (KC: MC) p. 384, verse 7
NIGHT HERDING SONG	Herding Row (KC: MC) p. 376, verse 2
OLD SMOKEY	Turtle Dove Place (KC: MC) p. 221, verse 1
SALLY GOODIN	Goodin Circle (KC: MC) p. 236, verse 1
STRAWBERRY LANE	Cambric Court (KC: MC) p. 17, verse 2
TALKING COLUMBIA	Hatbrim Terrace (KC: MC) p. 442, verse 2
THE DEER CHASE	Deer Chase (KC: MC) p. 164
TURKEY IN THE STRAW	Strawturkey Court (KC: MC) p. 95, chorus
WAY OVER IN THE HEAVENS	Wayover Way (KC: MC) p. 248, chorus

Henry Wadsworth Longfellow (1807-1882), American poet.

Longfellow, Henry Wadsworth. *The Complete Poetical Works of Henry Wadsworth
      Longfellow.* Cutchogue, NY: Buccaneer Books, 1993. [HCPL: 811.3L]

A SUMMER DAY BY THE SEA	Summer Day Lane (HC: Lo) p. 317
AN APRIL DAY	April Day Garth (HC: Lo) p. 7
AUTUMN	Harvest Moon Lane (HC: Lo) p. 69
DIVINA COMMEDIA	Beatrice Way (HC: Lo) p. 293
ELIOT'S OAK	Eliot's Oak Road (HC: Lo) p. 318
ENDYMION	Endymion Lane (HC: Lo) p. 15
EVANGELINE: A TALE OF ACADIE	Evangeline Way (HC: Lo) p. 72
JOHN ENDICOTT	Endicott Lane (HC: Lo) p. 465
MAD RIVER	Mad River Lane (HC: Lo) p. 358
RONDEL	Rondel Place (HC: Lo) p. 632
THE BROKEN OAR	Broken Oak Lane (HC: Lo) p. 323
THE CELESTIAL PILOT, PURGATORIA II	Celestial Way (HC: Lo) p. 633
THE EVENING STAR	Even Star Place (HC: Lo) p. 69
THE FIRE OF DRIFT-WOOD	Driftwood Court (HC: Lo) p. 107
THE IRON PEN	Iron Pen Place (HC: Lo) p. 344
THE LANDLORD'S TALE: PAUL REVERE'S RIDE	Mystic Court (HC: Lo) p. 208
	Paul Revere Ride (HC: Lo) p. 207
THE LIGHTHOUSE	Light House Court (HC: Lo) p. 106
THE OPEN WINDOW	Open Window (HC: Lo) p. 109
THE PHANTOM SHIP	Phantom Court (HC: Lo) p. 187
THE POET'S TALE: THE BIRDS OF KILLINGWORTH	Killingworth Way (HC: Lo) p. 240
THE SKELETON IN ARMOR	Fallriver Row Court (HC: Lo) p. 659, Appendix
	Gerfalcon Road (HC: Lo) p. 12
	Hildebrand Court (HC: Lo) p. 12
	Round Tower Place (HC: Lo) p. 13
	Windmill Lane [1] (HC: Lo) p. 659, Appendix
THE THREE KINGS	Three Kings Lane (HC: Lo) p. 339
THE VILLAGE BLACKSMITH	Blacksmith Drive (HC: Lo) p. 14
THE WRECK OF THE HESPERUS	Hesperus Drive (HC: Lo) p. 13

Other Longfellow sources used to track down the story behind *The Skeleton in Armor:*
Hattendorf, Ingrid M. and Christian-Albrecht Gollub. "From Longfellow's Journal." *The Old Stone
      Mill* (finding aid). Redwood Library & Athenæum.
            [http://www.redwoodlibrary.org/tower/longfellow.htm (accessed February 15, 2007)]

J. S. "Antiquities of North America." *The American Monthly Magazine (1833-1838)* 7 (January 1836): 67. In APS Online. [HCPL: database online (accessed February 15, 2007)]

Longfellow, Samuel, ed. *Life of Henry Wadsworth Longfellow: with Extracts from his Journals and Correspondence.* vol. 1. Boston: Ticknor and Company, 1886. [UMCP: McK PS2281.L6 1886 vol. 1]

Amy Lowell (1874-1925), American poet and critic.

Lowell, Amy. *The Complete Poetical Works of Amy Lowell.* Boston: Houghton Mifflin Company,1955. [UMCP: McK PS3523.O88 1955]

A CRITICAL FABLE	Slender Sky (HR: Ha) p. 424
A FAIRY TALE	Dusty Glass Court (HR: Ha) p. 13
A WINTER RIDE	Snow Crystal (HR: Ha) p. 5
AZURE AND GOLD	Centre Stone Ring (HR: Ha) p. 2
BEFORE DAWN	Cordage Walk (HR: Ha) p. 17
EAST WIND	East Wind Way (HR: Ha) p. 481
EVELYN RAY	Cricket Pass (HR: Ha) p. 438
MARKET DAY	Wicker Basket Court (HR: Ha) p. 20
MEMORANDUM CONFIDED BY A YUCCA	
TO A PASSION-VINE	Plaited Reed (HR: Ha) p. 246
	Scarlet Petal (OB: DG) p. 246
PANTOMIME IN ONE ACT	Satinwood Drive (HR: Ha) p. 475
POIGNANT GRIEF DURING A SUNNY	
SPRING, BY LI T'AI-PO	Sunny Spring (HR: Ha) p. 336
SONG	Misty Arch Run (HR: Ha) p. 5
SUGGESTED BY THE COVER OF A VOLUME OF	
KEATS'S POEMS	Branch Beech (HR: Ha) p. 2
THE FOOL ERRANT	Bridlerein Terrace (HR: Ha) p. 6
THE GREEN BOWL	Resting Sea (HR: Ha) p. 7
THE NOTE-BOOK IN THE GATE-LEGGED TABLE	High Beam Court (HR: Ha) p. 501
THE ON-LOOKER	Bright Plume (HR: Ha) p. 446
THE POET	Cloudland Court (HR: Ha) p. 17
THE WAY	Hawthorn (HR: neighborhood) p. 9
	The Hawthorn Center (HR: community center) p. 9
TOGETHER WE KNOW HAPPINESS, WRITTEN	
BY A DESCENDANT OF THE FOUNDER OF	
THE SOUTHERN T'ANG DYNASTY	Golden Hook (HR: Ha) p. 357

Note on Lowell works: *Poignant Grief . . .* (Sunny Spring) and *Together We Know Happiness . . .* (Golden Hook) are from a collection of Chinese poetry Lowell titled *Fir-Flower Tablets,* which she adapted and translated with the assistance from Florence Ayscough.

Ogden Nash (1902-1971), American poet.

Nash, Ogden. *Good Intentions.* Boston, MA: Little, Brown and Company, 1942. [UMCP: McK PS3527.A637G6]

DRIVE SLOW, MAN CHORTLING, OR APRIL 1941   April Journey 1 (DS: FH) p. 55

Nash, Ogden. *I Wouldn't Have Missed It: Selected Poems of Ogden Nash.* Boston: Little, Brown, 1975. [HCPL: 811.5N]

IT'S SNUG TO BE SMUG	Butler Court (DS: FH) p. 123
TARKINGTON, THOU SHOULD'ST BE LIVING	
IN THIS HOUR	Tarkington Place (DS: FH) p. 232
THE TALE OF CUSTARD THE DRAGON	Chase Lions Way (DS: FH) p. 100

Alexander Pope (1688-1744), English poet.

Pope, Alexander. *Collected Poems.* Edited by Bonamy Dobrée. Rutland, VT: Charles E. Tuttle Co. Inc., c1983. [HCPL: 821.5P]

EPISTLE TO THE SAME [MISS TERESA BLOUNT], ON HER LEAVING THE TOWN AFTER THE CORONATION
Morning Walk [2] (OB: Ho) p. 113 (SA: EPITAPH TO MR. C., ST. JAMES'S PLACE)

EPITAPH INTENDED FOR MR. ROWE IN WESTMINSTER ABBEY
Gentle Shade [2] (OB: Ho) p. 119

EPITAPH TO MR. C., ST. JAMES'S PLACE
Morning Walk [2] (OB: Ho) p. 117 (SA: EPISTLE TO THE SAME [MISS TERESA BLOUNT], ON HER LEAVING THE TOWN AFTER THE CORONATION)

ESSAY ON MAN, EPISTLE I, PART III
Solar Walk [2] (OB: Ho) p. 181

ESSAY ON MAN, EPISTLE I, PART V
Balmy Dew Way [1] (OB: Ho) p. 185
Constant Course [1] (OB: Ho) p. 185
Gracious End Court [1] (OB: Ho) p. 185
Nature's Road [1] (OB: Ho) p. 192

ESSAY ON MAN, EPISTLE II, PART III
TO ROBERT EARL OF OXFORD, AND EARL MORTIMER (EPISTLES)
Calm Sunset [2] (OB: Ho) p. 108

Other Pope sources consulted:

Pope, Alexander. *An Essay on Man.* Edited by Frank Brady. Indianapolis: The Bobbs-Merrill Company, Inc., 1965. [UMCP: McK PR3627.A12 1965]

James Whitcomb Riley (1849-1916), American poet.

Riley, James Whitcomb. *The Complete Poetical Works of James Whitcomb Riley.* New York: Grosset & Dunlap, 1978. [HCPL: 811.4 R]

A COUNTRY PATHWAY, POEM 26
Autumn Wind Circle (RH: PoR) p. 35
Bright Memory Drive (RH: PoR) p. 36
Towering Elm Terrace (RH: PoR) p. 36
Towering Oak Path (RH: PoR) p. 36

A DREAM OF LONG AGO, POEM 58
Mellow Twilight Court (RH: PoR) p. 62

A DREAM UNFINISHED, POEM 96
Folded Leaf Square (RH: PoR) p. 96

A SESSION WITH UNCLE SIDNEY: VII. AND MAKES NURSERY RHYMES: 5. THE DARING PRINCE, POEM 907
Daring Prince Way (RH: PoR) p. 697

A SUMMER SUNRISE, POEM 80
Gleaming Sand Chase (RH: PoR) p. 80
Summer Sunrise Drive (RH: PoR) p. 80

A WRAITH OF SUMMER-TIME, POEM 235
Enchanted Solitude Place (RH: PoR) p. 189
Velvet Path (RH: PoR) p. 189

AN OLD SWEETHEART OF MINE, POEM 24
Mellow Wine Way (RH: PoR) p. 28

AUGUST, POEM 34
Liquid Laughter Lane (RH: PoR) p. 45

DEAD LEAVES, POEM 38
Distant Melody Place (RH: PoR) p. 48, section Dawn

"DREAM", POEM 85
Radiant Gleam Way (RH: PoR) p. 85
Tender Mist Mews (RH: PoR) p. 85

DUSK SONG—THE BEETLE, POEM 153
Garden Walk (RH: PoR) p. 148 (SA: THE ROSE, POEM 76)
Golden Seeds Row (RH: PoR) p. 147

EVENSONG, POEM 898
Evensong Mews (RH: PoR) p. 688

I SMOKE MY PIPE, POEM 21
Drifting Cloud Mews (RH: PoR) p. 27

IF I KNEW WHAT POETS KNOW, POEM 23
Fairest Dream Lane (RH: PoR) p. 27

LIBERTY, POEM 93
Morning Light Trail (RH: PoR) p. 90
River Run (RH: PoR) p. 91

LOUELLA WAINIE, POEM 252
Waving Willow Path (RH: PoR) p. 199

OH, HER BEAUTY, POEM 201
Glorious Light Place (RH: PoR) p. 172

THE BEST TIMES, POEM 904
Best Times Path (RH: PoR) p. 690

THE EMPTY SONG, POEM 123
Empty Song Road (RH: PoR) p.130

THE EVENING COMPANY, POEM 786
Evening Company Circle (RH: PoR) p. 573

THE LOST PATH, POEM 105
Hazel Thicket Terrace (RH: PoR) p. 115

THE ONWARD TRAIL, POEM 827
Onward Trail (RH: PoR) p. 644

THE ROSE, POEM 76	Angel Rose Court (RH: PoR) p. 78
	Garden Walk (RH: PoR) p. 78 (SA: DUSK SONG—THE BEETLE, POEM 153)
	Waving Tree Court (RH: PoR) p. 77
THE SONG I NEVER SING, POEM 110	Waking Dreams Knoll (RH: PoR) p. 119
TO A BOY WHISTLING, POEM 4	Enchanted Key Gate (RH: PoR) p. 4
WHAT SMITH KNEW ABOUT FARMING, POEM 6	Ripe Apple Lane (RH: PoR) p. 5
WHAT THE WIND SAID, POEM 73	Forest Shade Trail (RH: PoR) p. 75
	Jeweled Hand Circle (RH: PoR) p. 75
	Old Romance Row (RH: PoR) p. 75
	Old Sea Place (RH: PhR) p. 74, poem 73
	Warm Sunshine Path (RH: PoR) p. 74
WHEN EARLY MARCH SEEMS MIDDLE MAY, POEM 376	Morning Time Lane (RH: PoR) p. 273
WHEN EVENING SHADOWS FALL, POEM 86	Evening Shadows Court (RH: PoR) p. 85
	Grateful Heart Gate (RH: PoR) p. 85

Other Riley sources consulted:

Riley, James Whitcomb. *The Complete Poetical Works of James Whitcomb Riley*. Bloomington, IN: Indiana University Press, 1993. [UMCP: McK PS2700.F93]

Carl Sandburg (1878-1967), American author.

Sandburg, Carl. *The Complete Poems of Carl Sandburg* (revised and expanded edition; introduction by Archibald MacLeish). New York: Harcourt Brace & Company, 1970. [HCPL: 811.5S]

AT A WINDOW	Dayshape Drive (OM: TS) p. 49
BALLOON FACES	Sargossa Place (OM: TS) p. 252
BASKET	Basket Ring (OM: TS) p. 266
BETWEEN TWO HILLS	Two Hills Court (OM: TS) p. 56
BIRD FOOTPRINT	Footprint Place (KC: Hu) p. 715
CABOOSE THOUGHTS	Caboose Court (OM: TS) p. 93
CHILD FACE	Early Spring Way (KC: Hu) p. 722
	Many Mile Mews (KC: Hu) p. 722
CHORDS	Black Velvet Lane (KC: Hu) p. 228
	Sea Shadow (KC: Hu) p. 227
CRISSCROSS	Crisscross Court (OM: TS) p. 341
DEEP SEA WANDERING	Wandering Way (OM: TS) p. 718
FAME IF NOT FORTUNE	Half Dollar Court (KC: Hu) p. 728
	Summer Park Court (KC: Hu) p. 728
FOG	Catfeet Court (OM: TS) p. 33
FOR YOU	Longlook Lane (OM: TS) p. 267
GOOD MORNING, AMERICA	Pinecone Row (OM: TS) p. 324, section 6
HALF MOON IN A HIGH WIND	Highwind Court (OM: TS) p. 213
HAZE	Corn Tassel Court (KC: Hu) p. 253
	Skyrock Court (KC: Hu) p. 254
HONEY AND SALT	Deep Smoke (KC: Hu) p. 708
	Honeysalt Row (OM: TS) p. 706 and p. 708
	Nightsong Lane (KC: Hu) p. 707
	Spring Water Path 1 (KC: Hu) p. 707
IF SO HAP MAY BE	Sohap Lane (OM: TS) p. 731
LAUGHING CORN	Cornsilk Court (OM: TS) p. 87
LESSON	Early April Way (KC: Hu) p. 733
	Moving Water Lane (KC: Hu) p. 733
	Summer Blossom Lane (KC: Hu) p. 733
LITTLE WORD, LITTLE WHITE BIRD	Polished Stone (KC: Hu) p. 739
	Red Apple Lane (KC: Hu) p. 736
	Sunfall Court (KC: Hu) p. 739
LOVE IS A DEEP AND A DARK AND A LONELY	Book Row (KC: Hu) p. 711
	Many Flower Lane (KC: Hu) p. 711
	Rainleaf Court (KC: Hu) p. 711
MOON RIDERS	Moonrider Lane (KC: Hu) p. 293, section 3
	Morning Mews (KC: Hu) p. 291, section 1
OLD DEEP SING-SONG	Old Deep Court (OM: TS) p. 699

OLD MUSIC FOR QUIET HEARTS	Mirror Light Place (OM: TS) p. 745
PANELS	West Window Way (KC: Hu) p. 263
PRAIRIE	Pinwheel Place (OM: TS) p. 83
REDHAW RAIN	Slow Rain Way (KC: Hu) p. 353
	Sweet Grass Ridge (KC: Hu) p. 353
SLABS OF THE SUNBURNT WEST	Cold Star Court (KC: Hu) p. 314, section 3
	Gray Mouse Way (KC: Hu) p. 308, section 2
	Green Moon Path (KC: Hu) p. 311, section 2
THE EVENING SUNSETS WITNESS AND PASS ON	Rainflower Way (KC: Hu) p. 717
	Tall Window Way (KC: Hu) p. 717
	Wild Grass Court [1] (KC: Hu) p. 717
THE WINDY CITY	Clocktower Lane (KC: Hu) p. 279, section 7
	Deerfoot Way (KC: Hu) p. 272, section 2
	Sandlight Court (KC: Hu) p. 280, section 9
	Softwater Way (KC: Hu) p. 275, section 4
	White Spring Way (KC: Hu) p. 281, section 10
TIMESWEEP	Timesweep Lane (OM: TS) p. 758
WALL SHADOWS	Shadowfall Terrace (OM: TS) p. 671
WITHOUT NOTICE BEFOREHAND	Lady Bug Row (KC: Hu) p. 353

John Ronald Reuel Tolkien (1892-1973), English author.

Tolkien, J. R. R. *The Hobbit, or, There and Back Again.* Boston: Houghton Mifflin Company, 2001. [HCPL: F Tol, Ya Tol and JF Tol]

THE HOBBIT . . .	Green Dragon Court [1] (HC: HG) p. 33; ch. 2, para. 10
	Hobbit's Glen (HC: neighborhood)
	Ravenhill Row [1] (HC: HG) p. 220; chapter 11, paragraph 5
	Rivendell (HC: HG) p. 52; chapter 3, paragraph 6
	Tooks Way (HC: HG) p. 5; ch. 1, para. 4

Tolkien, J. R. R. *The Lord of the Rings.* Boston: Houghton Mifflin Company, 1994. (Includes the three books of the trilogy: *The Fellowship of the Ring, The Two Towers,* and *The Return of the King*) [Columbia Archives]

THE FELLOWSHIP OF THE RING	Barrow Downs (HC: HG) p. 111; book 1, ch. 6, para. 34
	Buckleberry Path (HC: HG) p. 65; book 1, ch. 3, para. 18
	Goodbody Court (WL: RB) p. 28; book 1, ch. 1, para. 51 (SA: THE RETURN OF THE KING)
	Heathertoe Lane (HC: HG) p. 152; book 1, ch. 9, para. 45
	High Hay Drive (HC: HG) p. 97; book 1, ch. 5, para. 6
	Ivy Bush Lane (HC: HG) p. 22; book 1, ch. 1, para. 8
	Northern Fences Lane (HC: HG) p. 361; book 2, ch. 8, para. 31
	Oakenshield Circle (HC: HG) p. 10; prologue, para. 35
	Proud Foot Place (HC: HG) p. 28; book 1, ch. 1, para. 51 (SA: THE RETURN OF THE KING)
	Ridermark Row (HC: HG) p. 255; book 2, ch. 2, para. 75
	Rushlight Path (HC: HG) p. 152; book 1, ch. 9, para. 45
	Shadowmere Mews (HC: HG) p. 229; book 2, ch. 1, para. 147
	Southern Star Terrace (HC: HG) p. 8; prologue, para. 25
	Thistle Brook Court (HC: HG) p. 18; map
	Willow Bottom Drive (HC: HG) p. 18; map
	Wood Elves Way (HC: HG) p. 56; book 1, ch. 2, para. 138
THE RETURN OF THE KING	Cricket Hollow Court (HC: HG) p. 279; book 6, ch. 8, para. 36
	Elfstone Way (HC: HG) p. 853; book 5, ch. 8, para. 120
	Goodbody Court (WL: RB) p. 1074; Appendix C (SA: THE FELLOWSHIP OF THE RING)
	Lightfoot Path (HC: HG) p. 826; book 5, ch. 6, para. 41
	Proud Foot Place (HC: HG) p. 1074; Appendix C (SA: THE FELLOWSHIP OF THE RING)
THE TWO TOWERS	Silver Tree Place (HC: HG) p. 412; book 3, ch. 2, para. 18
	Straight Star Place [1] (HC: HG) p. 693; book 4, ch. 8, para. 38
	Watchwood Path (HC: HG) p. 573; book 3, ch. 10, para. 90
	Wellinghall Way (HC: HG) p. 459; book 3, ch. 4, para. 70
	Winding Star Circle [1] (HC: HG) p. 693; book 4, ch. 8, para. 38

Other Tolkien sources consulted:

Tolkien, J. R. R. *The Fellowship of the Ring: Being the first part of The Lord of the Rings.* Boston: Houghton Mifflin Company, 1993. [HCPL: T (paperback) and F Tol]

Tolkien, J. R. R. *The Two Towers: Being the second part of the Lord of the Rings.* Boston: Houghton Mifflin Company, 1982. [HCPL: F Tol and YA Tol]

Tolkien, J. R. R. *The Return of the King: Being the third part of The Lord of the Rings.* Boston: Houghton Mifflin Company, 1994. [HCPL: F Tol and JF Tol] Appendices (A-F) included. An index to *The Lord of the Rings,* divided into four sections (I. Songs and Verses, II. Persons, Beasts and Monsters, III. Places, and IV. Things), is found at the end of the book and was particularly helpful in finding lesser known names.

Tolkien, J. R. R. *The Annotated Hobbit: The Hobbit, or, There and Back Again.* Annotated by Douglas A. Anderson. Boston: Houghton-Mifflin Company, 2002. [UMCP: McK PR6039.O32H6 2002] The text is corrected in this volume and it is illustrated by the author. One schematic drawing of the Lonely Mountain is of particular interest since it identifies Ravenhill.

Mark Twain (pseudonym for Samuel Langhorne Clemens) (1835-1910), American writer.

Twain, Mark [Clemens, Samuel Langhorne]. *Adventures of Huckleberry Finn: An Authoritative Text, Backgrounds and Sources, Criticism.* Edited by Sculley Bradley, Richmond Croom Beatty, E. Hudson Long and Thomas Cooley. (A Norton Critical Edition). New York, NY: W. W. Norton & Company, Inc., 1977. [Columbia Archives; other editions at HCPL under following call numbers: F Twa, 813.4T, and JF Twa]

ADVENTURES OF HUCKLEBERRY FINN	
	Blue Arrow Court (HR: CC) p. 160; ch. 29, para. 57
	Currycomb Court (HR: CC) p. 45; ch. 9, para. 20
	Snuffbox Terrace (HR: CC) p. 15; ch. 3, para. 2
	Sternwheel Place (HR: CC) p. 97; ch. 19, para. 2
	Summergrape Way (HR: CC) p. 36; ch. 8, para. 12
	Tailcoat Way (HR: CC) p. 87; ch. 18, para. 1

Twain, Mark. *The Adventures of Tom Sawyer.* New York: William Morrow & Company, Inc., Books of Wonder, 1989. [HCPL: JF TWA; other edition in HCPL: F TWA and 813.4T]

THE ADVENTURES OF TOM SAWYER	
	Brass Knob (HR: CC) p. 62; ch. 7, para. 74
	Ferryboat Circle (HR: CC) p. 110; ch. 14, para. 14
	Frostwork Row (HR: CC) p. 220; ch. 31, para. 1
	Greatnews Lane (HR: CC) p. 230; ch. 32, para. 4
	Kiteline Court (HR: CC) p. 229; ch. 31, last para.
	Log Raft (HR: CC) p. 99; ch. 13, para. 6
	Quarterstaff Road (HR: CC) p. 69; ch. 8, para. 33
	Red Keel (HR: CC) p. 79; ch. 10, para. 25
	Schoolmaster Place (HR: CC) p. 148; ch. 20, para. 6
	Sixpence Circle (HR: CC) p. 203; ch. 29, para. 21
	Twinedew Place (HR: CC) p. 231; ch. 32, para. 5
	Whitewasher Way (HR: CC) p. 10; ch. 2, para. 2

Twain, Mark. *A Connecticut Yankee in King Arthur's Court.* New York: Bantam Books, 1981. [HCPL: F Tw; other editions at HCPL F Twa]

A CONNECTICUT YANKEE . . .	
	Eclipse Way (HR: CC) p. 11; ch. 2, para. 28
	Fortnight Court (HR: CC) p. 33; ch. 7, para. 3
	Launcelot Lane (HR: CC) p. 14; ch. 3, para. 2
	Oxhorn Court (HR: CC) p. 12; ch. 2, para. 37

Twain, Mark. *The Hidden Mark Twain: A Collection of Little-Known Mark Twain.* New York: Greenwich House, 1984. [HCPL: 818.4 T]

THE AMERICAN CLAIMANT	Half Crown Court (HR: CC) p. 389; ch. 1, para. 27
TOM SAWYER ABROAD	Caravan Court (HR) p. 28; ch. 6, title and para. 25
	Millet Seed Hill (HR: CC) p. 34; ch. 7, para. 43
	Pyramid Way (HR: CC) p. 57; ch. 12, para. 5
	Stray Camel Way 1 (HR: CC) p. 34; ch. 7, para. 35

Twain, Mark. *The Prince and the Pauper: A Tale for Young People of All Ages*. Pleasantville, NY: The
    Reader's Digest Association, Inc., 1988. [HCPL: F Twa; other editions at HCPL: F Twa]

THE PRINCE AND THE PAUPER	Buglenote Way (HR: CC) p. 70; ch. 11, para. 13
	Crossbeam Circle (HR: CC) p. 15; ch. 2, para. 2
	Maypole Way (HR: CC) p. 26; ch. 3, para. 51
	Triple Feather (HR: CC) p. 57; ch. 9, para. 6

Twain, Mark. *Roughing It*. Berkeley: University of California Press, 1973. [HCPL: 817.4 T]

ROUGHING IT	Glass Tumbler Path [1] (HR: CC) p. 311; ch. 48, para. 26
	Harpoon Hill [1] (HR: CC) p. 330; ch. 51, para. 7
	Steamboat Landing [1] (HR: CC) p. 44; ch. 1, para. 3

Twain, Mark, and Charles Dudley Warner. *The Gilded Age: A Tale of Today*. New York, NY:
    Meridian, 1994. [Columbia Archives]

THE GILDED AGE . . .	Buckstone Court (HR: CC) p. 250; ch. 35, para. 27
	Buttonhole Court (HR: CC) p. 180; ch. 24, para. 17
	Dovecote Drive (HR: CC) p. 114 ; ch. 14, para. 52
	Hawkeye Run (HR: CC) p. 66; ch. 7, para. 2
	High Bench (HR: CC) p. 42; ch. 4, para. 6
	Springing Step (HR: CC) p. 184; ch. 25, para. 7

Other Twain sources:

Railton, Stephen and the University of Virginia Library. *Mark Twain In His Times: An Electronic
    Archive* (1996-). [http://etext.lib.virginia.edu/railton/ (accessed October 17, 2007)] This
    website allows word searches across most of the titles used for Columbia place names; go
    to "Search," and then "Search Mark Twain's Works."

Twain, Mark. *The Gilded Age and Later Novels*. New York, NY: The Library of America, 2002. [HCPL:
    F Twa] This volume includes *The Gilded Age, The American Claimant,* and *Tom Sawyer Abroad.*

The University of Adelaide Library. *eBooks @Adelaide*. [http://etext.library.adelaide.edu.au/t/twain/
    mark/(accessed October 17, 2007)] This website offers information on Mark Twain and has
    online versions of *The Adventures of Tom Sawyer* (1881) and *The Adventures of Huckleberry
    Finn* (1884).

James Abbott McNeill Whistler (1834-1903), American painter and etcher.

Dodgson, Campbell. *The Etchings of James McNeill Whistler*. Edited by Geoffrey Holme. London: The
    Studio, limited, 1922. [UMCP: Art Folio NE2195.W6D6]

BILLINGSGATE	Billingsgate Row (HC: Sw) plate 21
MILLBANK	Millbank Row (HC: Sw) plate 37
"THE SWAN," CHELSEA	Swansfield (HC: neighborhood) K98
	Swansfield Road (HC: Sw) K98
THE TWO SHIPS	Two Ships Court (HC: Sw) K148

Lochnan, Katharine A. *The Etchings of James McNeill Whistler*. New Haven: Yale University Press in
    association with the Art Gallery of Ontario, 1984. [UMCP: Art NE2012.W45L6 1984]

MILLBANK	Millbank Row (HC: Sw) ill. 158
"THE SWAN," CHELSEA	Swansfield (HC: neighborhood) p. 279
	Swansfield Road (HC: Sw) p. 279
THE TWO SHIPS	Two Ships Court (HC: Sw) p. 280
THE WINE-GLASS	Wineglass Court (HC: Sw) p. 88
THE YOUNG TREE	Youngtree Court (HC: Sw) p. 282

Lochnan, Katharine A. *Whistler's Etchings and the Sources of His Etching Style, 1855-1880*. New York,
    NY: Garland Publishing, Inc., 1988. (Ph.D. thesis, University of London, 1982) [UMCP: Art
    NE2012.W45L63 1988]

| MILLBANK | Millbank Row (HC: Sw) ill. 190 |
| THE WINE-GLASS | Wineglass Court (HC: Sw) p. 71 |

Smithsonian Institution. Freer Gallery of Art. American Art Collection.
[http://www.asia.si.edu/collections/search.cfm (accessed February 20, 2007)]

BILLINGSGATE — Billingsgate Row (HC: Sw)
BROWN AND SILVER: OLD BATTERSEA BRIDGE — Battersea Lane (HC: Sw)
MILLBANK — Millbank Row (HC: Sw)
"THE SWAN," CHELSEA — Swansfield (HC: neighborhood)
  Swansfield Road (HC: Sw)
THE WINE-GLASS — Wineglass Court (HC: Sw)

Spalding, Frances. *Whistler.* Oxford: Phaidon Press Limited, 1979. [HCPL: 709.2S]
BROWN AND SILVER: OLD BATTERSEA BRIDGE — Battersea Lane (HC: Sw) p. 35

University of Glasgow [UK]. Hunterian Museum & Art Gallery. Whistler Collection.
[http://www.huntsearch.gla.ac.uk/ (accessed February 20, 2007)]

MILLBANK — Millbank Row (HC: Sw)
"THE SWAN," CHELSEA — Swansfield (HC: neighborhood)
  Swansfield Road (HC: Sw)
THE WINE-GLASS — Wineglass Court (HC: Sw)
THE YOUNG TREE — Youngtree Court (HC: Sw)

Other Whistler sources consulted:
Prideaux, Tom and the Editors of Time-Life Books. *The World of Whistler 1834-1903.* New York: Time-Life Books, 1970. [HCPL: 759.13P]

Walt Whitman (1819-1892) (orig. Walter), American poet.

Whitman, Walt. *Leaves of Grass.* New York: New American Library, 2000. [HCPL: 811.3W]

A BOSTON BALLAD — Clipper Lane (RH: PhR) p. 225 (SA: FACES, SONG OF MYSELF, SONG OF THE BROAD-AXE, and SONG OF THE OPEN ROAD)

A SIGHT IN CAMP IN THE DAYBREAK GRAY AND DIM — Daybreak Circle (RH: PhR) p. 259 (SA: SONG OF THE BANNER AT DAYBREAK)

A SONG OF JOYS — Drumbeat Place (KC: Hu) p. 153
A THOUGHT OF COLUMBUS — Fleets of Time Court [1] (RH: PhR) p. 55
AFTER THE SEA-SHIP — Whistling Winds Walk (RH: PhR) p. 224
AS CONSEQUENT, ETC. — Mystic Ocean Lane (RH: PhR) p. 300 (SA: TWO RIVULETS)
AS I LAY WITH MY HEAD IN YOUR LAP CAMERADO — Camerado Court (KC: Hu) p. 272
AS I WALK THESE BROAD MAJESTIC DAYS — Distant Bugles Court [1] (RH: PhR) p. 403
  Majestic Days Way [1] (RH: PhR) p. 402

AS THE GREEK'S SIGNAL FLAME [FOR WHITTIER'S EIGHTIETH BIRTHDAY, DECEMBER 17, 1887] — Signal Flame Court [1] (RH: PhR) p. 439
CROSSING BROOKLYN FERRY — Bright Flow Mews (RH: PhR) p. 136, section 3
  Hay Boat Court (RH: PhR) p. 136, section 3
  Summer Sky Path (RH: PhR) p. 136, section 3
  Sunlit Water Way (RH: PhR) p. 136, section 3
  Swift Current Way (RH: PhR) p. 136, section 3
DIRGE FOR TWO VETERANS — Ascending Moon Path (RH: PhR) p. 266
  Great Drum Circle (RH: PoR) p. 266
  Last Sunbeam Place (RH: PoR) p. 266
  Phantom Moon Walk (RH: PoR) p. 266
  Round Moon Circle [1] (KC: Hu) p. 266
  Silent Moon Run (RH: PoR) p. 266
FACES — Clipper Lane (RH: PhR) p. 384 (SA: A BOSTON BALLAD, SONG OF MYSELF, SONG OF THE BROAD-AXE, and SONG OF THE OPEN ROAD)

FACING WEST FROM CALIFORNIA'S SHORES — Western Sea Run (RH: PhR) p. 96
FANCIES AT NAVESINK: 1. THE PILOT IN THE MIST — Helmsman Way (RH: PhR) p. 423 (SA: O STAR OF FRANCE, THOU MOTHER WITH THY EQUAL BROOD, and WHILE BEHIND ALL FIRM AND ERECT)

WHEN LILACS . . . (continued)
    Lilac Bush Path (RH: PoR) p. 276, section 3
    Ocean Shore Lane (RH: PoR) p. 282, section 14
    Ranging Hills Gate (RH: PoR) p. 279, section 11
    Reedy Song Knoll (RH: PoR) p. 280, section 13
    Rising Waves Way (RH: PoR) p. 282, section 14
    Victorious Song Lane (RH: PoR) p. 283, section 16
    Welcome Night Path (RH: PoR) p. 280, section 12
    Western Star Run (RH: PoR) p. 276, section 2

Whitman, Walt. *The Neglected Walt Whitman: Vital Texts.* New York: Four Walls Eight Windows, 1993. [HCPL: 811.309W]

AFTER THE ARGUMENT	Rippling Water Walk (RH: PhR) p. 99
APOSTROPH	Pouring Glories Lane (RH: PhR) p. 82 (SA: O SUN OF REAL PEACE)
DEATH'S VALLEY	Rippling Tides Terrace (RH: PhR) p. 53
DEBRIS	White Pebble Path (RH: PhR) p. 89
NAY, TELL ME NOT TO-DAY THE PUBLISH'D SHAME	Hidden Waters Way (RH: PhR) p. 50
	Quiet Ways Court (RH: PhR) p. 50
O SUN OF REAL PEACE	Pouring Glories Lane (RH: PhR) p. 83 (SA: APOSTROPH)
ONE SONG, AMERICA, BEFORE I GO	Trumpet Sound Court [1] (RH: PhR) p. 93
ONE THOUGHT EVER AT THE FORE	Same Voyage Way [1] (RH: PhR) p. 48
PICTURES	Perfect Calm Court [1] (RH: PhR) p. 124
	Signal Bell Lane [1] (RH: PhR) p. 124
	White Marble Court [1] (RH: PhR) p. 116
RESPONDEZ (POEM OF PROPOSITIONS OF NAKEDNESS)	Floating Clouds Path (RH: PhR) p. 62
SUPPLEMENT HOURS	Indian Summer Drive (RH: PhR) p. 50
TWO RIVULETS	Eternal Ocean Place (RH: PhR) p.96
	Mystic Ocean Lane (RH: PhR) p. 97 (SA: AS CONSEQUENT, ETC.)
WHILE BEHIND ALL FIRM AND ERECT	Helmsman Way (RH: PhR) p. 48 (SA: FANCIES AT NAVESINK: 1. THE PILOT IN THE MIST, O STAR OF FRANCE, and THOU MOTHER WITH THY EQUAL BROOD)

Other Whitman sources consulted:

Whitman, Walt. *Poetry & Prose.* Edited by Shira Wolosky. [New Milford, CT]: The Toby Press, 2003. [HCPL: 811.3W]

John Greenleaf Whittier (1807-1892), American poet.

Whittier, John Greenleaf. *The Poetical Works of Whittier.* (Cambridge edition). Boston: Houghton Mifflin Company, 1975. [HCPL: 811.3W]

A SEA DREAM	Rising Moon (OB: DG) p. 160
BARBARA FRIETCHIE	Attic Window (OB: Ho) p. 343
	Broken Staff (OB: DG) p. 343
	Frietchie Row (OB: DG) p. 342
CHANNING	Deep Calm (OB: DG) p. 180
CHILD-SONGS	Open Flower (OB: DG) p. 454 (SA: DANIEL WHEELER and THE NEW YEAR)
COBBLER KEEZAR'S VISION	Cobbler Court (OB: DG) p. 77
DANIEL WHEELER	Open Flower (OB: DG) p. 182 (SA: CHILD-SONGS and THE NEW YEAR)
FLOWERS IN WINTER	Leafy Screen (OB: DG) p. 149
GONE	Setting Star (OB: DG) p. 179
HAZEL BLOSSOMS	Gay Topaz (OB: DG) p. 161
ICHABOD	Bright Soul (OB: Ho) p. 186
MEMORIES	Better Hours Court (OB: Ho) p. 387
	Melting Shadows Lane [2] (OB: DG) p. 387
MOUNTAIN PICTURES	Browsing Deer (OB: DG) p. 156
	Tinted Hill (OB: DG) p. 157
MY PLAYMATE	Sea Change (OB: DG) p. 77

William Carlos Williams (1883-1963), American writer.

Williams, William Carlos. *The Collected Earlier Poems of William Carlos Williams.* New York, NY: New Directions Publishing Corporation, 1966. [HCPL: 811.5W]

THE BIRDS	Topbranch Lane ☐1 (HR: CF) p. 218
THE BULL	Bright Passage (HR: CF) p. 336
THE DESCENT OF WINTER:	
10/29	Sleepy Horse Lane ☐1 (HR: CF) p. 302
10/30	Morningmist Lane (HR: CF) p. 303
11/2	Bonnet Brim Course ☐1 (HR: CF) p. 304
11/2, A MORNING IMAGINATION OF RUSSIA	Wild Ginger Court (HR: CF) p. 306
11/10	Shell Flower Lane (HR: CF) p. 309
THE FLOWERS ALONE	Lightfall Court (HR: CF) p. 90
THE TREES	Bridgehead Court (HR: CF) p. 66
	Winterlong Way (HR: CF) p. 67
THESE	Dark Fire Way (HR: CF) p. 433
	Lakewater Lane (HR: CF) p. 434
TREE AND SKY	Bare Bush Path ☐2 (HR: CF) p. 102
	Lone Tree Court (HR: CF) p. 102
TREES	Gray Star Way (HR: CF) p. 142
VIRTUE	Watch Chain Way (HR: CF) p. 153
WILD ORCHARD	Bare Sky Lane (HR: CF) p. 88
WINTER	Snow Patch Way (HR: CF) p. 89
WINTER SUNSET	Blue February Way (HR: CF) p. 127

Other Williams sources consulted:

Williams, William Carlos. *The Collected Poems of William Carlos Williams.* vol. 1. 1909-1939. Edited by A. Walton Litz and Christopher MacGowan. New York: New Directions Publishing Corporation, 1986. [UMCP: McK PS3545.I544A17 1986 vol.1]

Williams, William Carlos. *The Collected Poems of William Carlos Williams.* vol. 2. 1939-1962. Edited by A. Walton Litz and Christopher MacGowan. New York: New Directions Publishing Corporation, 1986. [Marina loan]

Andrew Newell Wyeth (1917-), American painter.

Pennsylvania Academy of the Fine Arts. *Andrew Wyeth: Temperas, Watercolors, Dry Brush, Drawings, 1938 into 1966; [exhibition] Pennsylvania Academy of the Fine Arts, Philadelphia, October 5-November 27, 1966; Baltimore Museum of Art, December 11, 1966-January 27, 1967; Whitney Museum of American Art, New York, February 6-April 12, 1967; the Art Institute of Chicago, April 21-June 4, 1967.* NY: Abercrombie & Fitch, Co., 1966. [Columbia Archives; UMCP: Art ND237.W93P4]

BENNY'S SCARECROW	Scarecrow Court (OM: TH) p. 52
BLUE COAT	Bluecoat Lane (OM: TH) p. 54
BRINTON'S MILL	Brinton Court ☐1 (OM: TH) p. 62
BUCKET POST	Bucketpost Court (OM: TH) p. 48
CREEK BED	Creekbed Court (OM: TH) p. 48
DELPHINIUM	Delphinium Court (OM: TH) p. 54 [b&w, p. 55]
DRY WELL	Dry Well Court (OM: TH) p. 64
ETTA	Etta Court (OM: TH) p. 72
FARM POND	Farm Pond Lane (OM: TH) p. 59
FLOCK OF CROWS	Crowflock Court (OM: TH) p. 46
GRAPE WINE	Grapewine Court (OM: TH) p. 108 [color, p. 109]
HAY LEDGE	Hayledge Court (OM: TH) p. 61 [b&w, p. 61]
HOUND	Hound Hill Court (OM: TH) p. 62
LIGHTNING ROD	Lightning View Road (OM: TH) p. 34
LOG CHAIN	Log Chain Road (OM: TH) p. 68
MARSH HAWK	Marsh Hawk Way (OM: TH) p. 96
MAY DAY	May Day Court (OM: TH) p. 76 [color, p. 77]
NETHER STONE	Netherstone Court (OM: TH) p. 96
ORCHARD RUN	Orchard Green (OM: TH) p. 56
RACCOON	Raccoon Court (OM: TH) p. 62 [b&w, p. 63]
RACE GATE	Racegate Run (OM: TH) p. 68
SLEEPING DOG	Sleeping Dog Lane (OM: TH) p. 62
SLIPPERS	Slipper Court (OM: TH) p. 74
SNOW SHOE	Snow Shoe Lane (OM: TH) p. 74

Section 2. Local History and Other Reference Sources.

Ackman, Richard. Discussion with Barbara Kellner [on The Kings Contrivance restaurant], April 15, 2006.

Ambrose, Steven E. "Go Hunt Someplace Else." *Columbia Today* 2, no. 4 (October/November 1969): 8-10. [Columbia Archives]

"American Obituary – 1834-1835," *The American Almanac and Repository of Useful Knowledge (1830-1861)* (1836): 297. In APS Online (accessed February 8, 2006). [HCPL: database online]

"Anecdote of the late Robert Oliver." *The Baltimore Literary and Religious Magazine (1835-1841)* 1, no. 2 (February 1835): 59. In APS Online (accessed February 8, 2006). [HCPL: database online]

Bedini, Silvio A. *The Life of Benjamin Banneker: The First African-American Man of Science.* 2nd edition. Baltimore, MD: Maryland Historical Society, 1999. [HCPL: B BAN-B and HCHS]

Benjamin Banneker Historical Park and Museum, Oella, Baltimore County, Maryland. http://lcweb2.loc.gov/cocoon/legacies/MD/200003116.html (accessed May 3, 2007).

Brugger, Robert J. *Maryland: A Middle Temperament, 1634-1980.* Baltimore, MD: The Johns Hopkins University Press, 1988. [Columbia Archives and HCPL: 975.2B]

Chesapeake Bay Program – A Watershed Partnership. "Bay Field Guide." http://www.chesapeakebay.net (accessed March 2007).

Chisolm, Evelyn (Menzies). Discussion with Barbara Kellner and Missy Burke, November 25, 2003.

Columbia Archives, Columbia, Maryland.
    Audio-Visual Collection.
        Chabon, Michael. Interview by Patrick Farrell and Josef Sawyer. December 2005. DVD. AV 665.
    Columbia Association. Records, 1968-present.
        "The Columbia Park and Recreation Association, Inc. Articles of Incorporation," 1965.
    Howard Research and Development Corporation. Records, 1963-present.
        Series 2 Work Group.
        Series 10.1 Development Directors.
        Series 14 Marketing.
        Series 15 Public Affairs.
        Series 21 Scrapbooks.
    James W. Rouse. Papers, 1914-1996.
        Series 1.5 The Rouse Company.
        Series 3 Columbia.
        Series 4 Mail-By-Month.
        Series 5 Speeches, Interviews and Writings.
    Kings Contrivance Community Association. Records, 1977–present.
        Series 3 Minutes.
    Oakland Mills Community Association. Records, 1968–present.
        Series 1 Histories.
    Owen Brown Community Association. Records, 1972-present.
        Series 13 News Clippings.
    Vertical files: Biographical File; Articles About Columbia; Columbia Builders and Developers; Columbia Place Names; and Howard County History.

Community Research & Development, Inc. / The Rouse Company. *Columbia* [newsletter].
    Baltimore, MD: The Rouse Company. [Columbia Archives]
    "First Lake Named for Frazar Wilde," 1, no. 1 (Winter 1966): 3.
    "River Hill In Second Season," 1, no. 1 (Winter 1966): 15.
    "Symphony Pavilion Named to Honor Mrs. Merriweather Post; Exciting Season
    Scheduled," 1, no. 4 (Winter 1967): 6.

Cramm, Joetta M. *Howard County: A Pictorial History.* Norfolk: The Donning Company, 1987.
    [Columbia Archives and HCPL: 975.281C]

Creighton, John W., Jr. "Shareholder Letters." *Weyerhaeuser 1997 Annual Report.* Weyerhaeuser
    Company.
    http://www.weyerhaeuser.com/annualreport/ar97/shareholder.htm (accessed July 20, 2006).

Dorsey, Caleb. *Original Land Grants of Howard County* [map] and *Index,* 1968. [Columbia Archives
    and HCHS]

Dorsey, Caleb. "The Original Land Grants of Howard County, Maryland," *Maryland Historical
    Magazine* 64, no. 3 (Fall 1969): 287-294.

Due, John. Discussion (phone) with Robin Emrich [on Trotter Road], May 22, 2007.

Feaga, Barbara W. et al. *Howard's Roads to the Past.* Ellicott City, MD: Howard County
    Sesquicentennial Celebration Committee, 2001. [HCPL: 975.281H]

Griffith, Dennis. *Map of the State of Maryland laid down from an actual survey of all the principal waters,
    public roads, and divisions of the counties therein; describing the situation of the cities, towns,
    villages, houses of worship and other public buildings, furnaces, forges, mills, and other remarkable
    places; and of the Federal Territory; as also a sketch of the State of Delaware shewing the probable
    connexion of the Chesapeake and Delaware Bays. June 20th, 1794.* Engraved by J. Thackara &
    J. Vallance. Philadelphia: J. Vallance, 1795. 2nd edition in 1813. [HCPL: R Md.912.752G;
    HCHS; LC: American Memory, http://memory.loc.gov/ammem/index.html (accessed
    September 11, 2007)]

Harris, Thomas G., Jr. Discussion with Barbara Kellner and Robin Emrich [on Howard County
    roads], March 6, 2007.

Hattendorf, Ingrid M. and Christian-Albrecht Gollub. "From Longfellow's Journal." *The Old Stone
    Mill* [online finding aid]. Redwood Library & Anthenæum.
    http://www.redwoodlibrary.org (accessed February 15, 2007).

Holland, Celia M. with updates from Janet P. Kusterer and Charlotte T. Holland. *Ellicott City,
    Maryland Mill Town, U.S.A.* Ellicott City, MD: Historic Ellicott City Inc., 2003 (original
    publication date, 1970). [Columbia Archives and HCPL: 917.5281H]

Hopkins, G. M. *Atlas of Fifteen Miles Around Baltimore including Howard County, Maryland, 1878.*
    Ellicott City, MD: Howard County Bicentennial Commission, Inc., 1975. 1988 reprint by
    Howard County Historical Society, with index and corrections. [HCPL: R Md.917.5281H]

Howard County Historical Society (HCHS), Ellicott City, Maryland.
    Oakland Manor Research Collection
    Map Collection
    Vertical Files: Mills, Howard County Roads, Howard County Historic Sites

Howard County Planning Commission. *Road Index.* Howard County, MD: the Commission, December 6, 1961. [HCHS: vfs]

Howard County Sesquicentennial Committee. Religious Subcommittee. *Profiles of Faith: Histories of Religious Communities of Howard County.* Howard County, MD: the Committee, 1999. [Columbia Archives and HCPL: R Md.277.52P]

Kenny, Hamill. *The Placenames of Maryland: Their Origin and Meaning.* Baltimore, MD: Maryland Historical Society, 1984. [HCPL: 917.52K]

Library of Congress (LC). America's Story from America's Library. "Mathematician and Astronomer Benjamin Banneker Was Born, November 9, 1731." *Jump Back in Time, Colonial America (1492-1763).* http://www.americaslibrary.gov (accessed May 3, 2007).

Library of Congress (LC). American Treasures of the Library of Congress. "Jefferson Responds to Banneker." http://www.loc.gov/exhibits/treasures/trr022.html (accessed May 3, 2007).

Mahoney, John F. "Benjamin Banneker's Mathematics – In His Own Handwriting." Paper presented at NCTM Annual Meeting, Session #1047. Philadelphia, April 24, 2004. http://web.mit.edu/qmahoney/ww/nctm/NCTM2004atalk.doc (accessed July 7, 2006).

Martenet, Simon J (surveyor). *Martenet's Map of Howard County, Maryland.* Baltimore, 1860. [Columbia Archives, HCHS, and lithograph by A. Hoen & Co., LC: *American Memory,* http://memory.loc.gov/ammem/index.html]

Maryland State Archives (MSA)
    Archives of Maryland Online, http://aomol.net/html/index.html
    (1) Volume 204, "Laws of Maryland 1785-1791." (accessed May 23, 2007).
    (2) Volume 547, "Session Laws, 1832." (accessed January 25, 2007).
    (3) Volume 570, "Session Laws, 1809." (accessed January 25, 2007).
    (4) Volume 628, "Session Laws, 1823." (accessed May 23, 2007).
    (5) Volume 630, "The Counties of Maryland" (reprint of Mathews, Edward B. "The Counties of Maryland, Their Origin, Boundaries, and Election Districts," *Maryland Geological Survey 6,* part 5 (1906): 419-572). (accessed May 19, 2005).

    "Governors Under Proprietary and Parliamentary Government, 1634-1689." Special Collections, MSA SC 2685. http://www.msa.md.gov (accessed July 25, 2006).

    Maryland Patents Index – Index 54. MSA, 2005. http://www.msa.md.gov (accessed July 12, 2006 and July 20, 2006).

    Reference and Research. "Land Records," MSA, 2007. http://www.msa.md.gov (accessed several times during 2006-2007, background information).

McGrain, John W. *From Pig Iron to Cotton Duck. A History of Manufacturing Villages in Baltimore County.* Towson, MD: Baltimore County Public Library, 1985. [HCPL: R Md.975.271M]

Menzies, Evelyn. "Piecing Together the Past," *Columbia Today 2,* no. 4 (October/November 1969): 4-7. [Columbia Archives]

Miller, Nancy. Discussion with Barbara Kellner, March 26, 2007.

Moon, Jean. E-mail to Barbara Kellner [on Ruth Keeton], October 31, 2005.

Moss, Paulina C. and Levirn Hill (eds.), with assistance of Laurence Hurst, Virginia C. Lee, and
Wylene S. Burch. *Seeking Freedom: A History of the Underground Railroad in Howard County,
Maryland.* Columbia, MD: Howard County Center of African American Culture, Inc., 2002.
[Columbia Archives; HCPL: 975.281S]

Murphy, Paige. Discussion with Barbara Kellner, January 10, 2005.

National Park Service. *National Register Information System (NRIS).*
http://www.nps.gov (accessed November 3, 2004).

Northwestern University Archives, Evanston, Illinois. "American Hospital Supply Corporation"
[online finding aid] and "Foster McGaw" [online finding aid].
http://www.library.northwestern.edu/archives/findingaids (accessed May 9, 2007).

Pappenfuse, Edward C. and Joseph M. Coale. *The Maryland State Archives Atlas of Historical Maps of
Maryland, 1608-1908.* Baltimore, MD: Johns Hopkins University Press, 2003. [revised edition
of the Hammond-Harwood House Atlas of Historical Maps of Maryland, 1608-1908, 1982]
[HCPL: R Md.911.752P]

"Reminiscences of Baltimore, or Baltimore Town in 1795," *The Bankers' Magazine and St. Financial*
3, no. 1 (July 1848): 9. In APS Online (accessed February 8, 2006). [HCPL: database online]

Science Resource Center. Thomson Gale. [HCPL: database online; search name in quotations]

> *Science and Its Times.* Detroit: Gale Group, 2000. (accessed May 1, 2007, except "Marie
> Curie" which was accessed August 2, 2007).
> Volume 4: 1700 - 1799. "Eli Whitney."
> Volume 5: 1800 - 1899. "Alexander Graham Bell."
>   "Marie Curie."
>   "Thomas Alva Edison."
>   "Robert Fulton."
>   "Samuel Finley Breese Morse."
> Volume 6: 1900 - 1949. "Albert Einstein."
>
> *World of Invention.* Edited by Kimberley A. McGrath. Detroit: Thomson Gale, 2006.
> "John Loudon McAdam." (accessed May 1, 2007).
> "James Rumsey." (accessed May 24, 2007).

Shipley, B. H. Jr. *Remembrances of Passing Days: A Pictorial History of Ellicott City and Its Fire
Department* (as told to William K. Klingaman, Ph.D.). Virginia Beach, VA: The Donning
Company, 1997. [HCPL: 975.281S]

Stein, Charles Francis Jr. *Origin and History of Howard County Maryland.* Baltimore, MD: the author in
cooperation with The Howard County Historical Society, 1972. [Columbia Archives and
HCPL: 975.281S]

Stevens, Phillip. Discussion with Missy Burke [on Sierra Villas street names], October 28, 2004.

Taylor, Pamela. E-mail on behalf of Mr. Melvin Anders to Missy Burke [on Harmel Drive], August 4,
2003.

Tennenbaum, Robert (ed.) *Creating a New City.* Columbia, MD: Partners in Community Building and
Perry Publishing, 1996. [Columbia Archives and HCPL: 711.4C]

Thompson, Cleora Barnes. *Historic Sites Survey: Howard County.* Crownsville, MD: Maryland Historical Trust, 1976-1979. [HCHS and http://www.mdihp.net/cfm/index.cfm]

Trinity Episcopal Church. "Trinity Episcopal Church History." http://www.trinity-waterloo.ang-md.org/history.html (accessed May 23, 2007).

Warfield, J. D. *The Founders of Anne Arundel and Howard Counties, Maryland.* Baltimore: Regional Publishing Company, 1967. [HCPL: R Md.929.1W]

Webster's Third New International Dictionary of the English Language Unabridged. Editor in chief, Philip Babcock Gove and the Merriam-Webster editorial staff. Springfield, MA: G. & C. Merriam Company, 1965. [note: used for call-out definitions]

Wehland, Granville. Discussion with Barbara Kellner and Robin Emrich [on Howard County road names], February 28, 2007.

White, Frank F. Jr. *The Governors of Maryland 1777-1970.* Baltimore, MD: Twentieth Century Printing Company, Inc., 1970. [HCPL: 353.9W]

Wilson, Mark R., Steven R. Porter and Janice L. Reiff. "American Hospital Supply Corp." *Dictionary of Leading Chicago Businesses (1820-2000) in The Electronic Encyclopedia of Chicago* [database online]. Chicago Historical Society. http://www.encyclopedia.chicagohistory.org/pages/2542.html (accessed May 9, 2007).

Wilson, Richard. E-mail to Missy Burke [on Sebring development], September 23, 2003.

Columbia Place Name Index

The Art of Black & White

PORTRAIT PHOTOGRAPHY

**TECHNIQUES FROM A
MASTER PHOTOGRAPHER**

Acknowledgments

Palabras para mi Mamá y Papá: Gracias por el Cariño, Inspiración, Apoyo y Disciplina. Words to my Mother and Father: Thank you for the Love, Inspiration, Support and Discipline.

To my children, Oscar II, Zoya and Jose: You are my strength, I love you.

A very special Thank You to Jessica Bartels for all the work and support in the making of this book.

I would like to thank:

Jose Almanza, Carol Andrews, Frank and Bertha Archibeque, Jim Baker, Willie Barela, Tom Benusa, Ernest Brooks II, Camera and Darkroom of New Mexico, Armando Chacon, Dr. Enrique Cortazar, Keith Drosin, Frank Eposito, Art Esquibel, Mario Fernandez, Jose and Luz Esther Galindo, Antonia Grijalva, IPSW, Jose Alfredo Jimenez, James Johnson, Felissa Garcia Kelly, Michele Lovato, Arturo and Maria Lozoya, Jennie Lozoya, Vicky Lozoya, Yolanda Abbud Lozoya, Mamiya America, David Marrujo, Amarante Martinez, Maxwell Museum of Anthropology, Frank McDaniel, Lucia Medina, Tony and Sylvia Nava, Daniel and Yolanda Parga, Rich Parker, Michelle Perkins, Photoflex Company, Portercase Company, PPA, PPA Minority Network, PPANM, Quantum Instruments Inc., Steven Michael Quezada, Natasha Riboni, Martin and Bernadette Rodriguez, Duke Salinas, Peter Skinner, Andrew Smith Gallery—Santa Fe, Yamel Soto, South Broadway Cultural Center, Speedotron Company, SWPA, John Tanguma, David and Susan Tompkins, Patricio Tlaelel Trujillo, Youth Development Inc., Yvonne Ulibarri

Published by:
Amherst Media, Inc.
P.O. Box 586
Buffalo, N.Y. 14226
Fax: 716-874-4508
www.AmherstMedia.com

Publisher: Craig Alesse
Senior Editor/Production Manager: Michelle Perkins
Assistant Editor: Barbara A. Lynch-Johnt

Preface, interview and editorial assistance by Peter Skinner.

ISBN: 1-58428-083-2
Library of Congress Control Number: 2002103395

Printed in Korea.
10 9 8 7 6 5 4 3 2 1

Table of Contents

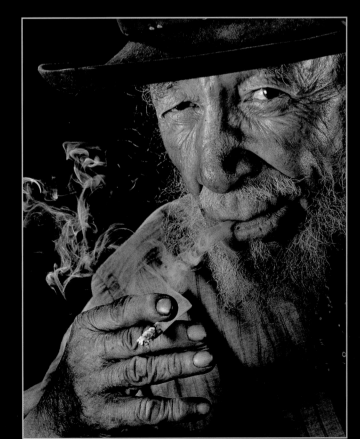

Preface and Interview

Oscar Lozoya: From Musician and Designer to Successful Portrait and Commercial Photographer

by Peter Skinner

Like many other leading practitioners, Albuquerque, New Mexico photographer Oscar Lozoya's interest in what would eventually become his profession began at an early age. "I've always enjoyed taking pictures. As a kid, I'd be the one taking the snapshots during family events and popping pictures whenever I could. About twenty years ago I started getting serious about my photography," he said.

Many visual artists are also musicians and Lozoya had been a professional musician for many years before embarking on a photographic career. "Though I loved playing music and being around other creative musicians, there came a time when I realized I was no longer comfortable with the lifestyle I was leading. I had to make a living, but I wanted to do something creative, challenging and rewarding — and be able to have more control over my life. At that time, one of my best musician buddies had been into photography for a while and the fun he was having got me interested. He had

researched equipment and helped me tremendously by giving me advice on it and I will always be grateful to him for his help," he said.

Lozoya had also studied design and had worked as a designer. The technical aspects of photography were mastered through a combination of intense studying of the theory and thus knowing how to predict the effects of what he was doing technically and how to analyze the outcome. In short, he was a good student of theory and had the inherent creative ability to convert mental images to reality. "I think that my attention to learning why things work like they do has been integral to my ability to advance quickly as a photographer," he said.

printing, which means I have complete control of a project from beginning to end."

He also is a strong proponent of low key lighting, especially in his personal work, which is strongly influenced by his Hispanic culture. "When I was getting started as a photographer, I was very resistant to having a 'style.' I worked in a lot of styles—and this gave me great experience, especially with lighting. Later, I started to see that having a recognizable style was important. I decided that if I had to settle on one style, it would be one that was going to continue to challenge me. Low key is one of the most technical styles of photography, since even small errors in lighting result in

> "I DECIDED THAT IF I HAD TO SETTLE ON ONE STYLE, IT WOULD BE ONE THAT WAS GOING TO CONTINUE TO CHALLENGE ME."

"My personal work tends to be in black and white because I have always seen black and white, properly executed, as an art. I love the tonalities and the timeless quality. I also like the fact that I can process the film and do the

loss of detail. Starting with a dark canvas also means that I can apply more light (and do more with it) before detail is lost.

"My work has been strongly impacted by going to art galleries and looking at the work of other photographers. It has particularly influenced my style and my choice of black and white. Additionally, I noticed that fine art photographers tended to work in themes or a series. At first I was a bit lost for what my own theme would be. As it turned out, it was right under my nose all the time: my culture. Hispanic culture has proved to be an endless source of inspiration. Additionally, I think that people like to learn about other cultures (like I do). Even if they misinterpret the imagery of my photographs at first, I think these images cause people to ask questions and to learn from the answers. I think that's good for people of all cultures."

Oscar Lozoya's work has been exhibited in numerous prestigious galleries and museums, both in his home state of New Mexico and in other US and international venues and is included in several permanent loan collections. Also, his images have been published in books, magazines, and corporate publications. And his list of selected awards runs the gamut from PPA, Best of Show, to Kodak Gallery Awards, and Fuji Masterpiece Awards—far too many to list here. He is a master of the black and white portrait and operates a busy and successful commercial studio.

LEARNING FROM THIS BOOK

As you read this book and scrutinize the images, Oscar has some advice that will help you develop your own lighting skills. Before looking at the accompanying lighting diagrams, study each image carefully and look for the direction and intensity of the

lighting. Look for where the shadows fall and then try to evaluate the lighting setup. And then study the diagrams. "A photographer's biggest asset is his or her eyes. Learn to look at light, both in photographs and in

"LEARN TO LOOK AT LIGHT, BOTH IN PHOTOGRAPHS AND IN NATURE, AND YOUR PHOTOGRAPHY WILL IMPROVE IMMENSELY."

nature, and your photography will improve immensely," he said.

In the following section, he answers some questions about his work and his approach to his craft.

INTERVIEW WITH OSCAR LOZOYA

Peter Skinner: *You seem to have a great way of working with people from all walks of life and social backgrounds. Is that a natural talent, or something that you worked on?*

Oscar Lozoya: People have always interested me. I've been able to get along with just about everyone I meet, so one might say that to an extent it is natural. In meeting and dealing with new personalities I am constantly learning about people and how to deal with them, so I guess you can say I am constantly working on developing people skills. I enjoy people-watching and studying behavior. I am very curious and enjoy learning about people's occupations, cultures, and experiences and can ask a lot of questions. By nature I can be very shy and in large social situations feel much more comfortable keeping a low profile and am content with listening and watching.

During a photo session, one-on-one or with a group of people, it is easier for me to converse and direct

the shoot. Talking is extremely important in my shoots for several reasons. It can help people to get to know each other and become more comfortable. I think people can see me more as a friend than a stranger with a camera. I ask many questions about them and have a sincere interest in what they have to say. This helps me understand how they see themselves, what their needs are and capture what they want to project, if that is the purpose of the shoot. If that is not the purpose of the shoot, it helps me know how to interact with them as a model to create and photograph a character. For many people, being in a dark studio with a bunch of strange looking equipment is a new experience and they don't know what to expect. I try to remain aware of this fact and not come across as intimidating. Working with different personalities requires different approaches. In an effort to keep them comfortable, spirits high and accomplish our goal, my approach is to generally follow their lead . . . so long as it does not stray too far from the objective.

P.S.: *Do you find it difficult asking interesting looking people to pose for you? Are people sometimes suspicious of your intent (perhaps a homeless person might feel you're "exploiting" their plight)? And how do you gain their trust?*

O.L.: I find some people are easier to ask to pose than others. If it is a person I know, I will not hesitate to ask. If it is a person I do not know, but they appear friendly and open, I can walk up to them introduce myself and talk with them about what I have in mind. If I know someone that knows them I will ask for an introduction. At times like this, I like to give them my card and have samples of my work with me to show them what I do. One thing I definitely do not enjoy doing is

taking a closer look at black and white prints created by masters in the medium and began recognizing differences in quality. I set up my own black and white darkroom and began learning how to have more control of the end results.

Ernest Brooks II, at the time president of Brooks Institute of Photography, was in Albuquerque to speak and judge at one of our IPSW (a pho-

familiar with the challenges, I can value successful results. While I do enjoy color photography very much, I feel that there is a classic, timeless quality to black and white. I enjoy the surreal state of mind it puts me in when I'm trying to visualize a final image. It can put me in a different world than the color world I live in.

photographing someone that does not want to be photographed. Some people can be suspicious and have a right to be, just like photographers should be careful about whom they approach. I rely on my gut feelings quite a bit and find when something doesn't feel right, it usually isn't. I feel homelessness is a problem that needs more attention. Looking away and pretending it doesn't exist is not going to help. If my photographs of the homeless help to shed light on this issue, I think it is a good thing. If I am exploiting a homeless person by photographing them, then I am exploiting everyone I photograph.

P.S.: This book is about black and white photography. Why did you focus on black and white? And did any particular person encourage you to concentrate on this?

O.L.: Early on, I used to think the only difference between producing color photography and black and white photography was using color film or black and white film. I started

tography association I belong to) conventions. Even though my early work was clearly a beginner's attempt, he was very encouraging and his work inspirational. From him I also learned that an encouraging word could make a world of difference. I will always be grateful to Ernie Brooks.

P.S.: Are there any major photographers/artists whose work you admired and who inspired you and your approach to photography?
O.L.: Ernest Brooks II, Yousuf Karsh and his printer, Robert Mapplethorpe and his printer, Tom Bari, Ansel Adams, and the imagery of William Mortensen.

P.S.: What is it about black and white that you really like? For example, some masters of the medium say that with black and white there are no distractions with colors and it handles dramatic lighting so well.
O.L.: I enjoy seeing a masterfully executed black and white print. Knowing a little bit of the process and being

P.S.: Your lighting is very controlled and also, in many cases, very dramatic. How do you determine what lighting patterns you are going to use for different faces? Are there times when you start with one thing in mind but can see a better way of bringing out the character/personality of a subject by doing something else? In other words, you might go into a session with a plan but are always open to lighting another way if things don't pan out as originally planned.
O.L.: When doing sessions with preconceived ideas, I have lighting designs in mind. We zero in on those ideas, and then we do variations (play). After looking at the originals, I decide which is the strongest image. Most of the time it is the preconceived idea. However, there are times I prefer one of the variations. Other times one of the variations has potential, but might need some fine-tuning. I will call the session a test and reshoot it at a later time and iron out the technical problems.

P.S.: What lighting systems do you use most, electronic or hot lights? What camera gear do you favor and what is your favorite camera/lens combination for portraiture?

O.L.: I mainly use strobe (electronic) lights. I've been using Speedotron brand for years. Speedotron lighting gives me not only power, but intensity range as well and is very reliable. They have many types of light heads and attachments that can be used to adjust the light quality. On location where there is no electrical power I use Quantum Qflashes® powered by the Quantum Qpaq®. They are compact and I can use them to create elaborate lighting setups. I also use the battery-operated Morris mini slaves. They are physically very small and besides having a PC socket they have a built-in photo sensor that detects other flashes going off and fires itself. Their size allows me to place them in very small spaces. They are great, especially when I want to accent and define. I've used them as mains also.

Mamiya cameras have been my choice since I started getting serious about photography. At first I used the Mamiya RB 67 Pro. For the past several years I've been using the Mamiya RZ 67 Pro II. The 6x7 negative gives me plenty of meat for high resolution, sharp prints. There is a lot of area on the negative should I decide I want to crop. The rotating film back is a feature that I consider very valuable. I can change from vertical to horizontal without having to rotate the camera and the lens axis doesn't move. The camera/lens combination I use most is the Mamiya RZ Pro II camera and the Mamiya 180mm lens.

P.S.: *Photography is, literally, writing with light—but photographers replace the pen with lights, sometimes one, but usually more. When you start to light a person, or situation, which light do you use first and how do you build from there? Is this a formula you use all the time, or do you "experiment" for different situations?*

O.L.: The main light is my anchor light, meaning all the other lights I use in a setup fall into ratio around it. For example: if I set my main light to f8 and I want to use a 5:1 ratio, I will set the fill light to f4. The fill light is now two under, or two f-stops less intense at the subject position than the main light. Say the subject was wearing a dark hat and I want to have separation between it and a dark background. I would set the hair light or top light at one f-stop more intensity at the subject position than the main light, or one over. So, if the main light were set at f8, the hair light would be f11. I use the main light as the reference for any other lights I might use in a setup. Even if I start the adjusting with another light in the setup, I always know what the main light needs to be putting out in terms of intensity.

P.S.: *How do you go about analyzing a person's facial structure to bring out the essence of that person's character and personality in the final photograph? Not necessarily how you disguise (cover up) perceived or so-called flaws, although these are all part of it, but how you really bring out the person's true self? Or at least, how you see that person.*
O.L.: When photographing a portrait of someone the best I can hope for is that I capture my interpretation of whom I think that person is. I think we each feel many different emotions and moods, and therefore have many faces. Because of this, I think it could be said that several different portraits with totally different looks and feel of the same person can accurately portray their personality at different times in different moods. In a portrait session arranged to please the sitter I might ask them what they like about themselves and what they don't. I will consider what they tell me while photographing them. I consider a shoot successful when a sitter is happy with the results from a session intended to please him/her.

When photographing someone for my purposes I will study their features to see what I feel are dominant. If the model is able, we play with expres-

> "THE MAIN LIGHT IS MY ANCHOR LIGHT, MEANING ALL THE OTHER LIGHTS I USE IN A SETUP FALL INTO RATIO AROUND IT."

sions, body language, and clothing while varying the lighting. In these types of sessions, the models' opinions of the end result are not my priority.

P.S.: *What do you see as more important in your personal work—portraying the person as you see them, or making them look good in a flattering way?*
I think the word "flattering" can be subjective. In my personal work, I feel it is more important to portray a person as I see them or portray a character through them. If I capture an image I feel comfortable with and it happens to be "flattering" in the gen-

erally accepted sense, fine, but that is not what I necessarily set out to do.

P.S.: What ratios of light do you typically use?

O.L.: Generally speaking, in a "flattering" session (a session in which I try to de-emphasize what some might consider flaws) I could use 1:1 to 3:1 ratios. In dramatic or personal work, I might use a 5:1 to an 8:1 ratio or more. This is just a general guide I use. There are exceptions, for example: a person might have features that would allow for dramatic ratios, yet produce a "flattering" image.

P.S.: How do you normally determine exposure—using a meter?

O.L.: For the type of work I do, I mainly use incident metering as opposed to reflective metering. I measure the light falling on the subject instead of measuring the light reflected from the subject. The exposure value the light meter reads from the main light is the aperture I set on the camera—unless I'm working with

a close main-to-fill ratio that can have a significant effect on exposure, in which case, I will compensate. Once in a while there are circumstances in which I will use reflective metering. I use the Sekonic 508 light meter because it is able to read both. After photographing and working with my lights for as long as I have, I have a pretty good idea what the exposure should be, but I always meter!

P.S.: Do you avoid overlighting a person or situation? In other words, do you keep lighting to the bare essentials to create the effect you want?

O.L.: I think overlighting or underlighting is a matter of personal opinion. I don't use more lights than I feel I need. I think the placement, intensity and quality of lights is more important than the number of lights.

P.S.: You are a master of black and white, but do you also work in color or digital?

O.L.: The majority of my commercial work is digital and in color.

P.S.: Do you do all your own black and white processing and printing and what developer/film/paper combinations do you like? Have you tried the Zone system, favored by fine art black and white shooters?

O.L.: I do my own black and white processing and printing. Depending on what I have in mind, I usually use Kodak Tri-X or Fuji Neopan. I use D76 for film developer, PolyMax

paper and Dektol paper developer. Years ago I read up on the Zone system to see what it was about. It seemed to me that it is a system based on one-stop increments. In that regard it is similar to the system I'd been using in the studio. I continued to use my system because it came more naturally to me. In the studio, I can set my exposure and tonalities with my lighting and the reflectance of

the components in my photographs. I think the Zone system is a great system, especially when working with available light and where there is less control of physical tonalities in the scene. Right now, if I were asked to accurately describe the workings of the Zone system, I would not be able to do so.

P.S.: What do you think it takes to become an expert practitioner in black and white—both photography and processing/printing?

O.L.: As with so many other things in life, a burning desire and genuine commitment to bettering one's skills. Not only to enjoy the completed results, but to also be willing to spend the time to learn the technical aspects—and long hours of practice.

P.S.: Are there any special developing and printing techniques you use—such as a lot of dodging and burning and other techniques? Obviously, you are very particular about the final result— would you say "perfectionist" describes you in that regard?

O.L.: I try to keep my darkroom work as simple and fast as possible. I try to get as much information in the negative as I can to prevent having to fight it in the darkroom. I dodge and burn when I feel it will enhance. I selenium tone for permanence. I use the same chemicals and times for all my prints. My enlarger is an Omega with a Chromega color diffusion head.

P.S.: It seems that you have a flair for injecting humor and irony into many of your photographs and you seem to

"I TRY TO GET AS MUCH INFORMATION IN THE NEGATIVE AS I CAN TO PREVENT HAVING TO FIGHT IT IN THE DARKROOM."

enjoy poking fun—in a nice way—at some of the more macabre or serious aspects of life (such as death). You obviously enjoy that. You must have a sense of humor about all this. Is it part of your Hispanic background?

O.L.: Yes, I believe I have a sense of humor. Sometimes I'll make serious images with a message. Other times I just want to have fun with the lighter side. On planned photographs it usually depends on my mood when the idea hits. Every memorable image I've seen has made me feel something. In addition to technique, viewer response is something I see as a vital element in a good image. The response can be positive or negative. Regardless of our intentions when making an image, we have no control over viewers' interpretations of our work.

Because of the traditional Mexican "Dia de los Muertos" or "Day of the Dead," I grew up seeing skeletal figures involved in many common and comical day-to-day situations. This definitely influenced my view and work with this sort of imagery that some might not understand and feel uncomfortable with. I see a difference in Death, the folklore, and Death, the reality.

P.S.: It is apparent from your portraits of less fortunate people, such as the homeless and other street people, that you respect them as people and individuals. Also, you bring out their personality and moods in a revealing and dramatic fashion. How do you do that and how do you get them to respond? Is it in your overall approach, your lighting, your empathy for their situation?

O.L.: Mutual respect and interaction must be present anytime I photograph anyone. As a photographer, I think if you're honest and sincere about what you're doing, people can pick up on it and reward you with their confidence. People from all different walks of life can have similar personalities. The very important personal approach will vary according to the personality. If, while looking at the person I'm photographing, I see them move into an interesting position, I will adjust the

lighting. When a person feels comfortable during the session, they can really get into it.

P.S.: You also work with youth groups and others. How are you trying to use your talent and expertise to benefit these people?

O.L.: Most of the youth groups I photograph come to me for publicity photographs to publicize their function or event. In this instance, you could say my photography is helping to get the word out. I also work with youth-at-risk programs. I think that observing someone working and enjoying what he or she does for a living can also help detour a young person from going down a less positive road. Many of the young people I work with are very artistic. Working together on a shoot gives them another and different creative outlet. I notice many of them ask a lot of questions and are fascinated by the photographic process. When I see young

people interacting and having fun, it brings back pleasant memories of my younger days. It also gives me a little insight into their interests and what some youth are into nowadays. It is very rewarding for me.

P.S.: Is the majority of your work in the studio? Do you do any location work? Which do you prefer and why?

O.L.: Yes, the majority of my work is done in the studio, but I do location work. My work is mostly done in the studio for many reasons. Studio work is what most of my clients desire and it is something that can be done at any given time or under any weather condition. My art is typically done after studio business hours. It is by far more time efficient to light and photograph in my studio than to set up on location. However, location work is something that I enjoy and would like to do more often.

P.S.: What advice would you give to young people interested in becoming professional photographers?

O.L.: Learn all you can about the theory behind photography and don't just memorize photographic formulas. Join photography associations. Practice, practice, practice!

P.S.: Have you learned a lot from being a member of PPA and similar associations and would you encourage young people to join it or similar trade organizations?

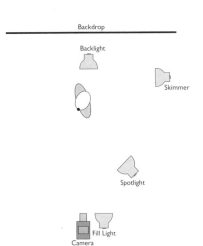

Backdrop

Backlight

Skimmer

Spotlight

Fill Light

Camera

Robin (Expecting)

The model in this photo (facing page) is a good friend who is also a photographer. She wanted some photos of herself while expecting, so we shot several art nudes, and several clothed images.

LIGHTING

Here, the model's body is silhouetted, but in low detail due to the low intensity of the fill light. Continuous light was provided by a theatrical spot placed to the camera right. This light was at a low angle to the subject, something evidenced by the horizontal nose shadow. A back light was placed behind the model's head, and a little below, to create the halo effect you see in this photograph. This same back light also silhouettes her stomach. A skimmer was used to the camera right.

Pam 1940s

THE SHOOT

This photograph (below) came out of another session in which Pam was a secondary character. Since she was dressed up so elegantly, we decided to shoot a few more images!

LIGHTING

Since the image mimics a 1940s style when popular lighting for glamour images was quite a bit harsher than that preferred today, I used a theatrical spot to accent her face.

PERIOD STYLE

1940s style is something that really appeals to me, and a look that you'll find in many of my images. I especially like the hats (of which I have a collection) and the baggy look of the suits (a style that is still popular). Capturing this period look convincingly also requires careful attention to lighting, as mentioned above.

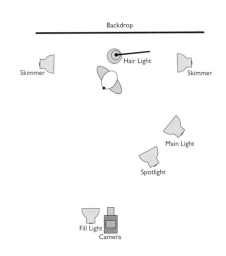

Backdrop

Skimmer

Hair Light

Skimmer

Main Light

Spotlight

Fill Light

Camera

Jan Vidra

For this photograph (right) I tried to create a very serious look. To this end, I used traditional hand posing.

LIGHTING

The main light was positioned to the right of the model and far back to create a split light effect (half the face is left in shadow). Fill light was used next to the lens. A skimmer was placed to the left of the model to add texture to the part of his face that was left in shadow by the main light. This skimmer also adds specular highlights to his fingers. A hair light was also used.

HAIR

The lighter the hair, the less light is needed on it. Even the fill light will pick up some detail on very light hair, while it will yield almost no detail on dark hair. With very light or white hair, the hair light should be equal to or less intense than the main light.

Vidra

CLOTHING AND HAIR

To create this image (facing page), we got rid of the patterned jacket completely and draped the model in black cloth all the way to his neck. We also played with his hair.

COMPOSITION

I shot this picture with only the face at first, but then decided that adding the hands helped give the photograph a stronger foundation. The basic compositional element here revolves around the positioning of the hair, pointing down, and the hands, pointing up. This arrangement, and the

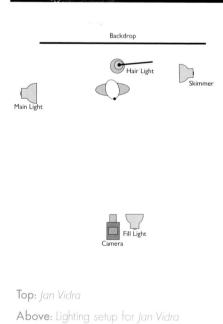

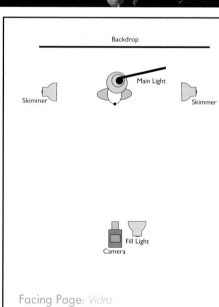

Top: *Jan Vidra*
Above: Lighting setup for *Jan Vidra*

Facing Page: *Vidra*
Above: Lighting setup for *Vidra*

overall symmetry of the image, create[s] a strong composition.

LIGHTING

The main light was positioned above the model's head to create a look of deep eye pockets and strong light on the brow and nose. A fill light used to the right of the camera functions almost as a second main. The hands are lit by the light from the main overhead and the fill light. Skimmers were used on either side of the subject.

Monongye

Monongye (facing page) is an Apache lady I met in my neighborhood. She has an interesting face that made her a great subject. I photographed her as part of a series on street people.

LIGHTING

The main light was positioned to the right of the model, and rather high. Fill light was used to the right of the camera. Two skimmers were used. The skimmer to her right helps to keep light on her dark hair and the fur she is wearing. The skimmer to the left creates specular highlights in the shadow due to the lack of illumination from the main light in this area. A hair light was also used.

PHOTOGRAPHING SENIORS

When shooting character studies such as this one, the images don't have to be flattering in the traditional photographic sense. These images aren't about perfect skin and youth, but rather they reveal the character of the subject in their lines, textures and tonalities.

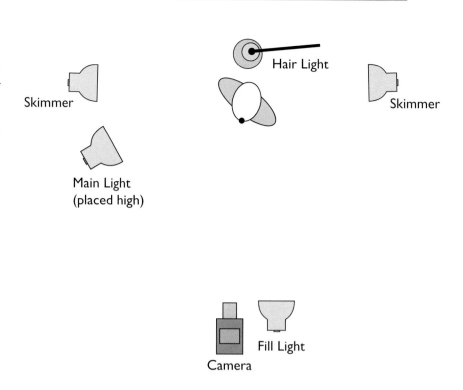

Facing Page: *Monongye*
Above: Lighting setup for *Monongye*

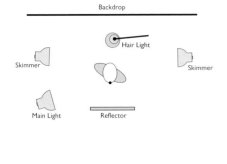

Backdrop

Hair Light

Skimmer

Skimmer

Main Light

Reflector

Fill Light
Camera

The Forgotten

This young man (facing page) had been on the street a couple of years when I met him. I had seen him on several occasions and asked if he would be interested in letting me photograph him. He stood me up several times, then showed up unannounced one day. I cancelled my appointments in order to shoot him. I gave him a neutral-tone shirt to wear (since he came in a light-colored sweater). It was only when I went to shoot that I realized he had buttoned it wrong. I decided not to fix it; after all, what I want to show in these images is people as they are. Fortuitously, the misbuttoned shirt also causes the collar to fall in a way that complements the composition of the image.

LIGHTING

The main light placed to the right of the subject creates split lighting on his face. A hair light was placed above the subject, and a fill light was used next to the lens. A reflector was placed under the model's chin to minimize the shadow in this area. Skimmers were placed to either side of the model. These cause the specular highlights on his nose. According to standard lighting rules, it's bad form to highlight a subject's nose. Although I'm certainly aware of rules like this, and know how to shoot that kind of photo if I want to, I find these rules can be too confining. Following the rules doesn't help you grow as a photographer, experimentation does.

Shadows of Society

This man (below) is someone I met in my neighborhood. When I approached him, he agreed to let me photograph him and came to the studio. The resulting photograph is now part of the PPA Loan Collection. Working with homeless people is something that stems purely from my love of

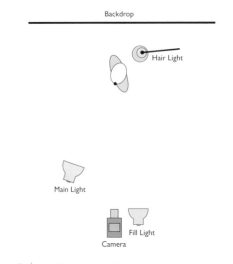

Backdrop

Hair Light

Main Light

Fill Light
Camera

photography. Although producing photographs for clients pays the bills, images of that kind don't always show the truth. Photographing the homeless allows me to capture images that are completely true and real; people being who they are. On a technical note, working on these images gives me an opportunity to play with more technical lighting. I also love the chance to talk with these subjects, hear their experiences, and get to know people from all different walks of life.

LIGHTING

Three lights were used to illuminate the model. The main light was placed to his right to create a loop pattern with strong shadows that give the face excellent depth and texture. A fill light was placed near the camera lens, and a hair light was used overhead.

Lifelines

I met this model, Jorge (below), when a friend of mine asked if he could sit in on a character study shoot. I agreed, and we went out and cruised around to find a subject. When we approached Jorge, who is also the subject of the following image (next page), he was on his way to the library. We gave him a ride there, then brought him back to the studio. Coincidentally, we

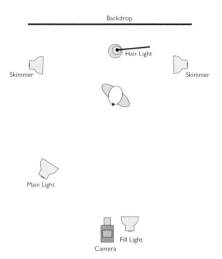

Left: *Lifelines*
Above: Lighting setup for *Lifelines*.

had much to talk about since he had been a photographer in the Army!

LIGHTING

The main light was placed to the right of the model and rather low (to get under the brim of his hat). A fill light was used to the right of the camera. Skimmers were placed to either side of the model, and a top light comes in on his head from above.

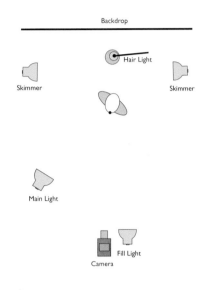

Right: *Jorge de la Plaza*

Above: Lighting setup for *Jorge de la Plaza*

Jorge de la Plaza (Downtown George)

LIGHTING

With minor adjustment, the lighting for the second image of Jorge (below) is very similar to the one used in the image on the previous page (a main light, skimmers, fill and hair light).

POSING

The previous image of Jorge is one that looks aggressive and outgoing.

While Jorge was certainly very sharp, the image shown here captures more of what he was really like. The camera was pulled back to show him as the short, slender man he is. It reveals a character that is much more mellow than in the previous image.

PAYMENT

When shooting figure studies with other models, usually I exchange pho-

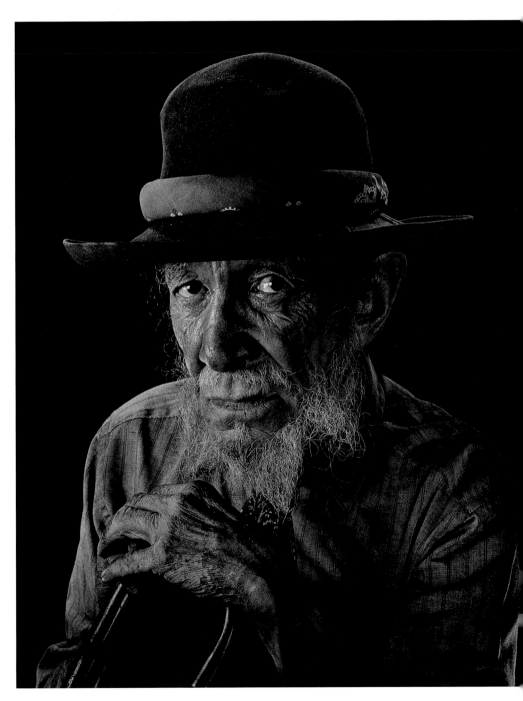

Power of Ages

My assistant knew this model (right) and brought her to the studio when I decided that I wanted to photograph more females for my character studies.

POSING

The pose developed organically from the tired look on the old woman's face, and the interesting way her hair fell forward. I draped the woman in black up to her neck and had my assistant hold her head up from below. The camera was tilted to position the arm at the corner of the image.

LIGHTING

The main light was positioned a little to the right and above the subject. It does not catch a lot in the eye area but shows up on the protruding areas of her face. A fill light was positioned next to the lens. Skimmers were used to either side of the subject and a hair light was positioned overhead.

Quiltman

The model for the image on the facing page (Patricio Trujillo) is my assistant, and an artist in his own right. He's been known to say "Anything for art!" This photograph certainly put that to the test, since he had to shave his head and eyebrows to make it! Using my assistant as a model was wonderful, since he knows the work it takes to shoot a great photo, and was willing to sit patiently while I took my time setting the lights.

LIGHTING

Since the fishing line in which the model was wrapped was pretty un-

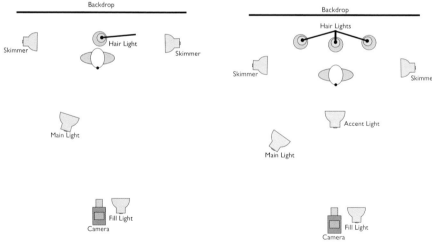

Top: *Power of Ages*
Above: Lighting setup for *Power of Ages*

Facing Page: *Quilt Man*
Above: Lighting setup for *Quilt Man*

comfortable, I posed him first and adjusted the lights. Then I wrapped the line around his face in such a way as to complement the lights that were set. A total of eight lights were used. Three lights were placed above the subject to pick up all the different tonalities, even on the top of his head. Skimmers were placed to either side of him and a fill light was used next to the lens. The main light was placed to the subject's right. Finally, an accent light was placed on the floor in front of him to separate his neck from his chin.

The Winker

Felipe (facing page) is someone from my neighborhood whom I've known for many years and, although we had talked about getting together for a photo session, it was only fairly recently that we managed to arrange it. He's a very funny man and has a face that is full of fun and mischief but it took a while before he relaxed in front of the camera and started to get comfortable with the shoot. But once he got going it was a photo party.

Felipe is a jokester with a lot of character, something that is emphasized by the lines in his face. I had him go through many poses and liked this one where he was holding his face in one hand, giving a wink and tightening up his mouth. As his face went into this expression the lines in his face were highlighted. It's really great when you can get someone who will play a role and have fun like this in a photo session. The hat was the ideal prop.

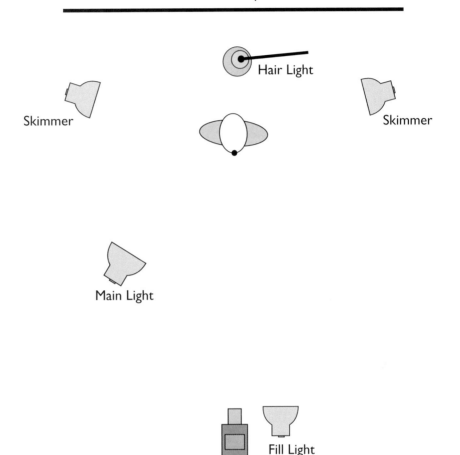

LIGHTING

I placed the main light in the basic Rembrandt position, which is one of my favorite forms of lighting. When using accent lighting such as skimmers, it is often more difficult to see the light pattern from the main light sharply defined. I have no problem with this, when I'm not going after a basic traditional look. A fairly standard setup with two skimmers, a hair light, main light, and a fill were used in this image. In the lighting diagram you will notice that the fill light is very close to the camera; I do this to fill more evenly and help prevent unwanted cross shadows.

Facing Page: *The Winker*

Above: Lighting setup for *The Winker*

Tijerina

Back in the 1960s there were major disputes about land grant rights in New Mexico and considerable political unrest over the issue. One of the principal activists during this period was Reies Lopez Tijerina (below), a very strong personality who fought for what he believed was right for his people. In most of the photographs of him, Tijerina is usually gesturing as he makes impassioned speeches and all the photographs I had seen were typical press or newspaper shots made many years ago. Recently, he was back in Albuquerque and I was fortunate enough to photograph him. I was honored that he trusted me to do this.

POSING AND CLOTHING

Mr. Tijerina came to my studio wearing casual clothes and a hat, but I wanted to capture the strength and personality of a powerful man who was also a politician. I had him put on a suit and adopt a pose that is more typical of a CEO of a major corporation or a statesman. I had him fold his hands, lean forward and look intently into the lens. The strength of character and the turbulent life he has led, evident by the lines etched in his face, are captured in this "executive portrait." Even his folded hands convey the strength of Tijerina's personality.

Reies Lopez Tijerina

This portrait of Tijerina (facing page) is closer to how most people remember him from his political days. At the height of the dispute over land rights, he was often at the forefront of demonstrations, making speeches and rallying people to the cause. He was a powerful leader but he dressed as one of the regular people he represented.

To create the image of how he is probably best remembered he wore his hat,

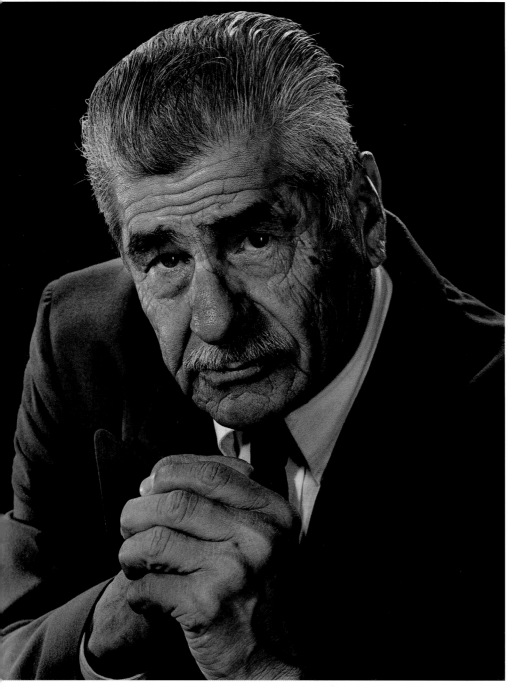

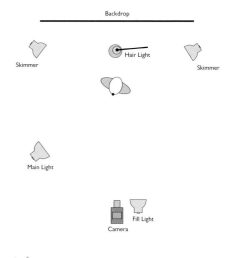

Left: *Tijerina*

Above: Lighting setup for *Tijerina*

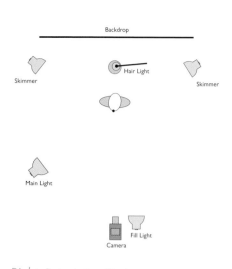

Backdrop

Hair Light

Skimmer   Skimmer

Main Light

Fill Light

Camera

Right: *Reies Lopez Tijerina*

Above: Lighting setup for *Reies Lopez Tijerina*

a denim jacket, and a bolo tie. I asked him to pose as if he were making one of his famous speeches. As he did this, it was almost as if we had stepped back many years and he was once again a dedicated political leader: there was a light in eyes and intensity in his face, which are portrayed in this portrait. The gesturing hands are also typical of his body language during his addresses to large crowds. In this portrait, and the previous one, I have captured the personality of a strong man but in two different environments and situations.

LIGHTING

One of the problems to be solved when photographing someone wearing a hat is to let enough shadow fall on the person's face to give a natural look but also to have enough shadow detail so that the shadow area of the face is not totally dark. Of course there are times when a mood or feeling is to be illustrated, such as a sinister or mysterious look, but in most cases I make sure the fill light throws just enough illumination into the shadows to maintain detail. Always remember that

film cannot record the same wide range of light that the human eye can, and photographers must be able to control the ratio of lighting. As is shown in the accompanying diagram, I used my standard portrait lighting setup. There is a great advantage to having a standard or favorite setup as a starting point—you are confident about the result and can concentrate on making the image and not worry about the lighting all the time.

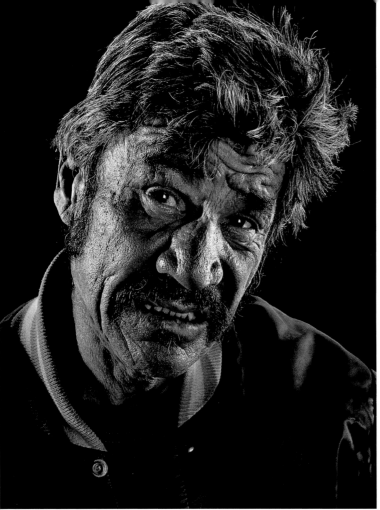

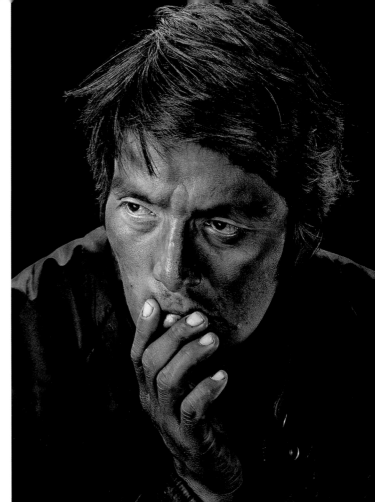

Ramon

At times we all work with models whose personalities are difficult to figure out. So it was with Ramon (top left), a homeless person I photographed because I also wanted to make a portrait of his companion, Betty. While Betty, also homeless, was a real character, Ramon was hard to deal with and kept asking why it was taking so long, why this was being done and so forth. He really put my human relations skills to the test. Ramon had a cynical nature that I think comes across in the portrait. It's almost as if he's sneering at the camera.

LIGHTING

The main light was set off to his right side (almost at a right angle to Ramon's face). The fill light was to the left of the lens. Two skimmers slightly behind the model and a hair light completed the lighting setup.

Rex

This is a homeless young man I have known for a long time and who is a good friend and very special to me

Backdrop

Hair Light

Skimmer

Skimmer

Main Light

Fill Light

Camera

Top Left: *Ramon*
Above: Lighting setup for *Ramon*

Backdrop

Hair Light

Skimmer

Skimmer

Main Light

Fill Light

Camera

Top Right: *Rex*
Above: Lighting setup for *Rex. Rusty* (facing page left) and *Robert Eagleman* (facing page right)

(facing page, right). Over the years he has worked around my studio and is part of the network of homeless people I have become associated with. I haven't seen Rex for a while now—a bit of a mystery because he used to come by quite often.

CAPTURING AN EXPRESSION

When I work with models I often direct the way they look or encourage an expression, but there are other times when I let them act as if I'm not there. As I use a waist-level viewfinder, my models are often not aware when I am actually composing a shot. So, when I see an expression I like, I pop the camera. This is what happened with this portrait of Rex. He was very contemplative and seemed completely unaware of what I was doing.

Rusty

Life is not easy for the homeless, as you can see in this portrait of Rusty (below left), a man I have known for many years—I photographed his wedding, long before he became homeless. I also know Rusty's family and my background with him has created a lot

of trust. Rusty lost his leg in a traffic accident and now relies on his wheelchair, which is integral to the portrait as it helps tell Rusty's story. Just before he came in for the session he had found a puppy, which he named Negrita, so we included Negrita. It's a very poignant photograph.

LIGHTING AND COMPOSITION

I had Rusty face directly at the camera and waited until the puppy was looking in the same direction. The details in the photograph tell the story. The main light was placed to the left, the fill on the right side of the lens, and

the skimmers and hair light provide detail and separation.

Robert Eagleman

Robert (below right) is from South Dakota and is a cousin of Bob Eagleman, who I had photographed previously. I met them through Jackson Longsoldier and they knew something about me and the kind of work I was doing, which made these portrait sessions go quite smoothly.

EYE CONTACT

I had Robert look directly into the lens—that results in his eyes looking

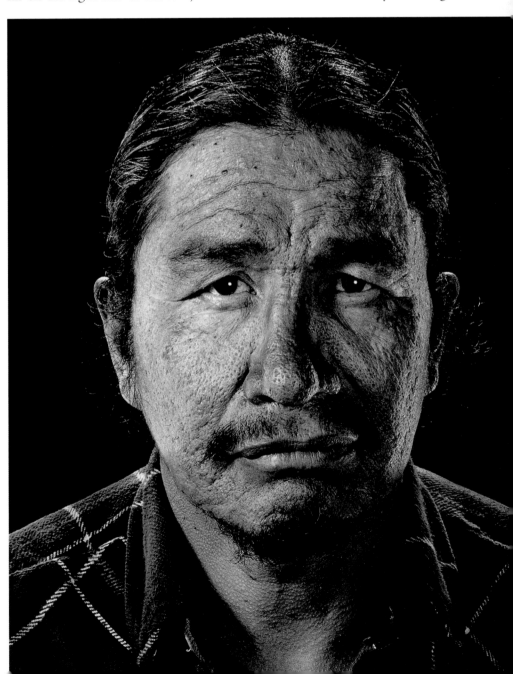

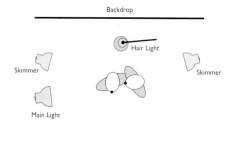

Right: *Betty and Ramon*

Above: Lighting setup for *Betty and Ramon*

straight into the eyes of the viewer. This very direct gaze also helps build trust between the model and the photographer. As I have noted, I take a keen interest in my subjects' lives and their stories. They are more than just models. I think that anyone who sets out on an ongoing project of personal work must be open and understanding. Though we come from different backgrounds we can usually find some commonality. Mutual respect really helps in this kind of a project.

Betty and Ramon

As previously noted, Ramon was not very cooperative, and I *really* wanted to photograph his companion Betty more than him. I made this portrait of the couple mainly to get Betty used to being in front of the camera, as she was a little shy and tentative at first.

LIGHTING AND COMPOSITION

I wanted Betty to be the principal subject and placed the main light so it would throw more illumination on her face. I also focused the lens on her

face with Ramon, almost a forbidding presence, receiving less light as his features merge into shadow.

Betty

Betty warmed up to the camera once she got used to the idea. She was a very sweet person with a playful personality and it started to shine through as she really got into the shooting session. Her companion, Ramon, was off to the side and he kept making comments, some of them quite mean, but that didn't faze Betty who was quick to respond. I really liked working with her. Sadly, about eight months after I made this portrait Betty died.

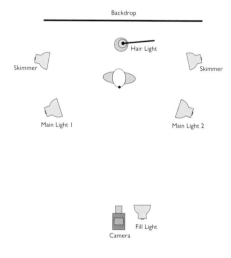

Facing Page: *Betty*

Above: Lighting setup for *Betty*

LIGHTING AND EXPRESSION

Betty had a great sense of humor and she would get this twinkle in her eyes

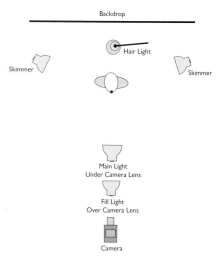

Backdrop

Hair Light

Skimmer   Skimmer

Main Light
Under Camera Lens

Fill Light
Over Camera Lens

Camera

Left: *Trust Me*

Above: Lighting setup for *Trust Me*

Trust Me

When I made the photograph above, I was involved in some business dealings and got the impression that, while some people will stab you with knives, there are many who will stab you with pens. My model, Bob Vokes, is a photographer buddy of mine. He has great features and has the ability to play different characters.

With the idea of making him look like a sinister wheeler-dealer, I placed the main light below the camera, then had him grasp a pen in his hand as one might hold a knife. A fill light above the lens softened the shadows without overpowering the effects of the main light. The hair light and skimmers outlined his shoulders and hair.

Abieta

Marvin Abieta (facing page, left) is another of the homeless people I have asked to pose for my series. He came to Albuquerque to perform at the Gathering of Nations, billed as the largest Pow Wow in North America, and ended up staying here. As he was also an artist, we got along very well.

He understood the importance of what we were trying to do, so he was most cooperative during the session.

DEVELOPING A RAPPORT WITH MODELS

Most people who sit for my personal portraits are easy to work with and are patient, or curious about the lighting and other technical aspects. But what makes them even more comfortable is when they see that I am interested in them as real people who have stories about their own lives. Everyone has a unique story and during each session I will chat with them about where they've come from, what they are doing, and often share stories of my own. It breaks the ice, helps build an understanding and rapport and so makes the shoot go a lot easier. This doesn't mean we talk endlessly throughout a shoot, and I try to be sensitive and avoid subjects the sitter might not be comfortable with. It takes experience to be able to do that but it pays off in getting great portraits.

I placed the main light on the left and just behind the model's face and the fill light was on the right of the lens. I used two skimmers, the one on the right was slightly higher than the model's head and closer to the camera in order to skim across the model's cheek on the broad side of his face, while the second, on the left, gives a subtle rim light to the short side of his face. I also used a hair light.

George Kiensuma

When I photograph people for my series on the homeless I never use makeup on the models. I photograph them the way you see them. George (below right) was a friend of another homeless person, Rex, who brought George over one day to help him do some work around my studio. The day I met George, he was a bit banged up, as you can see from the injury around his right eye. He said he'd fallen off a bus. George is originally from Laguna, New Mexico.

LIGHTING

As you can see from the diagram, I set up the main light on the left, used two skimmers positioned slightly behind the model and used a hair light. A fill light, used to the right of the lens, provided shadow detail. This is an example of the main light positioned on the broad side of the model's face.

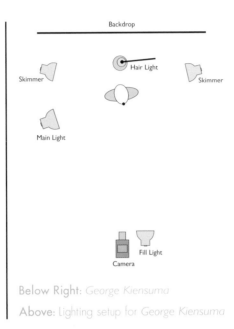

Below Left: *Abieta*

Above: Lighting setup for *Abieta*

Below Right: *George Kiensuma*

Above: Lighting setup for *George Kiensuma*

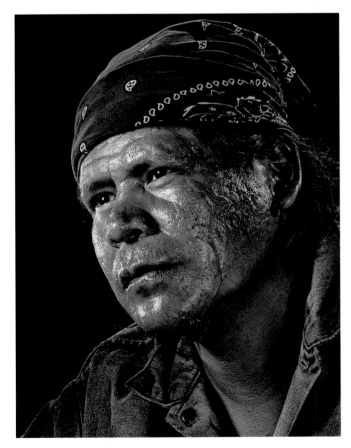

Gilbert

This is someone I have known from childhood (below); in fact I used to be a friend of his brother. Gilbert always wanted to travel and I hadn't seen him for a long time but on one of his recent return trips to Albuquerque he came to visit me at the studio and we did a portrait session.

LIGHTING

For this portrait I used a broad light, meaning the main light is positioned on the side of the face toward the camera, instead of short light, which I use more often. Occasionally I will use a broad lighting pattern depending on the shape of the model's face, as in this case. I also wanted more dramatic lines of separation and used the two skimmers to achieve that. The lighting ratio is very extended and though the short side of his face is dark, it does not merge with the dark background because of the rim light provided by the skimmer positioned on that same side. This same skimmer also edge-lights the side of his nose, accenting it in the process. The setup was completed with a hair light and a fill light.

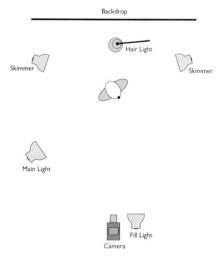

Left: *Gilbert*

Above: Lighting setup for *Gilbert*

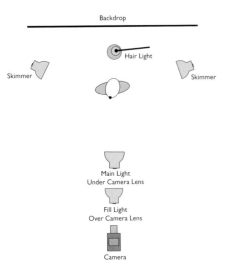

Backdrop

Hair Light

Skimmer   Skimmer

Main Light
Under Camera Lens

Fill Light
Over Camera Lens

Camera

Right: *Esposito*

Above: Lighting setup for *Esposito*

Esposito

Frank Esposito (above) is a photographer friend of mine from Massachusetts. He was in town doing a program for the Imaging Professionals of the Southwest. After the gig ended, we came to my studio for a photographic session/party and had fun creating this spooky and ominous feel.

LIGHTING

To achieve the effect we wanted I positioned the main light directly under the lens and put the fill light above it. To make it even more sinister, we had Frank cover his head with a hood with only part of his face exposed. To accentuate the texture of the hood I set up two skimmers and a hair light directly behind his head.

Face Without a Place (Paul Sanchez)
I was working on an exhibition to promote awareness of the homeless for The Maxwell Museum of Anthropology when I received a call from my son "O." He was a few blocks from the studio and told me he met someone I should photograph. I rushed over and met Paul. We started talking and I let him know about the project I was working on and asked if he'd be interested in being a part of it. He agreed, and immediately started doing exaggerated poses. It was obvious Paul liked joking around, and had a very open, approachable personality.

He knew where the studio was located and showed up a couple of days later as planned. Paul was a pleasure to work with. We talked a good long while before the shooting began. We were having so much fun that we started making things up just to top each other's stories. Once in front of the camera there was no stopping Paul, he would go from one overstated expression and pose to another. It really made me appreciate having lighting equipment with a recycle rate that could keep up with him. Even though we had a great time joking around during the session, we captured some very serious images.

SOMETHING TO CONSIDER
Generally, I have been very fortunate in meeting and asking people to pose for me. When approaching an unknown person to ask if they'd like to pose there is always a potential risk. Not everyone has good intentions or they could have problems beyond their control. When meeting someone for the purpose of posing, I assess the possibilities of working together. If I get good feelings, I continue; if I don't feel good about the situation, I know it's better to walk away.

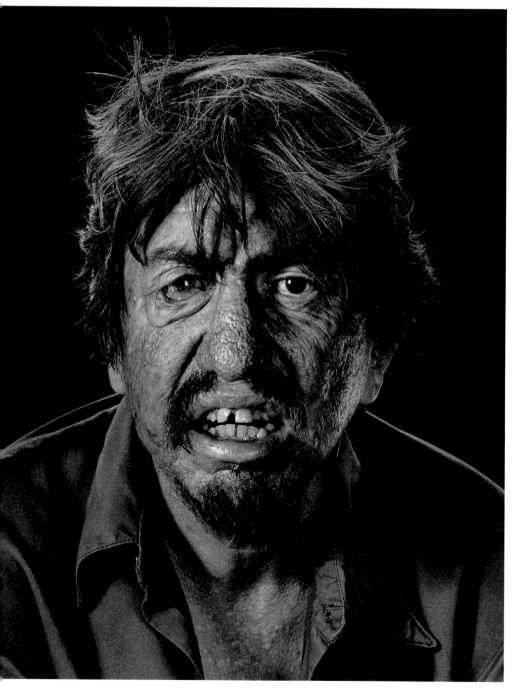

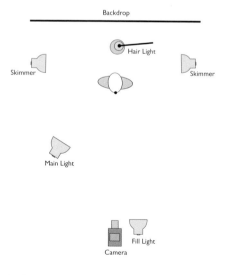

Left: *Face Without a Place*
Above: Lighting setup for *Face Without a Place*

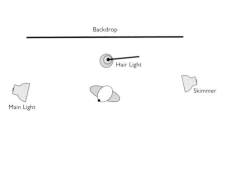

Backdrop

Hair Light

Main Light

Skimmer

Camera

Fill Light

Right: *Alan*

Above: Lighting setup for *Alan*

Alan

The portrait above is of my friend Alan Gelman, a photo equipment representative from Chicago. It's a classic illustration of the effectiveness of short lighting for portraiture. We set up the main light to camera left and behind Alan's face, and then set up one skimmer to provide separation. The positioning of the main light helped separation. A fill light to the right of the lens added just enough shadow detail without overpowering the effect of the main light. The image was made on location in a camera store where there was a lot of ambient light that made it impossible to see the lighting pattern cast by the modeling lights of the strobes. With practice, we can visualize the photograph in our mind, based on the position of the model and the position and intensities of the lights. To cancel out any of that extraneous ambient light, I simply used a faster shutter speed. Had I wanted any background detail in the image, I would have used a slower shutter speed.

Tri-diloxs

Patricio Trujillo (left), another member of the visual artists group Mezcla, has a great personality and is a wonderful model to work with—simply because he can play so many parts and will do anything to make a picture work. In this photograph, which is a spoof of Goldilocks we used discarded Tri-X film wrappers for "golden locks" and then had a lot of fun painting Patricio's eye makeup and gluing on fake fingernails and drawing the fake tattoo. The key to making photographs like this is to have models like Patricio.

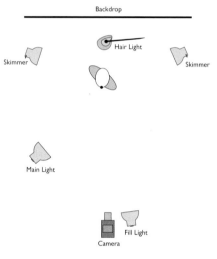

Left: *Tri-diloxs*
Above: Lighting setup for *Tri-diloxs*

Publicity Photos

Lozoya de la Muerte
(A Self-Portrait)

This untraditional self-portrait (facing page), which ties in with my "La Muerte" series, was made for the Andrew Smith Gallery in Santa Fe (which had requested portraits from the artists they represent). I applied the makeup, then had my assistant Jessica let her hair fall down over my shoulders so she became part of the portrait.

LIGHTING

I wanted a lighting effect that emphasized the Muerte aspect of my face, so I placed the main light under the lens to illuminate my blank expression and give an unsettling look. The fill light was directly above the lens and it softened the shadows from the low main light. I touched out the catch lights from the fill light, allowing only the low catch lights to remain, adding to the unnatural look. I also wanted Jessica's long hair to be evenly lit, so I placed the main light directly in line with the lens, not off to one side. The hair light illuminated Jessica's upturned face and the two skimmers outlined her arms and shoulders.

Stephan & KP

KP is a buddy of mine whose songwriting, singing and playing I really enjoy. He teamed up with another talented artist, Stephan, for this album project. This photograph (below) was made during the album cover session. Because they are entertainers it was quite easy to get them to play their parts and their very natural style helped a great deal.

LIGHTING AND MOOD

We wanted to create the look of a cozy nightclub, so my studio's brick wall was an ideal background. Many small nightclubs I have been to have a spotlight as the dominant light shining on the performers so I used a Speedotron zoom spot head directly over the camera for that purpose. I used the modeling lamp to see where the spot would hit and where it would fall off, which it does very quickly. While the

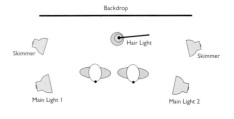

Below: *Stephan & KP*
Above: Lighting setup for *Stephan & KP*

Facing page: *Lozoya de la Muerte*
Above: Lighting setup for *Lozoya de la Muerte*

spot gave a well-defined look, it was not the main light (even though it looks that way). I used two main lights, one for each of the musicians, set quite close to them and off to the sides. A fill light was used to open up the shadow areas where the spotlight did not hit. Skimmers and hair lights gave separation and added to the look of a hot performance.

Marcos Devine

While doing a commercial shoot for Marcos (above), who is a singer and wanted a promo shot for a CD cover, my first priority was to nail down something that he liked and that would serve the purpose of the assignment. Once we had done that I asked him to go through a variety of poses.

Artists and performers are a pleasure to work with as they tend to be natural models—I asked Marcos to adopt a few poses and he worked with me.

PERSONAL AND COMMERCIAL WORK

This photograph evolved from a commercial assignment—which can often happen if the model is willing. However, photographers must be able to differentiate between the personal and commercial work, and be responsible for meeting the client's needs first. Marcos was a pretty cool-looking guy and I wanted to bring that across, through his expression and pose, and in the lighting. For even light on both arms, I placed the main light over the lens. A reflector under the chin, common in beauty headshots, defined his

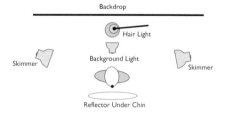

Top: *Marcos Devine*
Above: Lighting setup for *Marcos Devine*

chin and lips, while two skimmers and a hair light provided separation. I also used a background light that outlined the model's whole body and gave a theatrical look to the image.

Bodas de Sangre (Blood Wedding)

The photo below was a fairly complex one because it had to illustrate a story and also be lit in such a way that the central character stood out in relation to the others. The photograph was made during a session of publicity photographs for a theater presentation and this particular image had to tell the story of the intertwined relationships of the principal characters in the play. It can be quite hard to tell a story with a single image, but it's a challenge I enjoy.

WORKING WITH ACTORS

The task of telling a story with one photograph is made easier when you work with actors who know how to adopt the right expressions and can really play the part. Many times they have the experience to help set up the shot because, as in this case, they knew the story and were able to take on the personalities for the photograph in order to illustrate the relationships among the characters.

COMPLEX LIGHTING

As we had to pose the five models quite close together, I used a 50mm wide-angle lens on the Mamiya RZ Pro II to give the necessary depth of field and a feeling of greater distance between them—in effect, controlled distortion. Because of the way the characters were grouped I used two main lights set off to the left. Because the camera was so close to the subjects, I used a double fill system, with lights on either side of the camera, to give detail in the shadows on both sides of the bride and shadows cast by the bride onto the models behind her. Two accent lights, one off to the right and another behind the bride and pointing straight up, were also incorporated. Finally, two skimmers helped with separation of the pairs of models and a hair light and a selectively aimed background light were also used. The more lights that are used, the harder it is to make sure they all serve their purpose and complement each other and this is where modeling lamps are very helpful. A shot like this requires a lot of attention to detail.

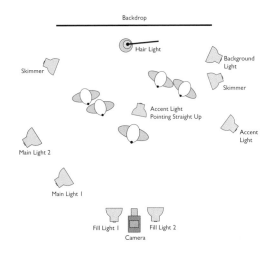

Below: *Bodas de Sangre*
Above: Lighting setup for *Bodas de Sangre*

Rey Lujan Gaytán

Rey Lujan Gaytán (facing page) is a very talented artist with a great look who came to me for a publicity shot.

COMPOSITION

We decided not to go with a traditional approach but to use a strong profile. When Gaytán spotted the bandolier in my studio, it struck his fancy, so we loaded it with his brushes. Above all, the image and its composition reflect the artist's personality: playful, comfortable, and not at all reserved!

LIGHTING

The lighting for this photograph was tricky since the model was wearing so much black, and because careful attention had to be paid to the brushes (mostly black) in his bandolier. We tried a few poses, then fine-tuned the position of the lights for this shot. A main light was placed almost in front of the model, but just slightly toward the background. Skimmers were used to either side of the subject. A hair light and a fill light on the camera lens axis were also used. The model's left hand picks up some nice specular highlights, the result of very careful positioning.

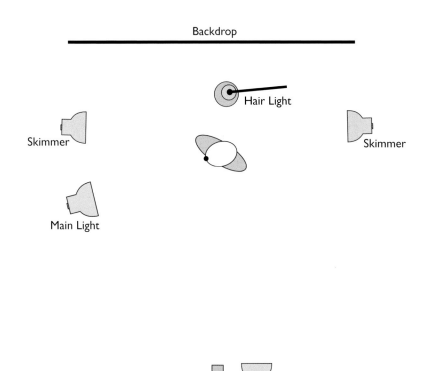

Facing page: *Rey Lujan Gaytán*

Above: Lighting setup for *Rey Lujan Gaytán*

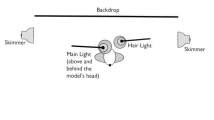

Facing Page: *Rick Maisel*

Above: Lighting setup for *Rick Maisel*

the subject. A low-power fill light left the shadows on the model's face quite dark. The main light was placed at a 45-degree angle to the model's right to create a Rembrandt lighting pattern, dividing the face and giving his features good shape and depth. A hair light completed the setup.

Rick Maisel (Escape Artist)

When you see photos of artists or musicians in this book, they are almost always depicted with their instruments or art. Shooting an artist with his work and in his environment tells something about his personality that goes beyond the face. Rick Maisel (facing page) is an escape artist and is depicted in his shackles, handcuffs, and chains. I met this interesting man when *New Mexico* magazine had me shoot color chromes for a story on him. Later, he came back for promotional shots. Although they look good in color, the "jewelry" of his trade is especially well suited to black and white photography.

The main light was positioned almost directly above and a little behind the model's head. It's a dramatic effect that complements the pose—both of

Micky Cruz

Micky Cruz (above) is a composer, musician, and bandleader whose publicity I have been doing for years. This image was shot for a CD cover.

CLOTHING

Since he had no concept in mind, I asked him to bring several outfits to the studio. Better to bring clothes you don't end up using, than to realize you don't have something you want!

LIGHTING

To create this dramatic look, a skimmer was used to the right and behind

Top: *Micky Cruz*

Above: Lighting setup for *Micky Cruz*

which seem to say "I want to be free!" Two skimmers were positioned to either side of the subject, and a fill light was used on the lens axis.

Eva Encinias Sandoval

MODEL

This model (below) is a well-known Flamenco dancer who also teaches dance. I photographed her for a calendar that was being created by the Hispanic Cultural Foundation. A major benefit of shooting artists is that they are hardly ever self-conscious and don't hesitate when you ask them to do something. They share a common goal with the photographer: the creation of art.

COMPOSITION

I had planned out this image well in advance, and had her bring her costume. I also arranged for an actor friend to play the guitarist—an important element in the composition since the eye starts here, moves up the neck of the guitar, toward the dancer and up her raised arm (at a similar angle).

This movement of the eye parallels the twirl of the dancer, movement captured in the uplift of her skirt.

LIGHTING

The main light was placed perpendicular to the dancer's face, just out of view of the camera. Two skimmers were placed on either side of the scene. A fill light was used close to the lens axis, casting the subject's shadow on the background and giving the background mixed tonalities. Very little light was allowed to fall on the guitarist since he is essentially a prop.

Foto Vato
(Foto Dude [A Self -Portrait])

I had originally been scheduled to shoot promotional pictures for a guitarist. When he couldn't make it, I figured there was no sense in letting a good setup go to waste! I put on my suit (purposely adding the bright white socks to throw white into the tonal arrangement), and used the pose for myself that I had had in mind for him. Of course, instead of a guitar, I shot myself with a camera (right).

SELF-PORTRAITURE

When shooting a self-portrait I generally set everything up and have a friend click the shutter. It take a few tries to get things right since I tend to be pre-occupied with all the technical considerations and have to "guess" what things look like through the camera. At first, I wasn't crazy about the idea of self-portraiture. I feel that I belong behind the camera and didn't want to seem conceited. Still, being in front of the camera has been a good experi-

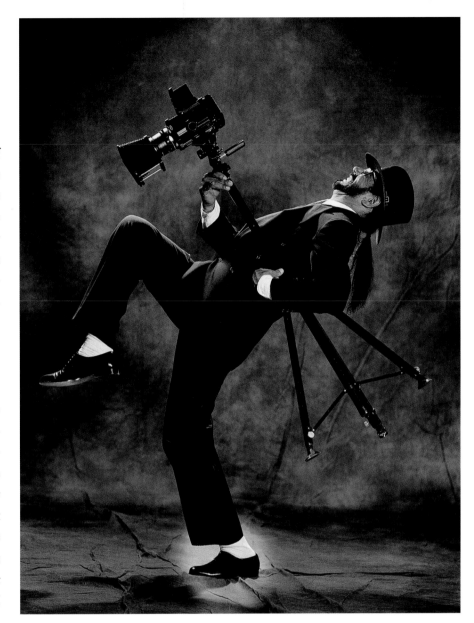

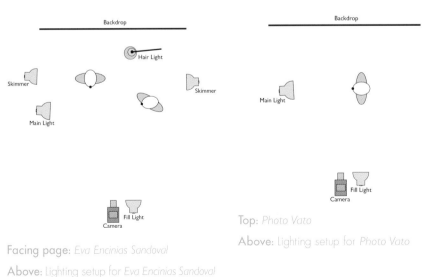

Facing page: *Eva Encinias Sandoval*
Above: Lighting setup for *Eva Encinias Sandoval*

Top: *Photo Vato*
Above: Lighting setup for *Photo Vato*

ence. First, there is a real collector's market for self-portraits, and I've been able to sell quite a few. More importantly, I get a chance to experience what it's like for my models, giving me a better understanding of how people feel as subjects. Finally, it gives me leverage, since I'm not asking models to do anything I wouldn't do myself!

Familia Pimentel

This group image (facing page) was also shot for a calendar featuring Hispanic artists. The Pimentel family runs a guitar-making shop, and manufactures high-quality guitars that are used by many famous performers. This image was shot in their shop, an intimate area in which the subjects were placed close together to show family unity. Guitars in various states of completion were used as props.

LIGHTING

Since we had a small space to work in, light was used to make the photograph more dramatic. Two main lights were placed on either side of the group. A hair light was added above and fill light was added close to the lens axis.

SHOOTING GROUPS

Taking pictures of groups is always harder than taking pictures of individuals simply because there is more to consider technically. There is also endless posing—the first person posed has moved by the time the last one has been posed. Therefore, it's almost impossible to get everything posed exactly right, so try to eliminate faults instead of seeking perfection.

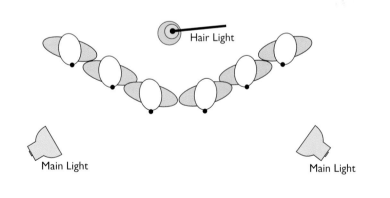

Facing Page: *Familia Pimentel*
Above: Lighting setup for *Familia Pimentel*

Federico Armijo

ON LOCATION

This image shown below was taken for a museum that was exhibiting Armijo's wood, steel, and stone sculpture. I shot the portrait on location, a challenge I love since it forces you to think on your feet. Although photography on location doesn't allow you the same degree of control you can have in the studio, the act of responding to the unknown can produce very interesting photographs. In this case, I shot the image on location in the artist's studio and had to work with the elements available. I saw this piece of unfinished sculpture and decided to use it in the image. It had to be placed in a vise to display it in the manner seen here.

LIGHTING

After selecting the art with which to shoot the subject, I placed him in front of it. Because the studio behind him was very cluttered, I used light falloff to remove all detail from the background of the image. The main light was placed almost in front of the model's face. Skimmers highlight the back of his shirt, his hair, and the front of his body. A hair light shines on the subject and a reflector also bounces this light onto the artwork. A fill light was added near the camera lens.

Rey

INSPIRATION

The artist (facing page) had brought with him to the studio a minifying glass, which I saw before the shoot. As we got to the end of the session, I kept thinking about the minifying glass, and for the last shot I put it in his hand and positioned it to catch a little face in a big face.

LIGHTING

Skimmers were used on either side of the subject, but were moved forward to create specular highlights on the noses and faces. This also helped keep light on the minifying glass and prevent it from shadowing the model's face. The main light was positioned above and to camera left. A hair light and fill light placed next to the lens completed the lighting setup.

Left: *Federico Armijo*
Above: Lighting setup for *Federico Armijo*

Facing Page: *Rey*
Above: Lighting setup for *Rey*

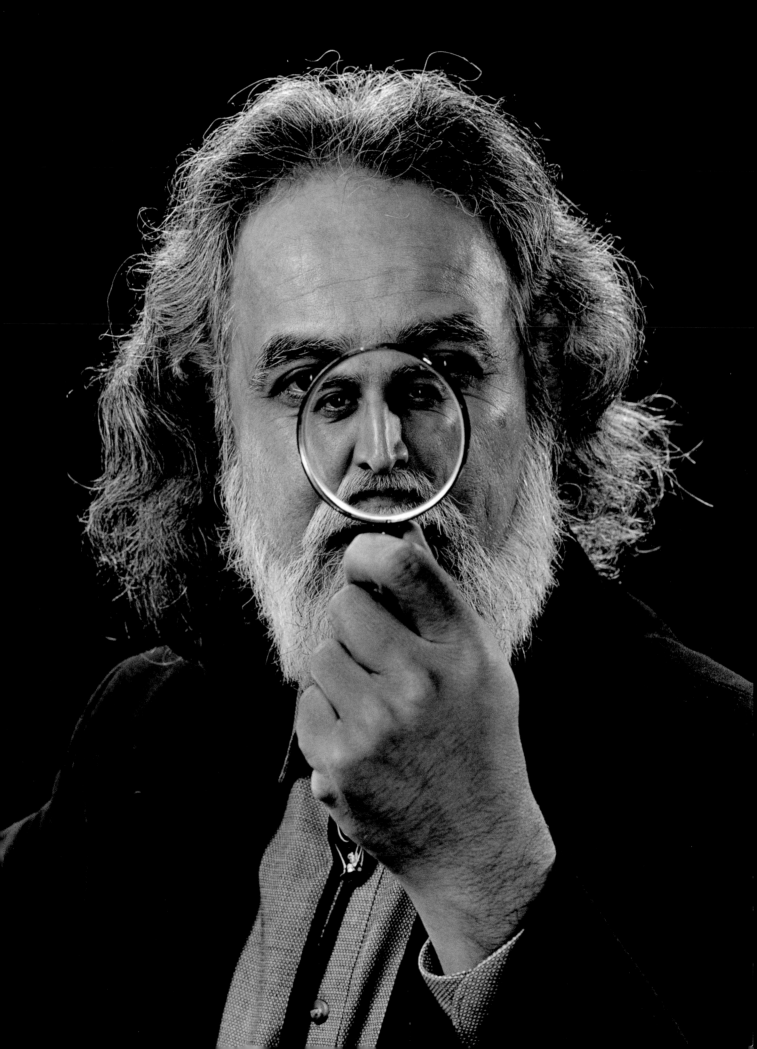

Luis Jiménez

This photograph (above) of artist Luis Jiménez was taken in his studio for the Albuquerque Museum. I used two assistants on this shoot. We would move the art around to set up a nice composition, then call him in periodically from where he was working to shoot a picture. The whole shoot took hours for us, but only a few minutes for the artist!

LIGHTING

The lighting for this image was especially complex since it involved lighting both the artist and large pieces of his work. The main light was placed to the left of the model, and a fill light was added at the lens. A strong skimmer was placed high behind the model to his right. Another was placed behind him and angled up to light the bottom of the horse sculpture. A third skimmer was placed behind the subject and to his left. The plant in the foreground was illuminated by a Morris mini slave, placed to light a dark spot. An additional accent light was placed on the camera left to highlight the edge of the plants. Another accent light hits the sculpture behind the model.

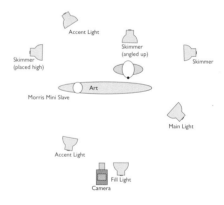

Top: *Luis Jiménez*

Above: Lighting setup for *Luis Jiménez*

Alia and Candles

WORKING WITH MODELS

This photo (below) was taken during a shoot for an album cover. The girl's mother was the singer of the band with which I was working. The band wanted a very dramatic image, and when I found out about their love of candles, I incorporated these for a high-impact look. One of my favorite parts of my job is getting to know the people I photograph. I love people (this is probably one of the reasons I like taking pictures of them), and most importantly, I like listening to their stories and learning who they are. I think this is an important element in creating great photos of them. First, it means that I'm no longer a stranger behind the camera, but a friend. This invariably puts people more at ease. Second, knowing my subjects helps me to capture more of who they are (if that is what's desired in the session). People photography, to me, is more talking to people than shooting them.

LIGHTING

Since strobe lighting was used, it had to be balanced out with the continuous light from the candles. A 3:1 light ratio was used on the skin, and the shutter was really dragged.

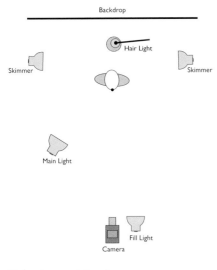

Right: *Alia and Candles*
Above: Lighting setup for *Alia and Candles*.

Diane the Magicienne

MODEL

Diane (below) came to me for publicity shots. She's a natural performer (as you can see in this photo!), and brought her own supply of tricks to the studio.

LIGHTING

Two skimmers were placed on either side of the subject. A hair light was used above, and a fill light was placed next to the camera lens. The main light was positioned to the camera left, just above head level. This creates short loop lighting on the subject's face (shadow from nose falls just below the nose).

HAIR LIGHT

The hair light should be geared to match the hair color of the subject you are photographing. Blond hair requires a rather low intensity, medium hair needs slightly stronger light, and dark hair requires the hair light to be quite intense.

Piador

THE SHOOT

Piador (facing page) is a very talented a cappella group (who treated me to a little concert prior to the session!). They came to the studio to shoot publicity photos for the group, and wanted a very simple shot.

LIGHTING

To photograph this rather large group, I used a broad main light centered above and in front of the subjects. A skimmer placed on either side

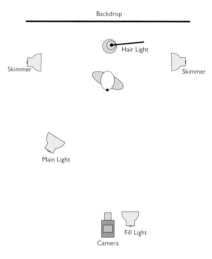

Left: *Diane the Magician*
Above: Lighting setup for *Diane the Magician*

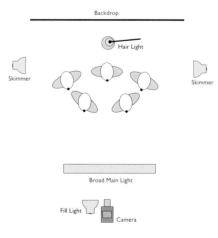

Facing Page: *Piador*
Above: Lighting setup for *Piador*

of the group helps to separate the group from the backdrop. A fill light was used next to the camera lens. A hair light was also used above the group.

LEARNING LIGHTING

Although I have studied design and worked professionally as a designer, I'm pretty much self-taught when it comes to photography. Lighting is one of the aspects of photography that has fascinated me the most, probably because it appeals to the technical, mathematical side of me, as well as the artistic side. Learning the theory of light and the laws of physics that govern illumination is something I did mainly by reading lots of books. Understanding these principles is crucial to using light creatively without being inefficient, since it helps to eliminate endless trial and error.

Sisters

MODELS

Twin sisters Didi and Dolly (facing page), a pair of singers and dancers, arranged this session as a publicity shoot. The image that resulted is reasonably like a regular portrait, but shows much more interaction.

POSING

This pose was selected to show the relationship between the two sisters. The models were photographed with their eyes closed, a facial expression that reflects intense emotion, but also mystery (it begs the question, "What are they thinking about?"). Adding this little element of mystery and emotion helps make the portrait more interesting.

LIGHTING

The main light was positioned to the camera left and kept relatively low (face level). This arrangement produces no loop on the nose. A fill light at camera level helps pick up the texture and adds definition to the subjects' black dresses. Two skimmers were placed to either side of the subjects, and a hair light was used above them.

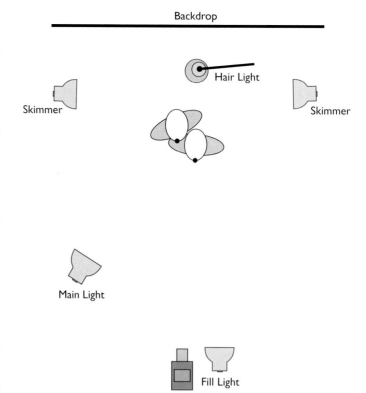

Facing Page: *Sisters*

Above: Lighting setup for *Sisters*

Gaspar Garcia

Gaspar (right) is a painter and sculptor, but also a very fine builder who has helped to restore historical buildings in my area. Knowing this, I decided to try to capture the "builder" side of my subject in this publicity shot.

LIGHTING

The main light was placed 90 degrees to camera left for loop lighting on the subject's face. The fill light was placed close to the camera. A hair light was used above the subject. Two skimmers were used: one behind the subject, and another weak one to the camera left.

Shooting subjects wearing hats can be tricky. If the main light is too high, the shadow from the hat brim can reduce definition in the shaded area. It was important not to let the light-colored hat overpower the subject, so a scrim was added in front of the main light to reduce the light falling on the hat.

Oscar Lozoya (Self-Portrait)

I do a lot of lecturing and often get requests for publicity shots. Most often I use *Foto Vato* (on page 67) but sometimes the request is for a head shot, which was why I made this image (facing page). I also made more traditional images, but after consulting with photographer friends about which to use, decided on this shot.

At the shoot, I took some mellow photos with my hair back, then decided to try a different look. I let my hair down and placed a fan under the lens. I put on a '70s-style, shiny shirt and

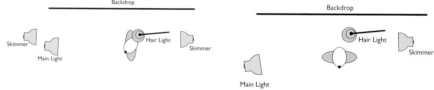

Top *Gaspar Garcia*

Above: Lighting setup for *Gaspar Garcia*

Facing Page: *Oscar Lozoya (Self Portrait)*

Above: Lighting setup for *Oscar Lozoya (Self Portrait)*

allowed my cross necklace to show (since people often wrongly associate some of my photos with the occult). I had my assistant trip the shutter.

LIGHTING

The main light was placed to the camera left, high and far back to create a split light effect. A skimmer was used to my left to add specular highlights. Fill light was used at a dramatic ratio with the main light, and a hair light was placed above.

Steven Maes

Steven Maes is a musician and producer who owns a recording studio. He came to the studio with his band for a publicity shot, but I also did some individual work with him afterwards.

LIGHTING

The main light was positioned high, back away from the camera, casting his eyes and face into shadow. A skimmer was used to his left, and a hair light was placed above him. Fill light was used close to the camera lens, and a little to the right, to add catch lights.

CONTACTS

As a former musician, I'm fortunate to have many contacts that were made during my career in that field. As a photographer, I draw on those contacts. Artists and musicians also learn about my work through photo credits. When people like what they see, they tend to seek it for themselves!

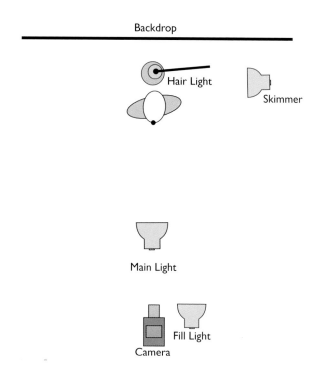

Facing Page: *Steven Maes*

Above: Lighting setup for *Steven Maes*

Duke and Pam

The subject, Duke, is a photographer and good friend who came in for a publicity shot. He had in mind a '40s-style image with a female model in the background and a camera as a prop.

LIGHTING

Both characters' faces were lit with theatrical spots. Skimmers light the edges of each subject. A fill light was placed to the right of the camera, and a hair light was used above.

NARRATIVE

Telling a story has become more and more important to me. Today, I find that just taking a "nice picture" isn't enough. Adding narrative to an image can make a controversial subject (such as a nude) more acceptable (especially in competition), but it also functions to make a picture appealing. People like to look at a photograph and see something there to interpret. Creating narrative can be as simple as the relationship shown in this image, where the viewer asks "Why is the woman walking away from him?" but even simple narrative devices attract (and hold) the viewer's attention.

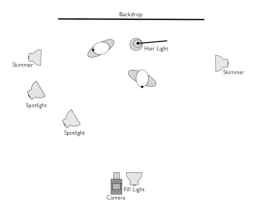

Top: *Duke and Pam*

Above: Lighting setup for *Duke and Pam*

Sol y Tierra (Earth and Sun)

This simple composition (below) reminded me of a tree with the limbs reaching up to the sun and the roots growing down into the ground. The model, Amaya, is a talented dancer and teacher. When we started the shoot, which evolved from a commercial assignment, we didn't have anything specific in mind. Amaya brought an outfit and mask she had made along with dried branches she had painted. We tried different poses and compositions. Amaya and I have been friends for years, I've always known she is very professional. In working with her and seeing her in action, only reinforces that fact. Amaya's face and body created something unique from a very simple composition.

LIGHTING AND POSE

The props, composition, and the pose adopted by Amaya fit in with one of my typical portrait lighting setups but with a slight difference in the location of the main light, which I placed high and quite close to one of the two skimmers. As you can see from the diagram, the skimmers were slightly behind Amaya and angled back towards her shoulders and head. This also helped outline the branches in stark relief against the dark background, adding a very graphic look to the whole composition.

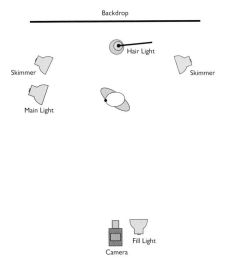

Right: *Sol y Tierras*

Above: Lighting setup for *Sol y Tierras*

David Crespin

MODEL AND POSING

The model in this image (facing page), which is also the cover photograph on this book, is a performer who works in carnivals, music videos, movies, etc.

He came in for a portfolio session and played with many different looks. He was a natural performer and really got into the shoot. For this image I told him to "Look pissed!"—as you can see he did a fine job of it!

LIGHTING

The main light was positioned to the right of the subject. Fill light was used next to the right side of the lens. Skimmers were placed to either side of the subject, and a hair light was used overhead.

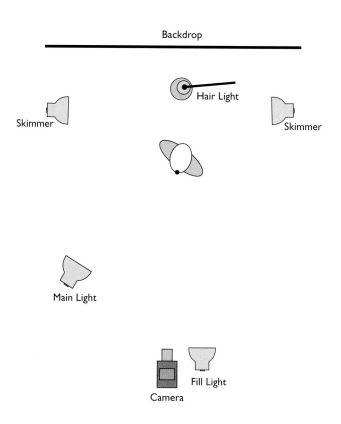

Facing Page: *David Crespin*

Above: Lighting setup for *David Crespin*

Killer Guitar

The model on the facing page is Will Patterson, who is a great guitarist and, as you can tell from his expression, has a great character that is a lot of fun to work with. Will came in for a commercial shoot for some publicity photographs, which were a bit more serious than this one. The custom guitars he uses are a bit scary—check out the "choppers" on the one in the photograph—so we decided to have a bit of fun with it.

WORKING WITH CHARACTERS

It's always fun photographing zany characters who will cooperate and go along with crazy ideas. In this case Will was very cooperative and played the role all the way. This is the great thing about working with artists—they are creative and will come up with poses and ideas and they are usually uninhibited.

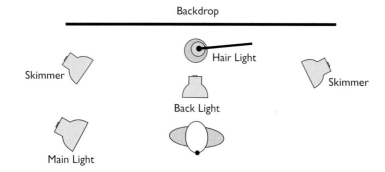

Backdrop

Skimmer

Hair Light

Skimmer

Back Light

Main Light

Fill Light

Camera

Facing page: *Killer Guitar*

Above: Lighting setup for *Killer Guitar*

La Muerte

The images in this section pertain to the Day of the Dead (Dia de los Muertos), an important festive Mexican holiday celebrated (in various forms) since the time of the Aztecs. The festival, celebrated on All Saints' Day, honors the dead, but also mocks death and has fun with it, all the while aware that death in folklore is not the same as death in reality. The use of these images also has political meaning; artist José Posada popularized the skeleton imagery in the 1800s as a poke at the government during the Mexican Revolution. Having grown up around this imagery, I decided to use the skeleton imagery popularized by Posada, with my own characters. Rather than depict a complete skeleton, I chose to paint only the face of my subjects. This preserves the human element and helps suggest that this folklorish imagery is not meant to be frightening.

The Muerte series began several years ago. A local cultural center was seeking material for an exhibition on the Day of the Dead. The deadline for submission was in two days, so I worked fast and contacted local performing academies to arrange for models, costumes, and props. The very first shoot was a success, and since then the series has continued to grow. Now, even when I'm working on commercial shoots, if a particular model inspires an idea (or seems appropriate for an image I've preconceived), I ask them to do it. If they consent, we go ahead and shoot!

Muñequitas de la Muerte (Death's Dolls)

LIGHTING

This photograph of my daughter (above) was taken using a five-light system. Two skimmers were placed as accent lights on either side of the subject, a hair light illuminates the scarf on her head, a fill light was placed next to the camera lens, and a main light was positioned to place light on the side of the model's face that is away from the camera (short loop lighting).

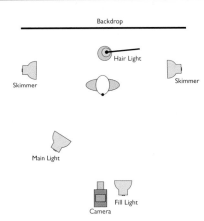

Top: *Muñequitas de la Muerte*
Above: Lighting setup for *Muñequitas de la Muerte*

Muerpatinetito

This is one of those images that can result when you let the model decide what he or she would like to do (above left). My son José decided that his favorite prop would be his scooter. In this photograph I wanted to illustrate the belief that the dead have a parallel existence to the living. A boy riding a scooter seemed to convey that message. We wanted to have a bit of fun with this shot and add a lighter touch. The slight grin and twinkle in José's eyes help achieve that. In addition to prop selection, José also directed the application of makeup, which was done by my assistant Jessica.

LIGHTING

I used two skimmers slightly behind José to provide edge light separation,

The feeling of motion was achieved by rotating the camera on the tripod.

Disco esta Muerto (Disco is Dead)

My daughter Zoya is something of an actress and played the disco role well (above right). She's very creative and in addition to doing her own makeup, also selected the props. We decided to do a spoof on disco dancing and Zoya knew how to do the pose made famous in *Saturday Night Fever*.

LIGHTING AND PROPS

The mirror ball appears to be balanced on the tip of Zoya's finger, but actually it's held in place by a boom stand covered with black cloth, and Zoya simply put her arm up and touched the ball with her fingertip. Because I wanted to light everything evenly, we

positioned the main light to the front and used a fill light next to the camera. Two skimmers and a hair light helped outline Zoya and separate her from the background.

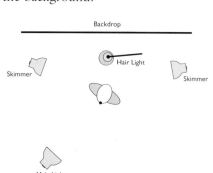

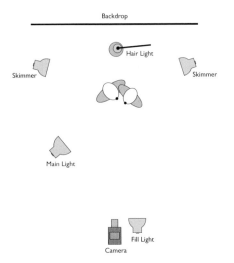

Backdrop

Hair Light

Skimmer   Skimmer

Main Light

Fill Light
Camera

Right: *Madona de la Muerte*

Above: Lighting setup for *Madona de la Muerte*

Madona de la Muerte

This is a more serious portrait made during one of my earlier La Muerte sessions (above). In it I wanted to capture the strong, loving bond between mother and child that continues beyond life. Because of the somber lighting and the realistic expressions of both models, this treatment is more solemn than other photographs in the series. This bond between the models shines through the photograph for a very good reason; in real life they are mother and daughter.

LIGHTING

When photographing people I try to be aware of the catch lights in the eyes. These add life. Here, I was not concerned about the catch lights, as their absence adds to the theme.

This low key image and the dark clothing require very careful lighting to ensure that the detail in the dark material is not lost and the more reflective parts of the image, the faces and makeup and eyes, also contain necessary detail. I built the lighting around one main light and then used a fill light, two skimmers, and a hair light. If you examine this low key photograph you will see that even in the darkest areas of the dark clothing there is detail.

Se Ve Muernífica

Like many other images in the series, the title of this image (right) is a play on words where "muerte" (meaning "death") is substituted for part of another word. Here, I imagine the little girl whispering, "Isn't she lovely!" ("Se ve magnifica!"), but the "magnifica" has been changed to "muernifica" to reflect the content of the image.

SUBJECT

I've had lots of experience shooting weddings and this is a spoof of the "typical" wedding portrait. After all, if death is a parallel existence to life, it seems reasonable to assume they do what we do. Thus, we have a wedding from the "other" side!

LA MUERTE SERIES

Although the series began as a fine art collection, it has been well accepted in the professional world. Images from the series have won Kodak Gallery Awards. They have also scored very well in PPA (Professional Photographers of America) competition, and have earned a place in the National Loan Collection.

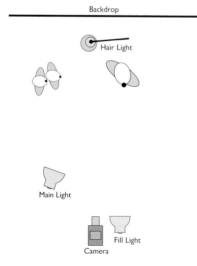

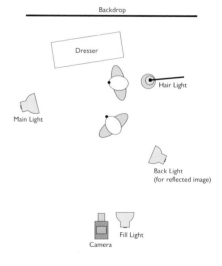

Top: *Se Ve Muernifica*

Above: Lighting setup for *Se Ve Muernifica*

Facing page: *Diva de la Muerte*

Above: Lighting setup for *Diva de la Muerte*

Diva de la Muerte (Death's Diva)

PLANNING

The idea behind this photo (below) was to show that death is lurking everywhere. I planned about six images to shoot during this session. Thus, when preparing with my models, we were able to approach it as a commercial assignment.

Attention to detail and being prepared are vital to the success of any assignment. In this case, I needed to have this dresser on hand. Often I make detailed plans for shoots like this, and find it's an efficient way to create images. Still, there are also many times when I go in without a preconceived shot. With a great model (or group of models), this is usually no problem and can be fun—we just play around, then adjust the lights and shoot!

EXPOSURE

A double exposure was used to create the effect of death in the mirror. The figure of death was backlit and her reflection photographed with the right side of the camera covered. Then the image of the young woman brushing her hair was shot with the left side of the camera covered.

Carmen Muertanda

The portrait below, obviously enough, is a spoof of Carmen Miranda and was made for a performance by members of the Expresiones Academy of Arts,

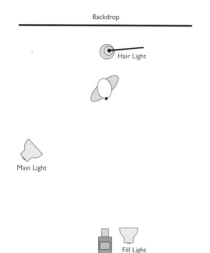

which is owned by friends of mine, Martin and Bernadette Rodriguez. This talented couple has helped me in many of my other projects.

LIGHTING AND POSING

We had discussed with the dancers the type of photograph that would work and having an accomplished dancer to model made my job quite easy. I set up a main light, to the front and left, the fill light was to the right of the lens and a hair light helped to illuminate the very ornate hat (made by Martin) worn by the model, Sharon. The key to the success of this image is the spontaneity and flair of the dancer's pose and her animated expression. She was having fun, and so were we.

Jugando con la Muerte (Playing with Death)

This is another cautionary tale in the La Muerte series (facing page, top) and the message is self-explanatory with examples of vice illustrated: gambling, boozing, drugs, smoking and sins of the flesh. At the apex of the triangular composition is a portrait of the patron of vice, "Dona Vismuerte." The model on the right is Martin Rodriguez, a gifted artist in many mediums and he did the makeup. We put him in the photograph as a living person playing with the dead.

LIGHTING AND COMPOSITION

As noted, I used a triangular composition incorporating the wall portrait. Fortunately, the rising smoke cooperated and drifted in the right direction to fit the composition. I'd like to say I planned it that way, but at times luck plays a part. I placed the main light directly above the camera and a fill light under the lens to direct light under the man's hat and provide shadow detail. A spot light to the right was directed at the photograph on the wall. A hair light and two skimmers illuminated the models' shoulders and hair, and also backlit the cigar smoke to make it stand out against the darkness of the unlit areas of the room.

Paranda de la Muerte

This parody of life after death (facing page bottom) was a promotional photograph for Mezcla, a group of visual artists that exhibits paintings, poetry, installations and photography based on themes from the Chicano culture. I am a member (that's me standing on

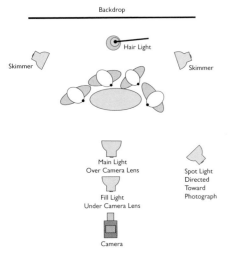

Backdrop

Hair Light

Skimmer

Skimmer

Main Light
Over Camera Lens

Spot Light
Directed
Toward
Photograph

Fill Light
Under Camera Lens

Camera

Right: *Jugando con la Muerte*

Above: Lighting setup for *Jugando con la Muerte*

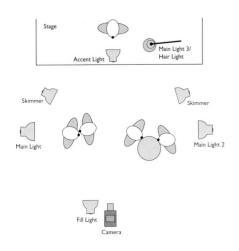

Stage

Main Light 3/
Hair Light

Accent Light

Skimmer

Skimmer

Main Light

Main Light 2

Fill Light

Camera

Right: *Paranda la Muerte*

Above: Lighting setup for *Paranda la Muerte*

the right) so I played director, model, *and* photographer. A member's six-year-old son, Isaac (an up-and-coming young artist) was gracious enough to hit the shutter on the count of three.

Paranda means party or fiesta and we wanted to have fun with this shot. We intended to shoot in a cemetery but had to change our plan due to unco-operative weather. One member sug-gested we shoot at a bar in town. We

called the owner to ask permission and she was gracious enough to allow us to do the shoot on very short notice. Once there, I had to set up a complex lighting situation. This is where hav-ing technical knowledge makes the difference between depending on a situation to be able to produce an image and producing an image

regardless of the situation. This is valuable in both personal work as well as commercial photography.

LIGHTING AND COMPOSITION
Composing, lighting, and photo-graphing a group like this requires planning and execution—especially when there is considerable distance

between the models in front and those at the back. To light the group I used two main lights, each set on opposite sides. The main light on the left was just behind the two dancers, throwing their shadows across the floor. Two skimmers provided separation from the stage and the guitar player in the background. The fill light, on the left of the camera, added shadow detail to the group of four in front. The guitar player and the stage required separate lighting and I used a third main light, which also doubled as the hair light for the front group, to illuminate the guitar player. Finally, a Morris mini slave, hidden behind a potted plant, was used as an accent light to add

more illumination on the guitarist and stage. Once everything was in place, I had Isaac trip the shutter.

Diversión de la Muerte (Death's Diversion)

PROPS AND COSTUMES

The photograph above draws on the political imagery of the Day of the Dead, depicting soldiers of the revolution having fun during a free moment. While I tend to minimize props (since I'm more interested in lighting), here the props (such as the cards and bandolier) as well as the period clothing add to the sense of narrative in the image. Fortunately, my subjects for this photograph, a group of Mexican

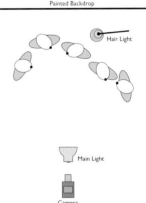

Top: *Diversión de la Muerte*

Above: Lighting setup for *Diversión de la Muerte*

dancers from the Expressiones Academy of Arts, had all the costumes on hand. The cemetery backdrop was also provided by the same academy.

MAKEUP

The skull makeup for the images in this series was created with regular theatrical products. When shooting images with stage performers, I have had the benefit of professional makeup work, but at other times the makeup has been applied by my assistant, myself, and even my babysitter! In the end, it's not important to me that the makeup be consistent from image to image. After all, as individuals we all look different in life, so the dead probably all look different too.

Sociedades de la Muerte (Death's Societies)

CHARACTERS

The image below, a publicity shot to promote a Day of the Dead event, was influenced by using models based on the characters created in the artwork of José Posada. These characters included, to the far right, a female general (of which there were unofficially several during the Mexican Revolution) and, to the far left, Doña Catrina, a high society lady. Doña Catrina's escort, seeing all the fun being had at the bar, looks back over his shoulder as if to say, "Give me a second to dump this priss, and I'll be right back!" Look at the bottle being poured by the bartender and see how well it fits in with the theme.

LIGHTING

The lighting setup for this image included six lights. Two skimmers were placed to either side of the subjects, and a fill light was used next to the camera lens. A broad strip light was used as the main to illuminate the large group of figures, and two hair lights add specular highlights to the models' hair and faces.

CLOTHING

In black and white you have to be careful of certain tones. For low key images this is especially true, since light-colored clothing tends to steal all the attention. In this picture, Doña Catrina's dress was too light, so to cut down on its brightness I wrapped a black lace scarf around the skirt.

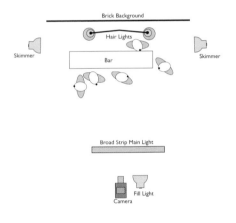

Right: *Sociedades de la Muerte*
Above: Lighting setup for *Sociedades de la Muerte*

El Mueriachi

This image (facing page) pokes fun—in its content and its title—at stereotypes of the mariachi. When shooting this model, a talented musician and composer, I had him bring in a selection of his guitars. I chose the smallest one, in order to emphasize his size. The composition of the image is very simple because sometimes "simple" is exactly what catches your eye.

LOW KEY IMAGES

I selected low key as my signature style because I liked the lighting challenge. In low key, the quality of the image is extremely dependent on lighting. If the lighting is a little off, it will translate immediately into lack of detail. (Of course, it didn't hurt that black is also my favorite color!)

San Francisco de Muersisi

This image (left) is a good-natured spoof of St. Francis of Assisi and his love of animals. The model, Patricio Trujillo, and his dog, named "Take it Easy," were real troopers on this 3 a.m. shoot. (The rooster and crow, on the other hand, couldn't have cared less, since both were stuffed!)

LIGHTING ON LOCATION

I used the same basic setup as I use in the studio: a main light on the right, fill light close to and on the left of the camera, two skimmers, and a background light to create separation and throw some light onto the trees in the background. I also placed a back light behind St. Francis to illuminate the grass behind and outline the subjects against the black background.

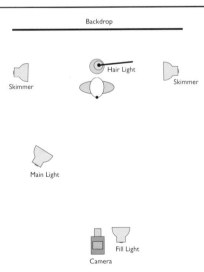

Facing page: *El Mueriachi*

Above: Lighting setup for *El Mueriachi*

Top: *San Francisco de Muersisi*

Above: Lighting setup for *San Francisco de Muersisi*

Winos de la Muerte

The "dead end" image (facing page) was shot in an alley behind a bar. It seemed ideal for showing the deadly side of bad habits but in a humorous way. The photograph resulted from a shoot we were doing for a publicity photograph for an independent movie that was going to be filmed. All the props were there—the dumpster, the old tire, litter, and also the graffiti. All we had to do was light the scene and put the models in place.

LIGHTING

This photograph was made after midnight. I used the Quantum Qflashes with the main light to the right, two skimmers placed to give some separation, an overhead hair light on the upper right, and a fill light. I dragged the shutter enough to let the streetlights in the background add to the mood and shine through the fence.

Proposición de la Muerte (Deadly Proposition)

This image (left) is one of the cautionary tales from the La Muerte series based on the temptations that people face—in this case it is prostitution—and was shot on location outside of a bar. The central characters obviously are the woman and the man offering the money but in the background are the pimp and in the lower left the pimp's dog, both of whom are watching the scene unfolding before them. In real life, the dog is owned by the man playing the pimp and kept getting into the shot (uninvited) so eventually we decided to put some makeup on him and let him be part of the

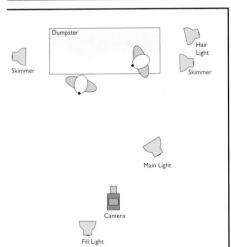

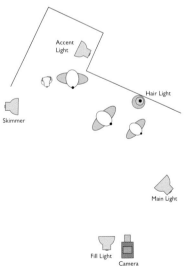

Facing page: *Winos de la Muerte*
Above: Lighting setup for *Winos de la Muerte*

Top: *Proposición de la Muerte*
Above: Lighting setup for *Proposición de la Muerte*

action. This also helped add a touch of humor. The man propositioning the woman is a musician friend of mine and is a great model because he really enjoys playing different roles.

LIGHTING AND LOCATION

Because the photograph was made on location outside of a bar I had to create the lighting from scratch. To do this, I used Quantum Qflash lights, my favorite on-location lights. Setting the mood was very important. The accent and background light provided enough illumination so there is separation and detail in the shadows. The hair light was also the light over the door sign, and the main light was placed quite close to the principal characters. A single skimmer was all that was needed to separate the propositioner from the background.

Justicia de la Muerte (Deadly Justice)

I made this image as a satire about the legal system that is inspired from observation. Many viewers have also given me their own unique interpretations. Once after a competition I had a judge approach me to tell me he thought the word "justice" in the title was not appropriate. He told me he could not see it as justice because some people in the image had lots of money and were happy, while others appeared poor and humble. He went on to tell me that Blind Justice herself was not being fair because she was peeking through her blindfold. At first I thought he was joking by stating the obvious, but when I looked at his face I realized he was dead serious. This

encounter once again reinforced the fact that we have no control of other's interpretation of our work. It also confirmed to me what some people take for granted: justice for one is injustice for another.

FAMILY

This image is special to me, not only is it a personal expression, but all the models are my family members. In preparation for the shoot we had lots of fun making and finding wardrobe and props. The session itself was a family event. When I see this print I get a warm feeling and remember the special time we all spent together.

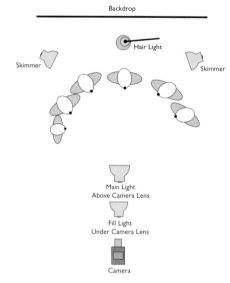

Top: *Justicia de la Muerte*

Above: Lighting setup for *Justicia de la Muerte*

El Diablo
and Folklore

El Diablo (The Devil)

The idea of the devil is strong in Mexican culture, and it was with that in mind I planned the images in this section. For this photograph and the two that follow, I chose three models to portray three characters: the devil, a priest, and a young woman. While shooting the scenarios I had planned between the actors, I also took this portrait (facing page) of my good friend and actor Steven Michael Quezada as the devil alone.

MAKEUP

After Halloween I always keep my eyes open for specials on theatrical make-up, masks, unusual props, and anything else that might someday be useful in the studio. In this case, the subject was photographed wearing horns cut off a Halloween mask and applied with theatrical adhesive.

LIGHTING

The bottom lighting is appropriate to the subject and makes him look unnatural. The effect is amplified by the fact that he is wearing contact lenses, giving his eyes an unusual tone.

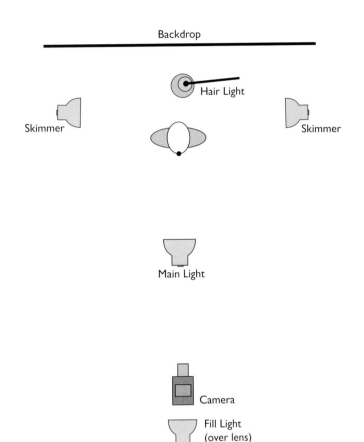

Facing page: *El Diablo*

Above: lighting setup for *El Diablo*

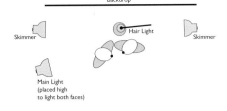

Facing Page: *Pasion del Diablo*

Above: Lighting setup for *Pasion del Diablo*

Pasion del Diablo
(Passion of the Devil)

LIGHTING

This image (facing page) was one that I preplanned for the session. The positioning of their bodies and faces created a great potential for dramatic illumination, and the spreading of the devil's fingers allowed interesting light patterns to be created on his hand (emphasized by the dramatic fake nails). The faces of both the devil and the girl are lit by the same main light. However, because of the posing of the shot, the lighting effect is different for each character. The devil's face shows a Rembrandt lighting pattern, while the girl's face displays a loop pattern.

Tentaciones (Temptations)

LIGHTING

In my take on the classic battle between good and evil (above), lighting was supplied by seven sources. I metered from the main light and geared the other lights in ratio to this. The first light used is a spotlight, which was turned to illuminate the girl's face. Two skimmers were placed on either side of the models.

Two main lights were also used: one, placed behind the devil, illuminates his back and the face of the priest; the other, placed behind the priest, illuminates his back and the face of the devil. Finally, a top light was used to highlight the hair of the models, and a fill light was used near the camera lens.

PRINTING

I am a printer by necessity only. Although I would love to have more time to experiment in the darkroom, when I'm in there, I'm effectively losing money. Fortunately, shooting chrome really teaches you how to expose film, so my strategy is to use my shooting skills to cut the time I need to spend in the darkroom fighting with poor negatives.

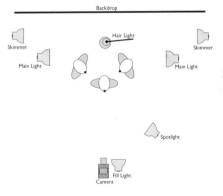

Top: *Tentaciones*

Above: Lighting setup for *Tentaciones*

Doing my own printing also assures me of getting across my artistic vision in the final prints (something I have had problems achieving with other printers). When necessary, I sometimes will expose my prints, stick them in a black bag and have my assistant run them through the chemicals.

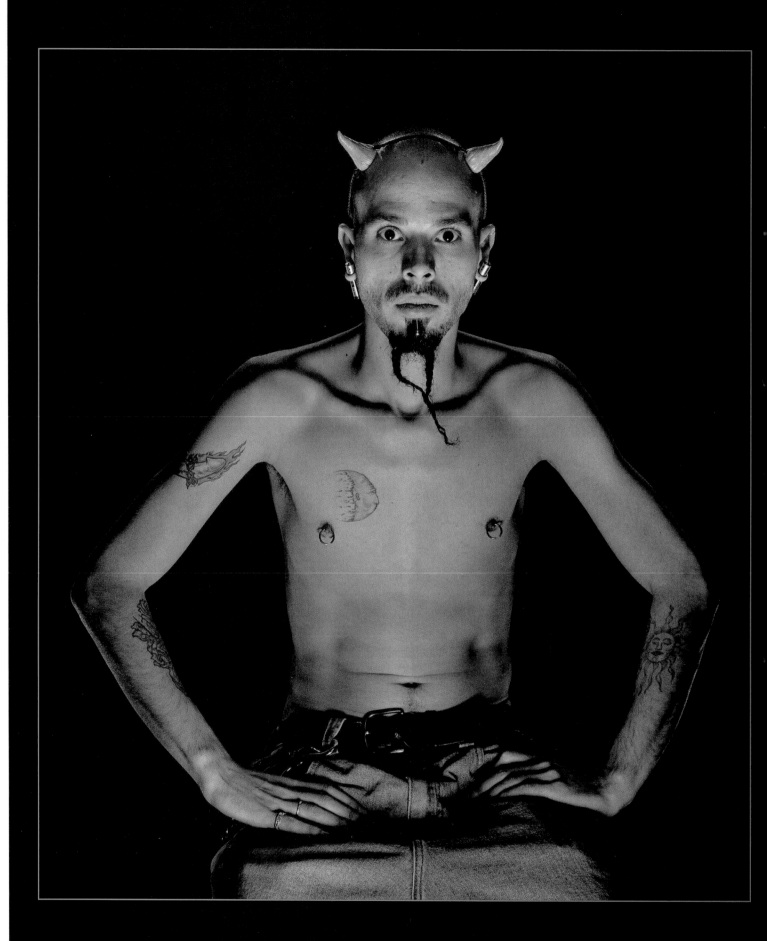

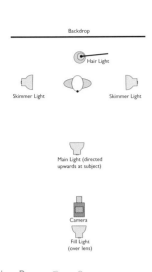

Hair Light

Skimmer Light   Skimmer Light

Main Light (directed
upwards at subject)

Camera

Fill Light
(over lens)

Facing Page: *Goat Boy*

Above: Lighting setup for *Goat Boy*

Goat Boy

This was my first shoot with Goat Boy (facing page) and I didn't know what he looked like, so it wasn't possible to preconceive the images I would want to create with him. So, when he arrived at the studio wearing devil's horns, I simply set about to shooting a variety of angles, working with his features and trying to capture him in a very dramatic way. I have since used him as a model in other sessions.

LIGHTING

The bottom lighting in this image adds to the dramatic effect I was attempting to convey. Combined with the very symmetrical composition, this helps to accentuate his piercings and tattoos. A slight edge light also helps to define the figure.

La Llorona (The Weeping Woman)

FOLKLORE

La Llorona (above) is a character from Mexican folklore who drowned her own children. After death she was denied entry into heaven and was condemned to walk the earth in search of

her lost offspring. She is often used as a discipline tool ("Be good or La Llorona will get you!"). Here, she is depicted at the window of a house, looking in on a mother and child. Images like this have consistently sold well for me through museums and exhibitions, and also through PPA seminars.

LIGHTING

Two main lights were used, one directed at the old woman from her right and slightly behind her, one directed at the mother and child in the background. Two skimmers relatively close to the camera help light the side of the old woman's face. A hair light and a fill light complete the setup.

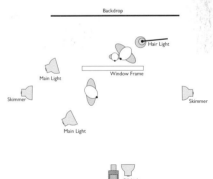

Backdrop

Hair Light

Window Frame

Main Light

Skimmer   Skimmer

Main Light

Fill Light

Camera

Top: *La Llorona*

Above: Lighting setup for *La Llorona*

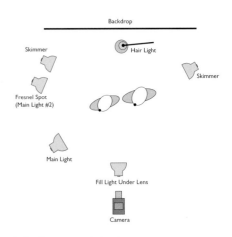

LIGHTING

I used two main lights, both placed to the left of the photograph. The first main light illuminated the woman. The second main light, a fresnel spot, was focused precisely on the Cucui's face. I like to use this fresnel when I want to pinpoint light and not have it spill over onto unwanted areas. A fill light, placed under the lens, threw some shadow from the woman onto Cucui's chest to give a more threatening look. Finally, two skimmers and a hair light provided separation.

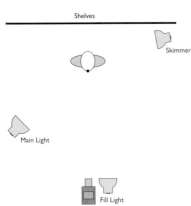

La Curandera (The Healer)

La Curandera (facing page) is a practitioner of folk medicine who uses herbal remedies in her healing. The image was shot for a calendar that featured Hispanic artists of all media. This woman is definitely an artist, and one closely tied to Hispanic culture.

ON LOCATION

Since it obviously wouldn't have been practical to move all of her supplies to the studio, I shot La Curandera on location in front of her shelves of herbs. Shooting on location is something I don't get to do as much as I would like to. I particularly enjoy working with people in their own environment, as well as the challenge of dealing with unknown conditions and having to think on my feet to create the right pose and lighting.

Beauty and the Feast

This photo (above) is a takeoff on "Beauty and the Beast" featuring an attractive damsel in distress and a character from Mexican folklore, El Cucui, who is sort of a boogey man. Parents will sometimes use him as a disciplinary tool and warn their kids that if they misbehave, "El Cucui will get you!" Speaking from experience, I can tell you it works! In this case El Cucui is feasting on the distressed woman's arm while she's screaming for help.

Santos, Diablos y la Muerte (Saints, Devils and Death)

This is another photo created to publicize an exhibit and performance by the group Mezcla. The characters are the same ones we portrayed in the performance. The performance piece, titled "An Encounter Along the Way," was written by Jimmy Santiago Baca and premiered at the National Hispanic Cultural Center of New Mexico. The group's 2001 lineup, all are founding members, are (from the left): Cecilio Garcia Camarillo, Bernadette K. Rodriguez, Patricio Trujillo and sitting Oscar Lozoya.

This session is very special to me because it was the last time I photographed Cecilio Garcia Camarillo. He passed away within months of this shoot, leaving behind a large, beautiful body of work. He worked unselfishly in our community and was always willing to help someone, he is greatly missed.

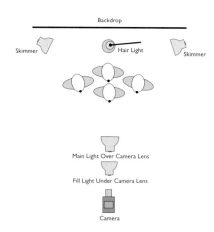

Top: *Santos, Diablos y la Muerte*
Above: Lighting setup for *Santos, Diablos y la Muerte*

Index